IMAGES
of America

INDIANA'S HISTORIC NATIONAL ROAD

THE EAST SIDE, RICHMOND TO INDIANAPOLIS

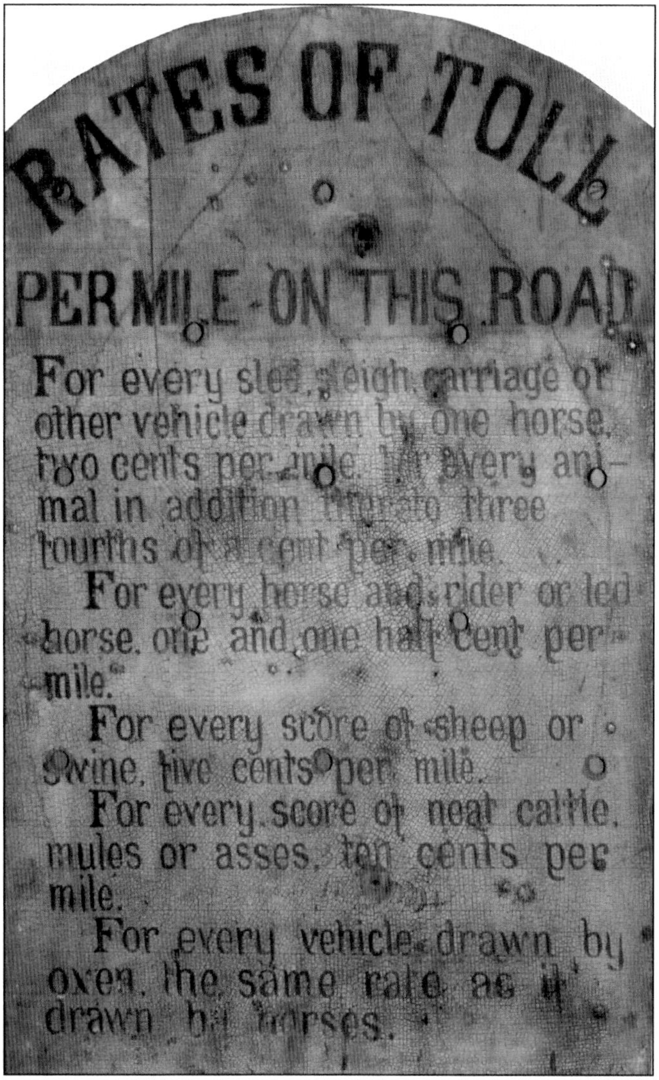

This faded, tombstone-shaped wooden sign once rested on the National Road in Henry County. The sign reads, "Rates of toll per mile on this road. For every sled, sleigh, carriage or other vehicle drawn by one horse, two cents per mile. For every animal in addition thereto three fourths of a cent per mile. For every horse and rider or led horse, one and one half cent per mile. For every score of sheep or swine, five cents per mile. For every score of neat cattle, mule or asses, ten cents per mile. For every vehicle drawn by oxen, the same rate as if drawn by horses." (Courtesy Henry County Historical Society.)

On the Cover: The Huddleston Farmhouse Inn of Mount Auburn, Indiana, is a historic inn that once served travelers along the National Road. This c. 1890 image shows the descendents of John Huddleston, including his wife, Susannah, and several of the couple's surviving 12 children posing proudly in front of their ancestral homestead. An assortment of young Huddleston grandchildren can be seen playing on the sloping hill on the northeast side of the home. The main house is three stories high. Before renovations, the basement consisted of three separated rooms that could only be entered from the outside; two of the rooms were lodging for guests, and the middle room was John's shop where he would sell items to travelers passing through. On the middle level there is a kitchen, a family room, a dining room, and a formal parlor. The third floor was where the bedrooms would have been. It was purchased by Indiana Landmarks in 1966 with funds provided by the organization's founder, Eli Lilly. The house, barn, and other outbuildings have been restored and serve as the Indiana National Road Heritage Site and the eastern regional office of Indiana Landmarks. (Courtesy Huddleston Farmhouse Museum archives.)

IMAGES
of America

Indiana's Historic National Road

The East Side, Richmond to Indianapolis

Alan E. Hunter and Joseph M. Jarzen for
the Indiana National Road Association

ARCADIA
PUBLISHING

ISBN 978-0-7385-6055-7

Published by Arcadia Publishing
Charleston, South Carolina

Printed in the United States of America

Library of Congress Control Number: 2011932837

For all general information, please contact Arcadia Publishing:
Telephone 843-853-2070
Fax 843-853-0044
E-mail sales@arcadiapublishing.com
For customer service and orders:
Toll-Free 1-888-313-2665

Visit us on the Internet at www.arcadiapublishing.com

This book is dedicated to the members of the Indiana National Road Association, past and present, for keeping the spirit of the road alive. The mission of the Indiana National Road Association, or INRA, is to preserve, protect, and promote the Historic National Road across the Hoosier state to save our history, interpret our heritage, develop tourism, and boost economic development. With an eye on its future and a firm grip on its historic past, the INRA strives to preserve, protect, and promote the Historic National Road.

Indiana
NATIONAL ROAD ASSOCIATION

Contents

ACKNOWLEDGMENTS

The idea for a roadway linking Eastern manufacturers with Western markets is as old as the country itself and was first broached by George Washington as early as 1755. It took until 1802, however, for the idea to take shape. Congress, in the act creating Indiana, required that five percent of funds received from public land sales in the Hoosier state be used to build public roads connecting the Atlantic Ocean to Indiana. In 1803, Congress made the first appropriation for a highway across the Allegheny Mountains to Ohio—the National Road. Beginning in Cumberland, Maryland, and running through six states, the road cost approximately $7 million and is known by many names: National Road, National Pike, Old Pike, Cumberland Road, Cumberland Pike, Highway 40, and Washington Street.

By the time the road reached Indiana, its national significance was well documented and many of the state's future leaders and budding politicians realized that it would be in their best interest to help build this thoroughfare. It is not uncommon for researchers to find the work crews littered with the names of Hoosier antebellum leaders. Just as we can never properly thank every one of those bygone pioneers for their contributions to the National Road, we can never properly thank all of the researchers, historians, documentarians, and collectors who have furnished material, past and present, for this volume. The best that we can do is to try and acknowledge a few of them here.

The authors would like to thank many people who contributed images for this book. Individuals or organizations that deserve recognition are Sue King, Historic Knightstown, Cambridge City History Room, Rick Newton, April and Mark Riggle, Norma and Jim Bertsch, Jim Orr, Rhonda Hunter, Ron Sanders, Steve Barnett, Bill Raney, Mick Kissick, Tom Saunders, Kathy Miller, Western Wayne Heritage, Irvington Historical Society, Vigo County Historical Society, and Indiana Landmarks.

INTRODUCTION

The National Road is the nation's first federally funded interstate highway commissioned by Pres. Thomas Jefferson in 1806. Today, it is among a select number of designated All-American Roads within the National Scenic Byways program. These roads are considered the most distinguished of all nationally designated byways. However, the story of the road is about the people who traveled it, settled along it, and lived along it over the past 200 years. This road is defined by the built environment and footprints of millions of Americans whose lives have been impacted by their interaction with it.

A traveler along Indiana's Historic National Road, which follows US Route 40 between Richmond, Indianapolis, and Terre Haute, will find today a landscape little changed since the heyday in the 1940s. Historic towns with traditional main streets and tree-lined residential districts still give way to productive fields and tranquil pastures that brought Indiana prosperity. From the Federal-style architecture of the 1840 Huddleston Farmhouse to the 1940s Plainfield Diner, one can literally track the westward migration of the nation in the buildings and landscapes previous generations left as testimony to their hard work and creative spirit. From famed literary figure James Whitcomb Riley to cultural icons, such as Madame Walker, Hoosier Pete gas stations, the Hulman family and motor racing, and the Indiana School of Artists, they are all part of the story of this important road.

A history that spans 200 years provides a very unique story to be told and experienced. The use of federal tax dollars and the fact that tree stumps were removed made the National Road different from other roads. Experiencing the road introduces local lore, such as the fact that Dublin was not named after the city in Ireland, but because travelers were "doublin' up" their oxen to pull their wagons up the hill that led into town. Even religious figures found their way along the road, like Henry Ward Beecher, whose first church was located just north of the National Road in Indianapolis.

Much of the pop culture of the 1920s had its founding along the road, including the Clabbergirl Flour Company and the original glass Coca-Cola bottle in Terre Haute. Of course, in Richmond, many outsiders may only know about Tom Raper and see the slew of billboards promoting the RV King along I-70, but when one gets off the highway and drives the byway, they may learn that jazz music found its early roots in the Richmond Gorge. Famed musicians Louis Armstrong and Hoagy Carmichael first recorded at the Starr-Gennett Studios in Richmond, and today there is a Walk of Fame that honors the well-known artists who recorded there. Also in Richmond, visitors will find the rehabilitated Richmond Depot designed by Daniel Burnham, the famed American architect who also designed the Flatiron Building in New York City and Union Station in Washington, DC, and was the chief architect for the Chicago World's Exposition in 1896 (also featured in the best selling novel *Devil in the White City*). This building sat vacant for almost three decades before Indiana Landmarks, the Indiana National Road Association, and the City of Richmond worked with Roger Richert, owner of the Richmond Furniture Gallery, to invest the needed money into restoring the building so that it may be adaptively reused.

Efforts such as these can be seen across the road still today with buildings and landscapes being protected, preserved, and reused to promote the National Road heritage. Festivals and events, such as the Lewisville Stoplight Festival, the Irvington Halloween Festival, and the National Road Yard Sale, are all events centered on the National Road.

The combination of sharing these stories beside historic photographs provides a unique opportunity to tell the story of the road and hopefully encourage appreciation and energy to preserve the buildings that laid the background for the stories. This book is intended to orient the reader to the heritage of the road through historic photographs of the architecture built along it and to showcase the common people whose ancestors were the early pioneers who settled the towns and farmed the fields. These were the people who were photographed living their daily lives and building a better future for their children.

This book also aims to open a window of understanding—to look at these structures not just as old buildings, but also as artifacts of the past, of which we are only custodians. The landscapes that separate these towns are not necessarily fields for future development of houses and big-box development, but they are part of local heritage steeped in farming and early settlement. We are responsible for the continued existence of these resources for people in the future to learn from and use.

By driving the Historic National Road, one may still experience firsthand a bit of the history that began when the United States was young. By reading these pages and viewing the photographs, hidden and unknown stories may reveal themselves and allow the history of the National Road and the United States to become richer.

The National Road is seen here as it appeared in 1816. Indiana's first roads were little more than paths made over time by the ramblings of wild animals leading to and from waterways. As the settlers entered the new frontier territory, these paths were expanded into roads. (Alan E. Hunter collection.)

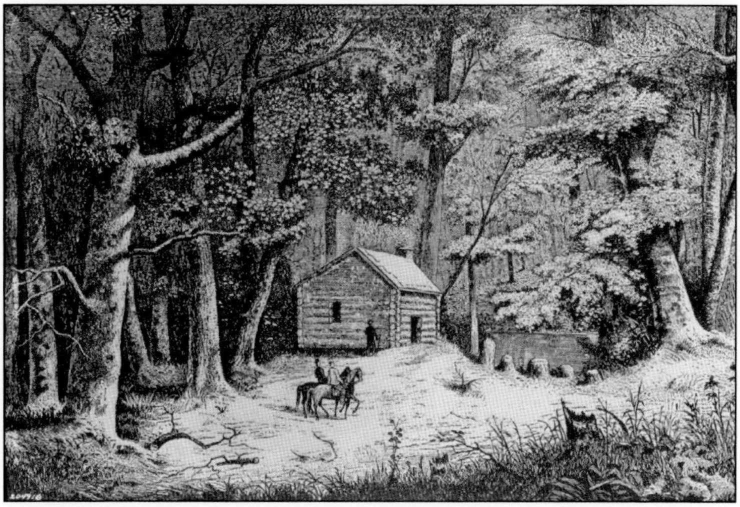

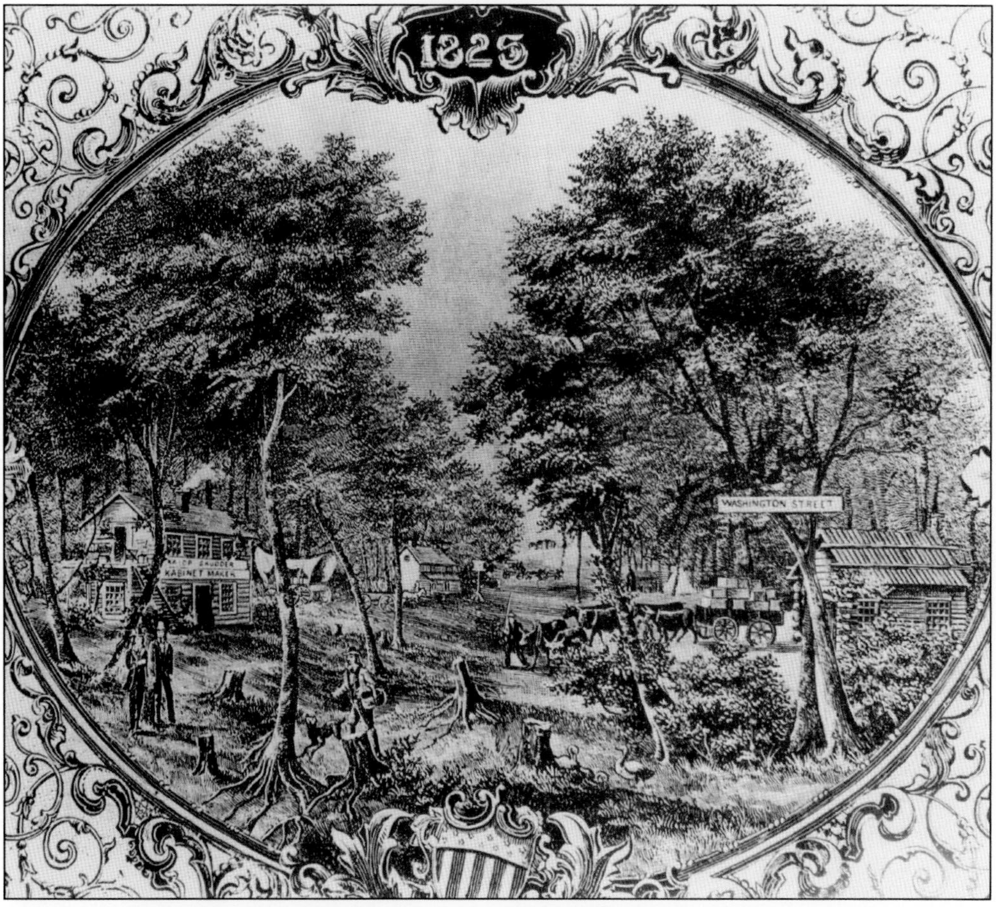

This is the National Road in 1825. Stories of pioneers literally cutting their way through the woods to build their homesteads are nearly as common as those decrying the "rivers of mud" that the few trails existing would become outside of summer months. (Alan E. Hunter collection.)

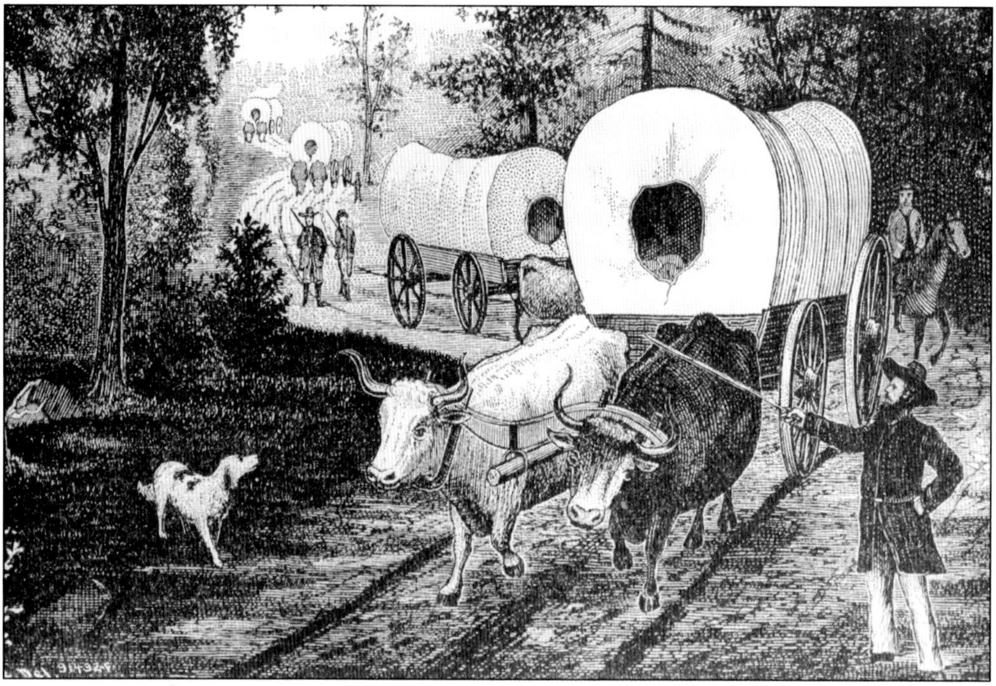

This view of the National Road is from 1827. The earliest roots of the Historic National Road can be traced to Richmond pioneer Robert Morrisson, founder and namesake of the Morrisson Library in Richmond. Morrisson created a gravel road from Richmond to Dayton, Ohio, known as the Richmond and Short Line Pike that roughly traced the early route of the National Road. (Alan E. Hunter collection.)

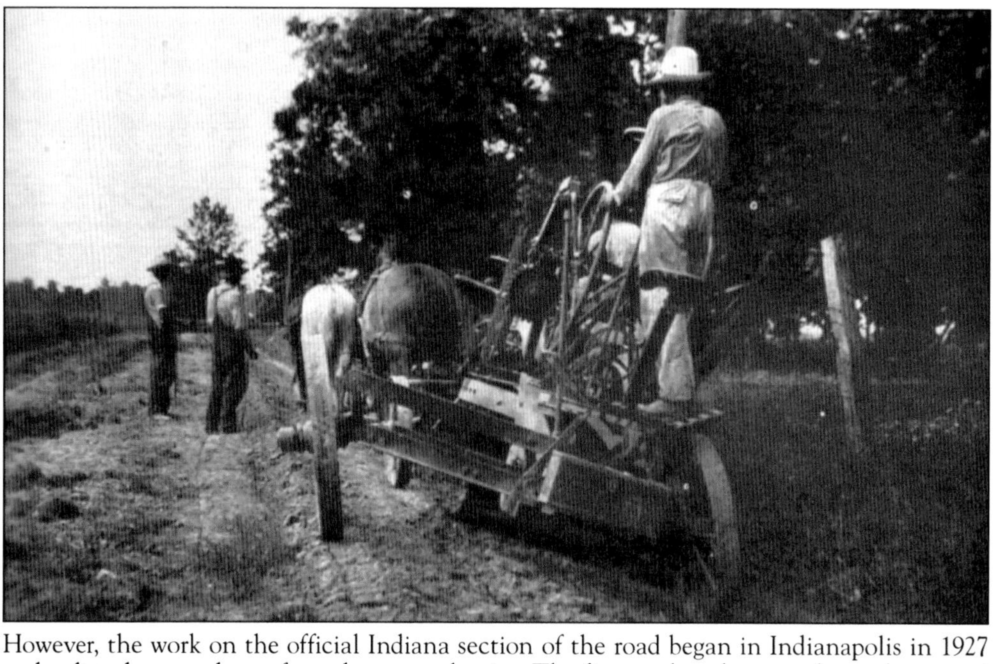

However, the work on the official Indiana section of the road began in Indianapolis in 1927 and radiated east and west from that central point. The first road graders were horse drawn and operated by two men with a team of horses. (Alan E. Hunter collection.)

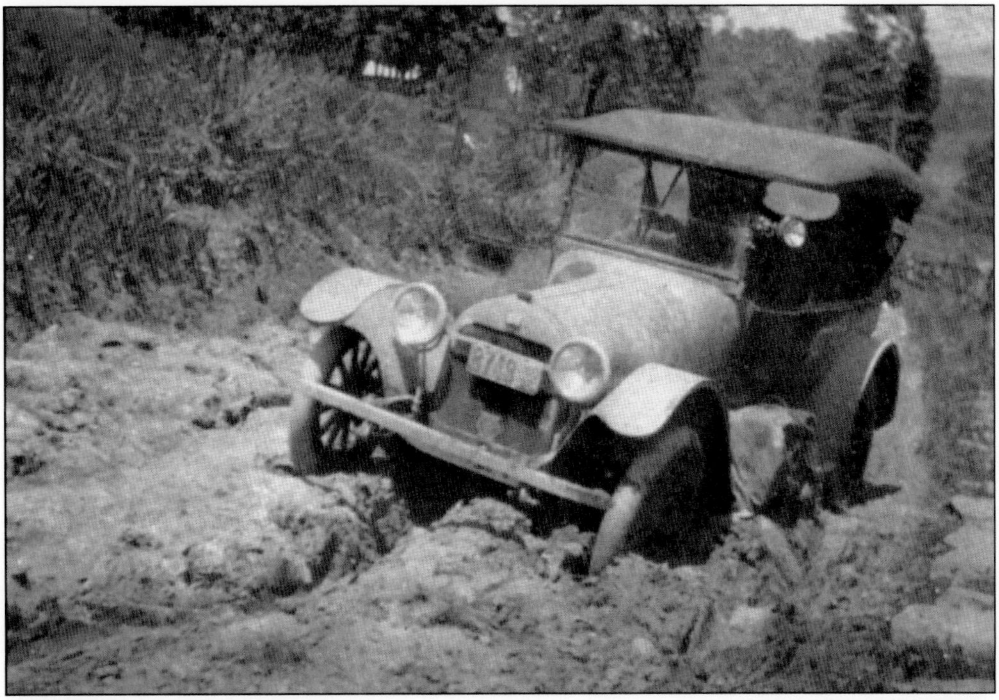

Early Indiana roads were simply ruts carved into the ground by generations of horses and wagons. Travel was brutal at best, and inclement weather often made roads impassable. The dawn of the 20th century saw the horse and buggy replaced by the automobile, and it was readily apparent that the old road was well past due for a major renovation. (Alan E. Hunter collection.)

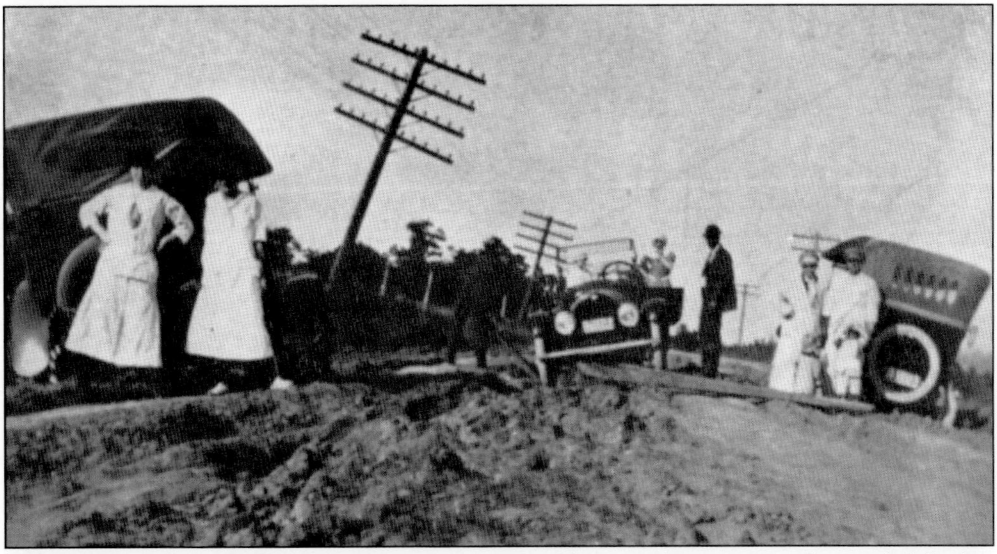

Before 1927, most of Indiana's roads were maintained by township trustees who graded ditches and did some dragging of the roadway bed to form a primitive grade but little else. In many spots along the pike, the wagon-wheel ruts were so deep that cars struggled to navigate them in fair weather and became hopelessly stuck whenever it rained. A popular chant about the National Road in Indiana went, "The roads are impassable, Hardly jackassable; I think those that travel 'em, Should turn out and gravel 'em." (Alan E. Hunter collection.)

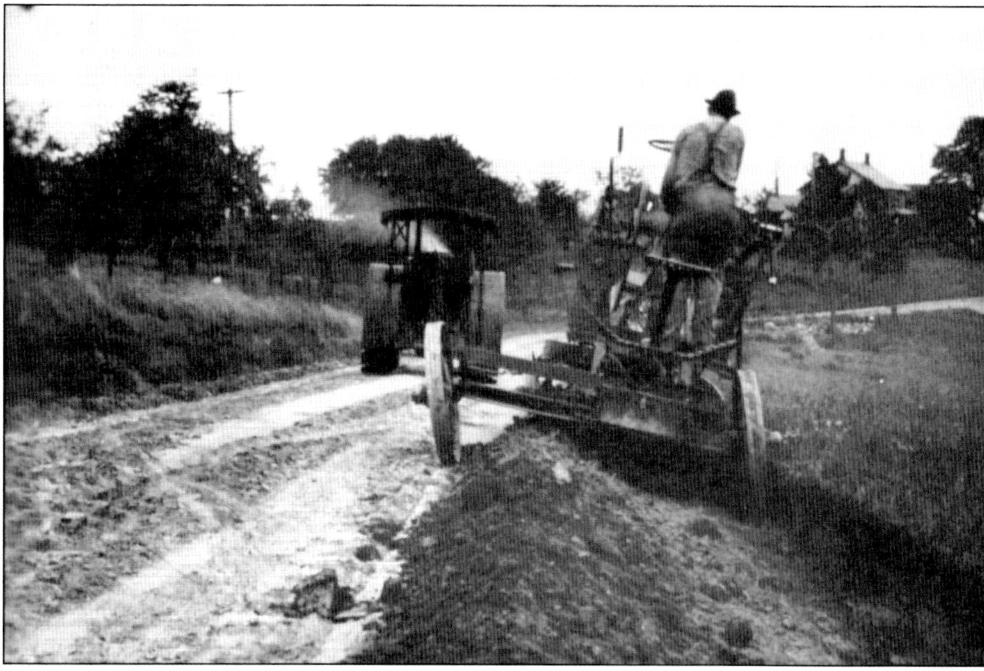

The rural National Road grading took place in the 1930s. The design of the road grader did not change much in a decade, with the only discernible change being a hitch welded to the tongue so that it could be pulled by a tractor instead of a team of horses. (Alan E. Hunter collection.)

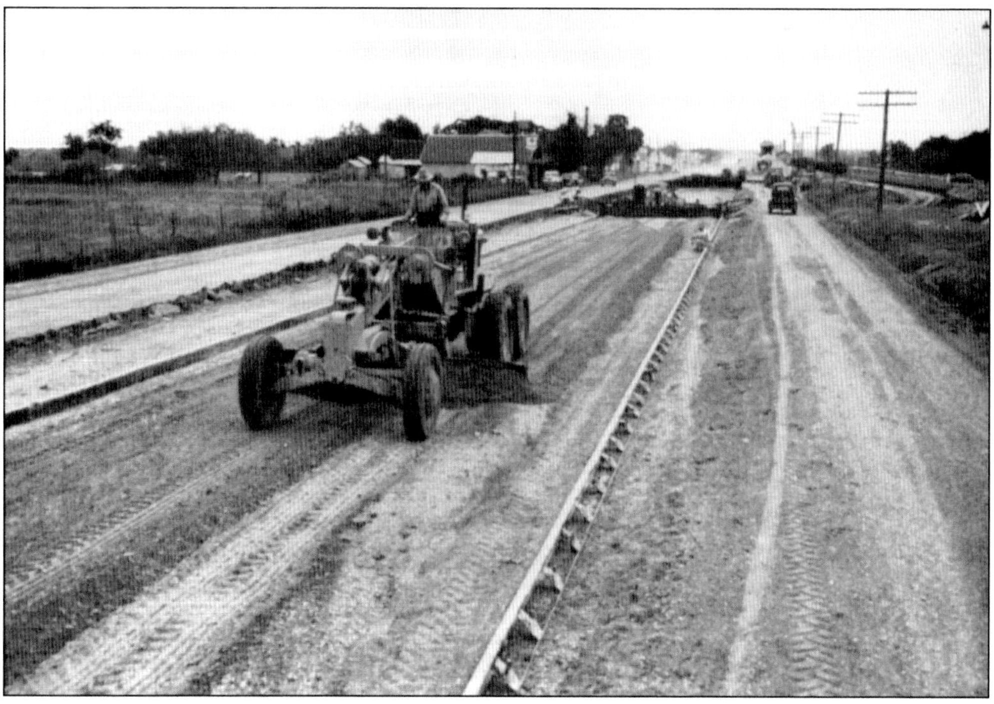

The urban National Road grading occurred in the 1940s. The Depression-era public works programs like the WPA and CCC stepped in to insure safer travel by rerouting and grading the National Road using the designs of trained civil engineers. (Alan E. Hunter collection.)

This is a World War II–era Highway 40 car window decal. (Alan E. Hunter collection.)

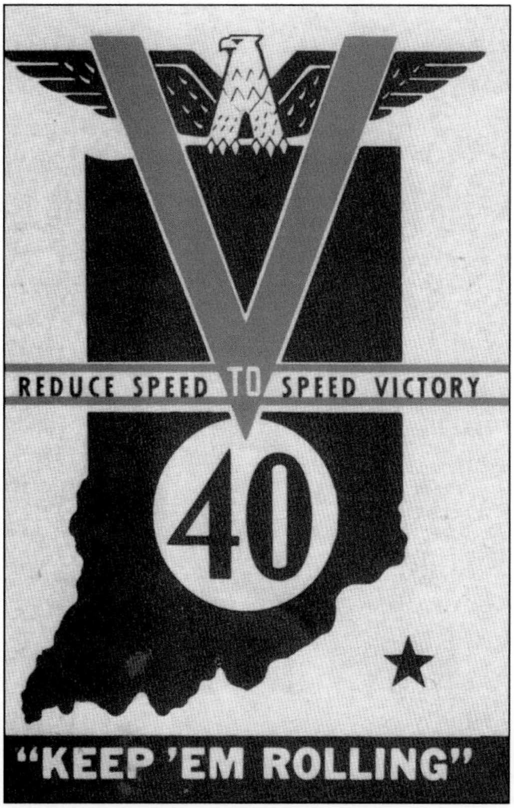

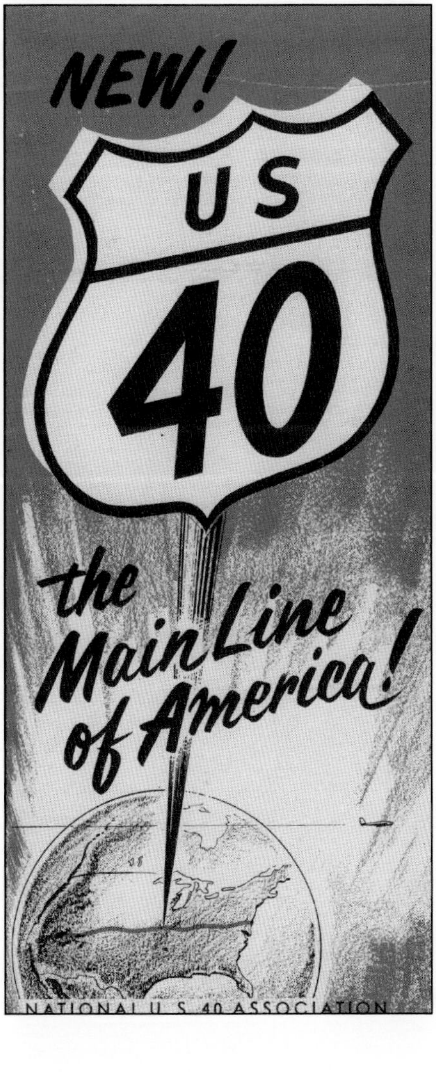

A 1950s traveler's brochure promotes the new coast-to-coast Highway 40. In 1926, US Highway 40 extended from San Francisco, California, to Atlantic City, New Jersey. The route was built on top of several older highways, most notably the National Road and Victory Highway. The western end has changed several times, and the route now ends just outside of Salt Lake City, Utah. (Alan E. Hunter collection.)

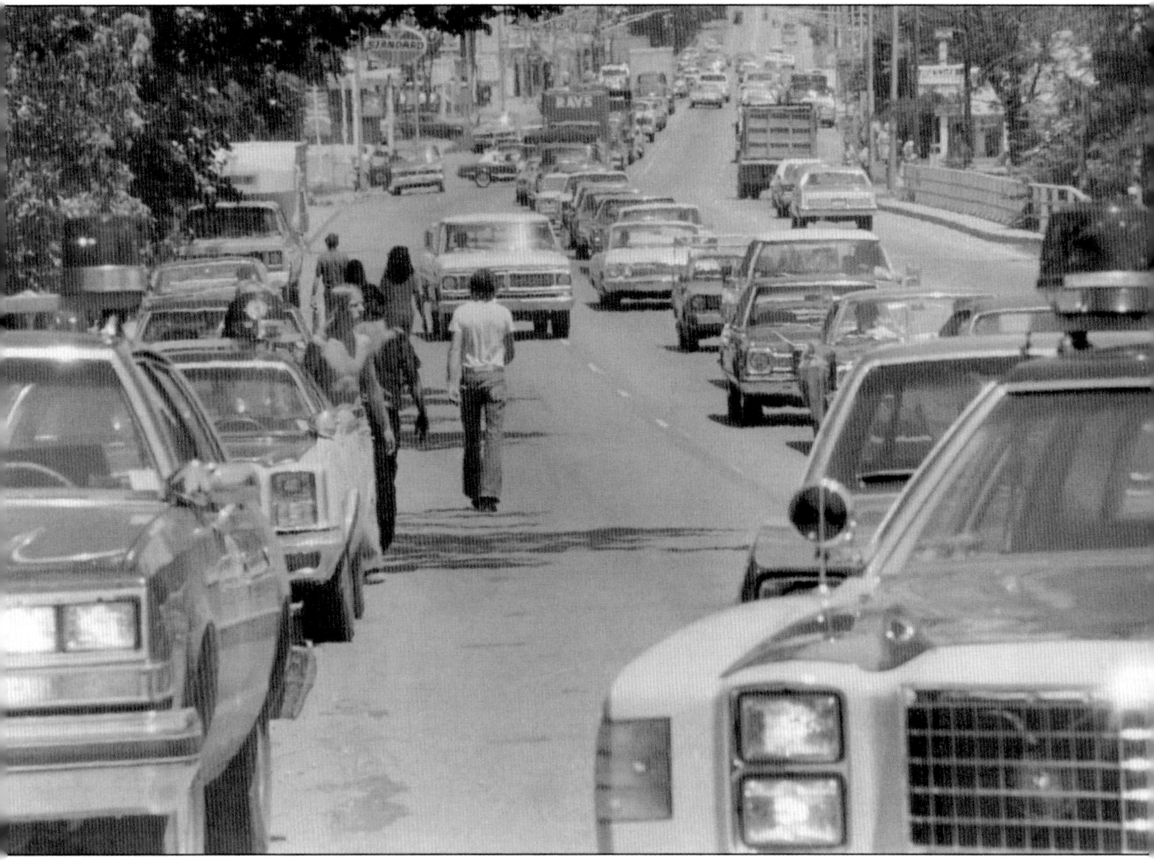

Traffic is seen flowing on the new National Road in the 1970s. True to its motto, "Cross Roads of America," Indiana has more miles of interstate highway per square mile than any other state. The Indiana state motto can be traced back to the early-1800s National Road. Today, more major highways intersect in Indiana than in any other state. (Alan E. Hunter collection.)

One

Richmond to Centerville

Once the cradle of early jazz recordings at the Starr-Gennett recording studio, the home of the Daniel Burnham–designed railroad station, and the Eli Coffin House, the site of an elaborate history of the Underground Railroad with Quaker roots, Richmond's past runs deep and offers much more than the billboards that one would see as he or she passed Richmond on Interstate 70. While some landmarks have been lost, such as the natural and cultural landscape of Hayes Arboretum along the Historic National Road, this community has an incredible amount of historic architecture remaining. Advocacy efforts by merchant owners and preservationists in the Depot District and along downtown Main Street have been preserving and developing the economic viability of the community.

Platted in 1814, Centerville is the town of arches and remains one of the best examples of a historic pike town along the Historic National Road. Between 1820 and 1836, buildings originally constructed farther off the road were added on to bring the front of the homes right up to the edge. This was done in an effort to have businesses serve travelers along the National Road. In order to access the original buildings in the rear, owners constructed arches for access, and these have become a strong part to the town's identity. The town was also the county seat for a time until the decision was made to move it to Richmond. Citizens of Centerville did not appreciate this, and evidence of their attempt to stop officials from moving the county records remains today at the old sheriff's residence, where one can see cannonball holes from "Black Betty," the town's three-pound cannon. Despite their attempts, the county seat was moved to Richmond in 1873, but the community remains an important stop along the Historic National Road.

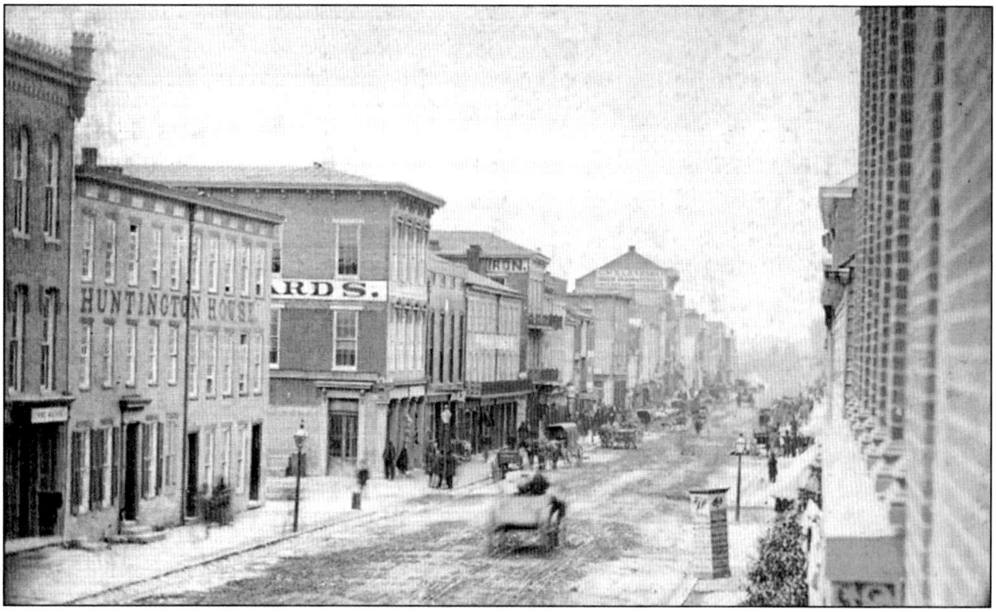

An early carte de visite of the National Road in Richmond is depicted here. The sign atop the tallest building in the distance, at 31 Main Street, reads, "G.W. Barnes & Co. Seeds, Grains & Produce-Groceries." The Galt House and a billiards parlor are to the right of the Huntington House. A four-sided kiosk, with two Union eagles near the top and headlines from the Civil War, is seen in the lower right. The stamp on the back reads, "Specaltie [*sic*] Mote & Swains Star Gallery 102 & 104 Main Street, Richmond, Ind." (Courtesy Mick Kissick.)

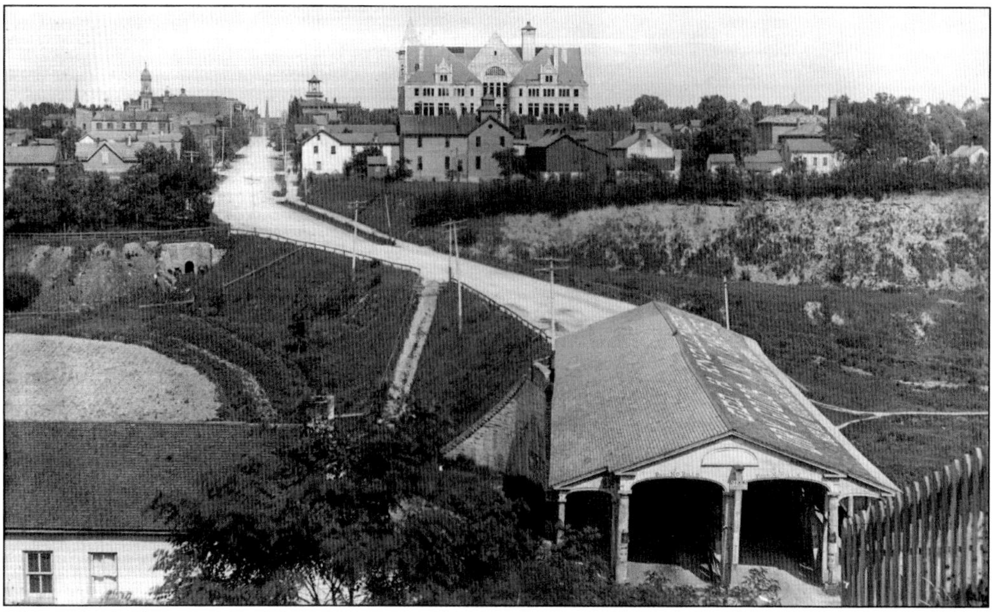

This c. 1893 photograph of the Wayne County Courthouse is from the west bank of the Whitewater Gorge with the cupola of the old courthouse visible behind it. In the foreground lies the distinctive covered bridge featuring two-way tunnels, as well as a covered pedestrian walkway attached to the side. An ad for the "George H. Knollenberg Dry Goods Store" in Richmond can be seen on the wooden shingles atop the roof of the bridge. (Courtesy Morrisson-Reeves Library.)

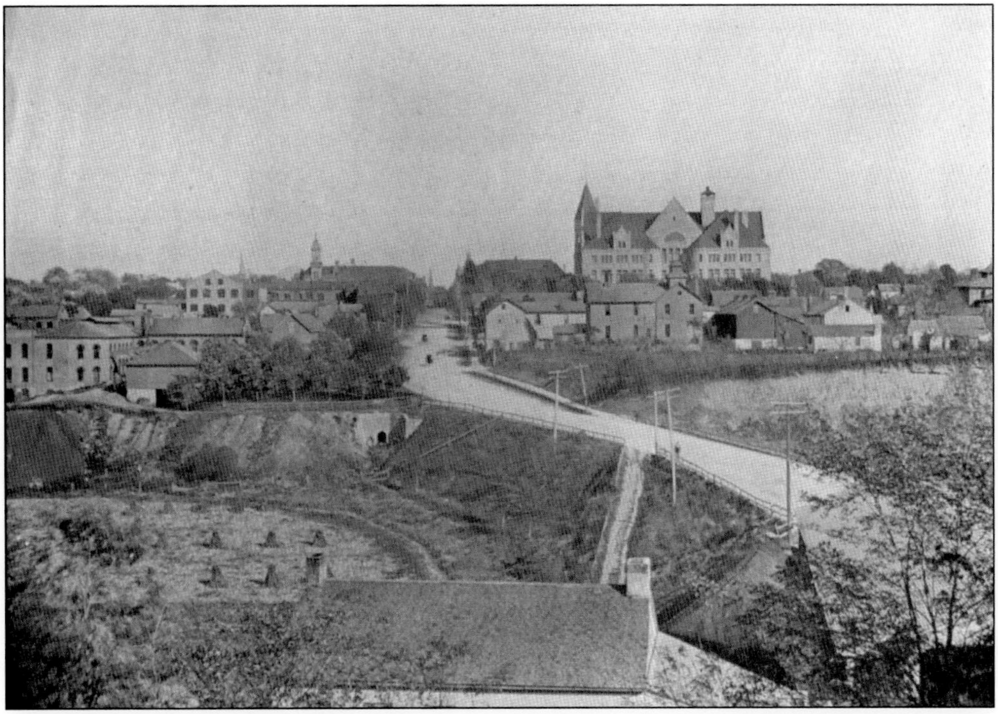

This Dalbey photograph of Main Street, or the National Road, and the Wayne County Courthouse was taken from the west bank of the Whitewater Gorge in 1896. (Courtesy Morrisson-Reeves Library.)

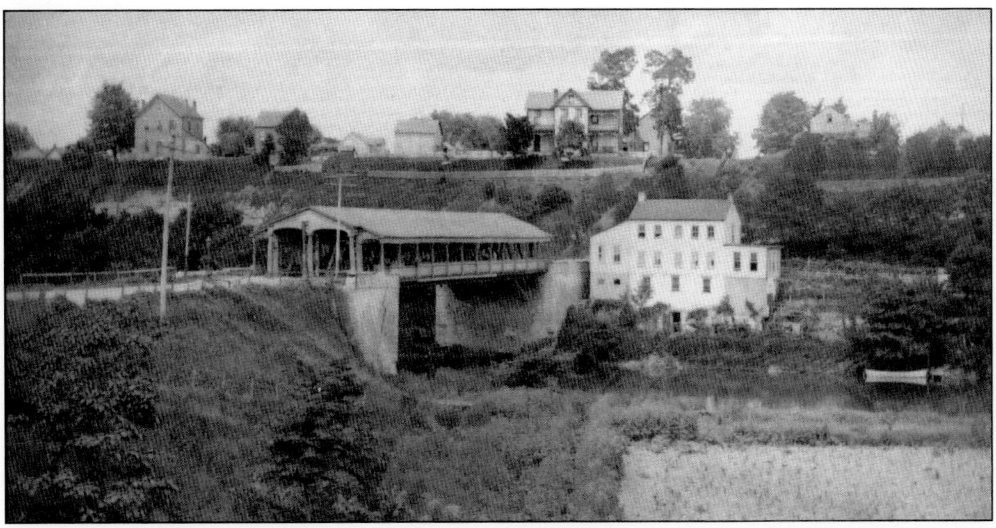

The National Bridge over Whitewater Gorge is pictured from the east bank looking west around 1893. (Courtesy Morrisson-Reeves Library.)

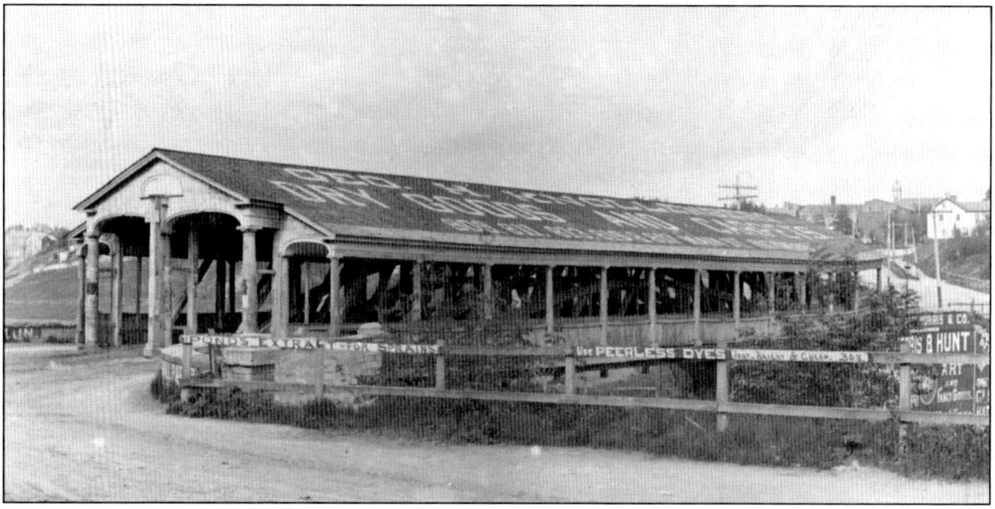

This c. 1893 photograph of the National Bridge looks out at the Whitewater Gorge and back towards Richmond with the cupola of the old courthouse visible in the background. Ironically, above each entrance are signs reading, "Post No Bills," yet the pillars are festooned with posters pasted onto the front, and the rails of the fences leading up to the bridge are covered with ads and hand-painted signs. An ad for "George H. Knollenberg Dry Goods Store" is visible atop the bridge's roof. (Courtesy Morrisson-Reeves Library.)

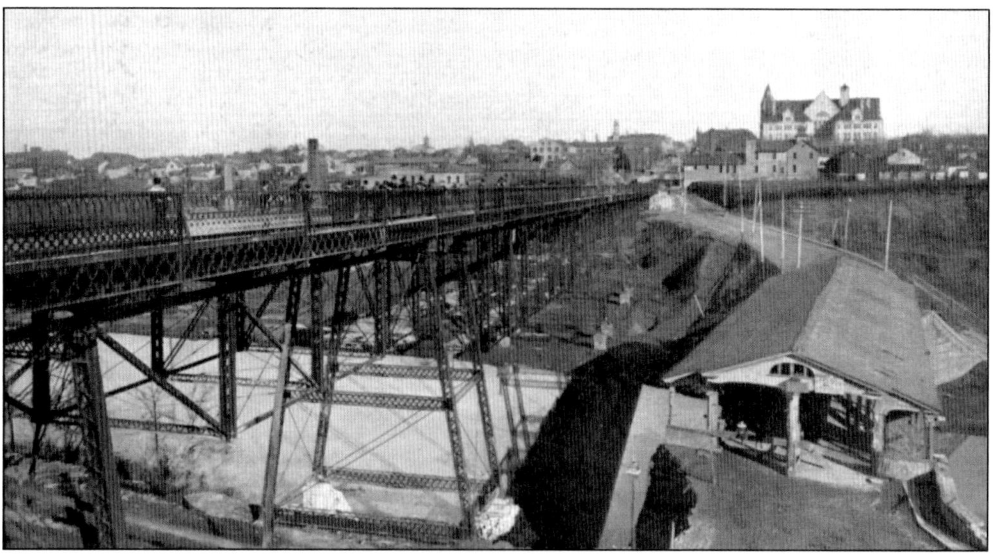

This 1906 Dalbey photograph is captioned, "Main Street Bridge-Old National Bridge," and overlooks the Whitewater Gorge. The bridge replaced the double-tunneled covered bridge that can be seen to the right. (Courtesy Morrisson-Reeves Library.)

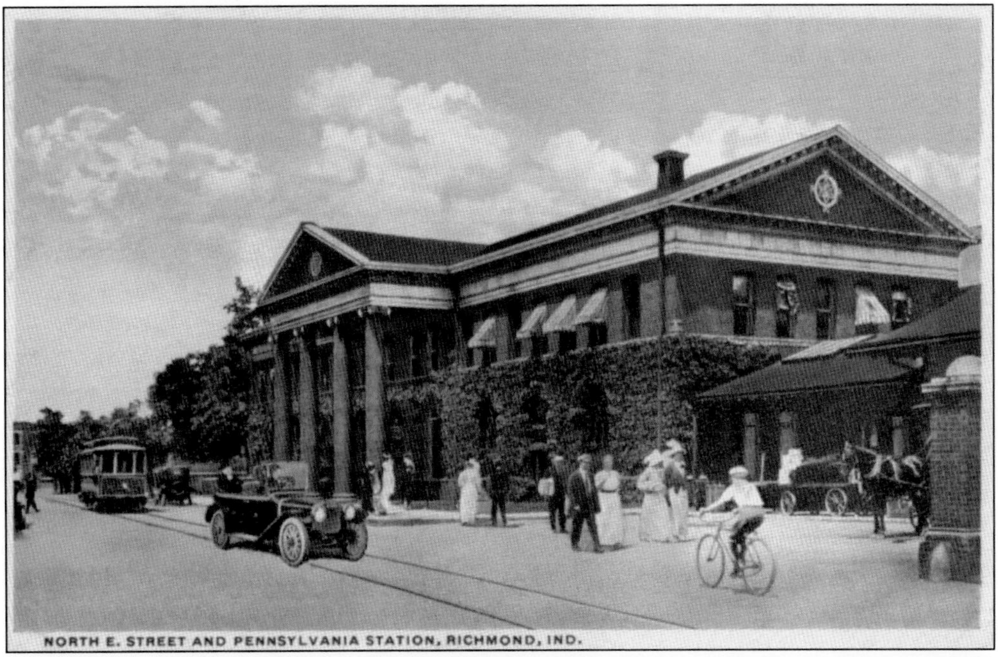

Pictured is a c. 1915 postcard of "North E. Street and Pennsylvania Station, Richmond, Ind." Known as the Richmond Depot, the building was designed by Chicago architect Daniel Burnham, who was perhaps best known for designing the Rookery Building in Chicago and the Flatiron Building in New York. The depot is the focal point of the Depot District. Roger Richert, owner of the Richmond Furniture Gallery, rehabilitated the depot in 2010–2011 after the landmark sat vacant for over 25 years. (Courtesy Morrisson-Reeves Library.)

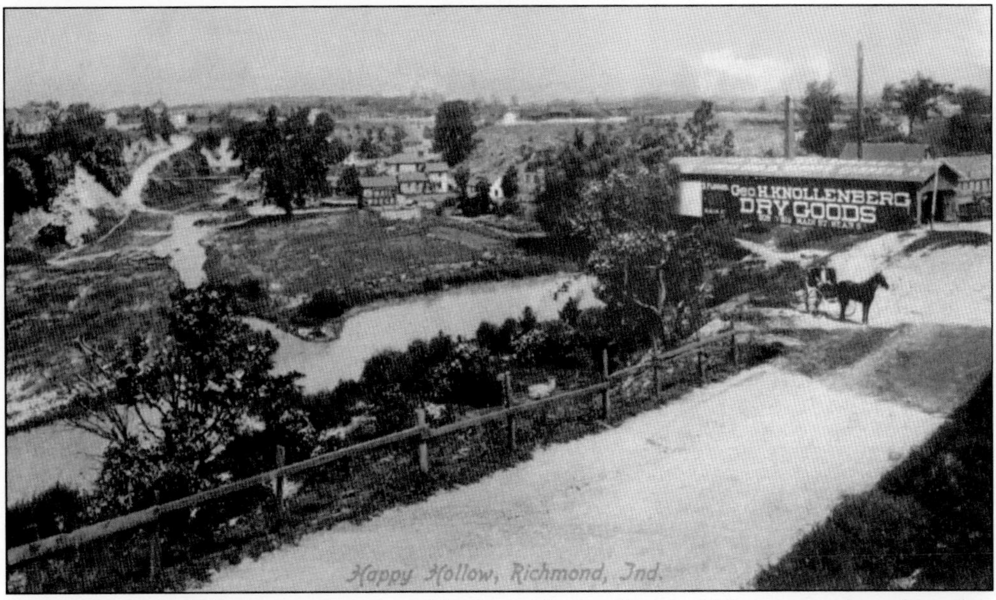

A c. 1910 postcard, displaying the covered bridge at the confluence of the west and east branches to form the west fork of the Whitewater River that flows through downtown Richmond, Indiana, is captioned, "Happy Hollow, Richmond, Ind." The bridge has advertising for the "George H. Knollenberg Dry Goods Store" at 809 to 815 Main Street. (Courtesy Morrisson-Reeves Library.)

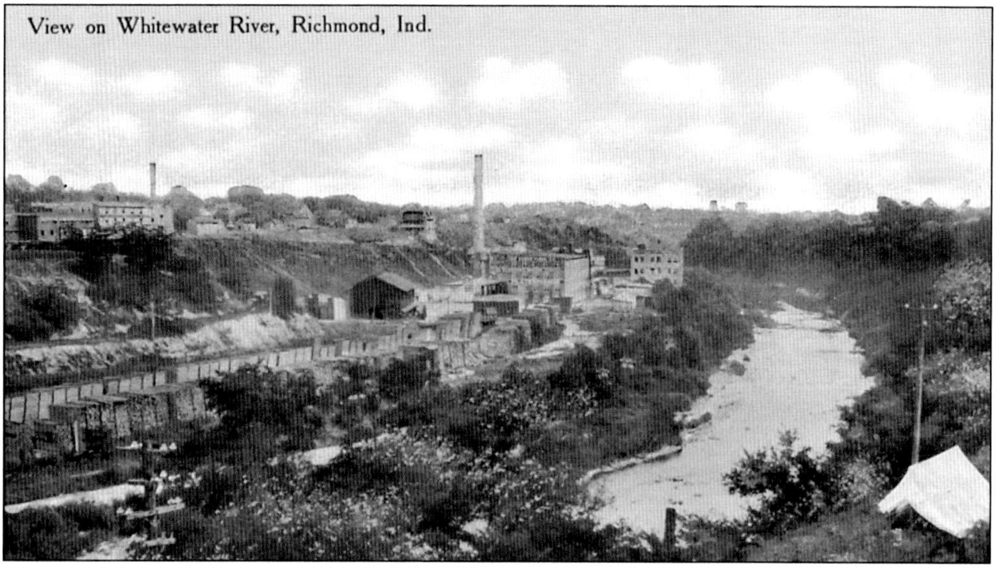

This c. 1910 postcard states, "View on the Whitewater River, Richmond, Ind.," shows the Starr Piano Company in the center. (Courtesy Morrisson-Reeves Library.)

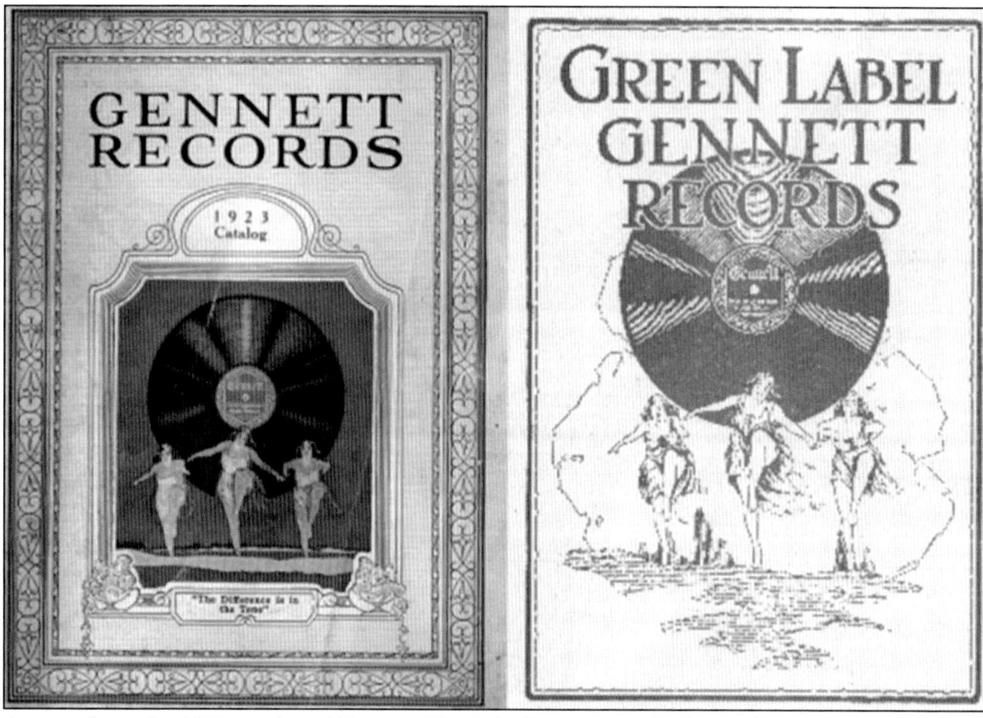

A cover from the 1923 catalog of Gennett Records Company in Richmond reads, "The difference is in the tone." Gennett Records was founded by the Starr Piano Company and released its first records in October 1917. Gennett is best remembered for the wealth of early jazz talent recorded on the label, including sessions by Jelly Roll Morton, Louis Armstrong, and Hoagy Carmichael. Gennett also recorded early blues artists such as Blind Lemon Jefferson, Charlie Patton, and Big Bill Broonzy, as well as early "hillbilly" or Country performers such as Fiddlin' Doc Roberts and Gene Autry. (Alan E. Hunter collection.)

A c. 1906 postcard shows the "Reid Memorial United Presbyterian Church Richmond, Ind." The church, located at Eleventh and North A Streets in Richmond, was dedicated on May 13, 1906. Daniel G. Reid gave it in memory of his parents, Daniel Reid and Anna Gray Dougan Reid. The building cost $295,000 (approximately $7 million today) to build. All of the windows were created by Louis Comfort Tiffany. Reid is thought to be one of 10 churches in the country with all Tiffany windows, which cost between $2,000 and $3,000 each at the time of installation. (Courtesy Morrisson-Reeves Library.)

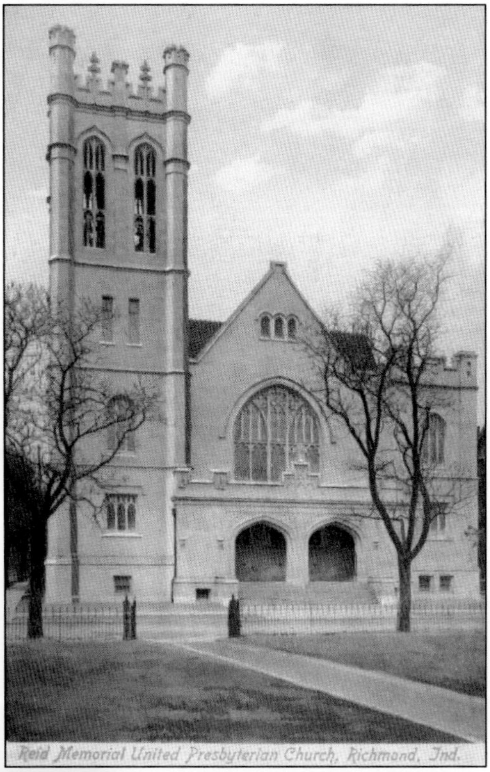

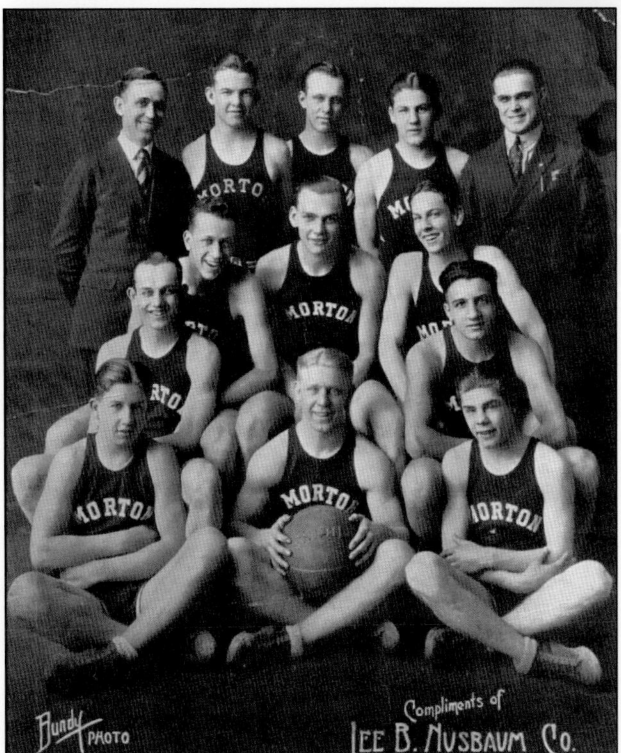

The back of this sepia cabinet photograph states, "Morton Basket Ball Team 1923–24" from "Bundy Photograph Compliments of Lee B. Nusbaum Co." The well-made premium photograph was given away to customers of Nusbaum's Department Store in Richmond. It identifies the players as, from left to right, (first row) Porter, Kessler, and Ewbanks; (second row) Price, Plasterer, Krueger, Johanning, and Rizio, captain; (third row) manager Clevenger, Williams, Muey, Reeg, and coach Little. It is a perfect example of just how important basketball has been, and still is, to Indiana. Prior to 1939, the Richmond Red Devils were known as Morton High School in honor of Indiana Civil War Gov. Oliver P. Morton. (Alan E. Hunter collection.)

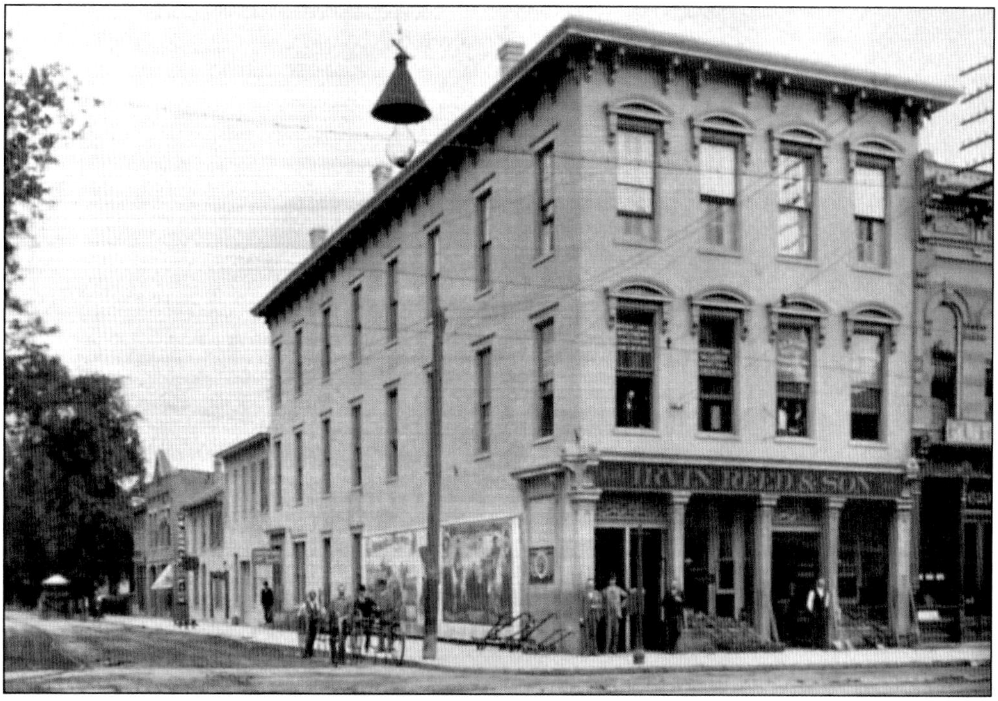

This 1896 Dalbey photograph shows the Irvin Reed & Son store specializing in, according to the back, "Hardware, Glass & Farming Implements-Established 1857." It was located at 631 and 622 Main Street in Richmond. The side of the building has two large posters promoting the upcoming May 7 appearance of the Buffalo Bill Wild West Show. (Courtesy Morrisson-Reeves Library.)

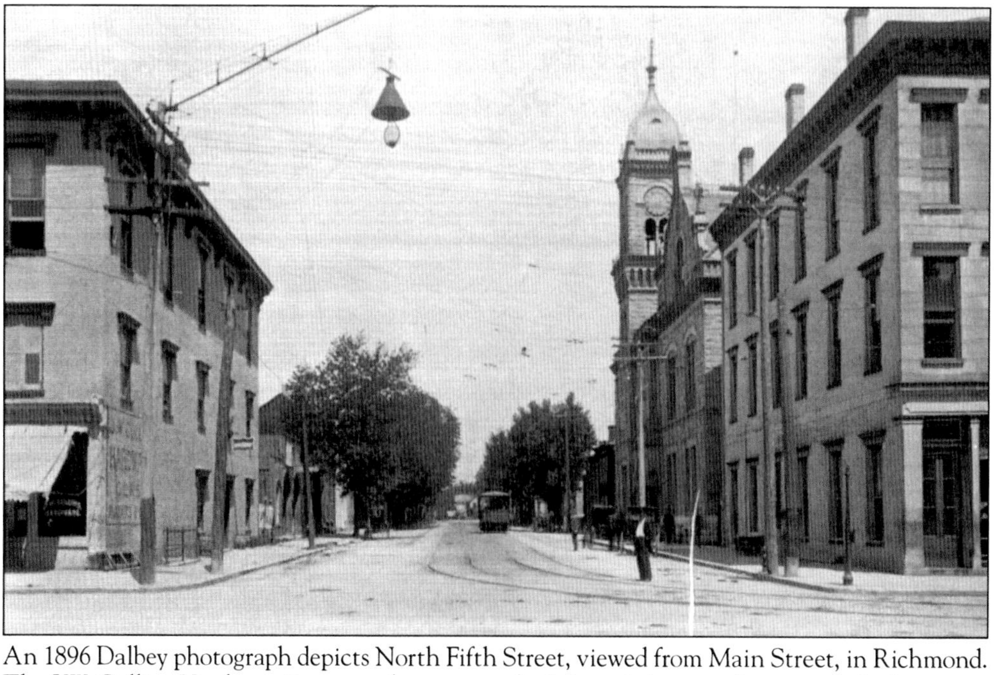

An 1896 Dalbey photograph depicts North Fifth Street, viewed from Main Street, in Richmond. The J.W. Collins Hardware Store can be seen on the left, and the courthouse and clock tower is visible on the right. (Courtesy Morrisson-Reeves Library.)

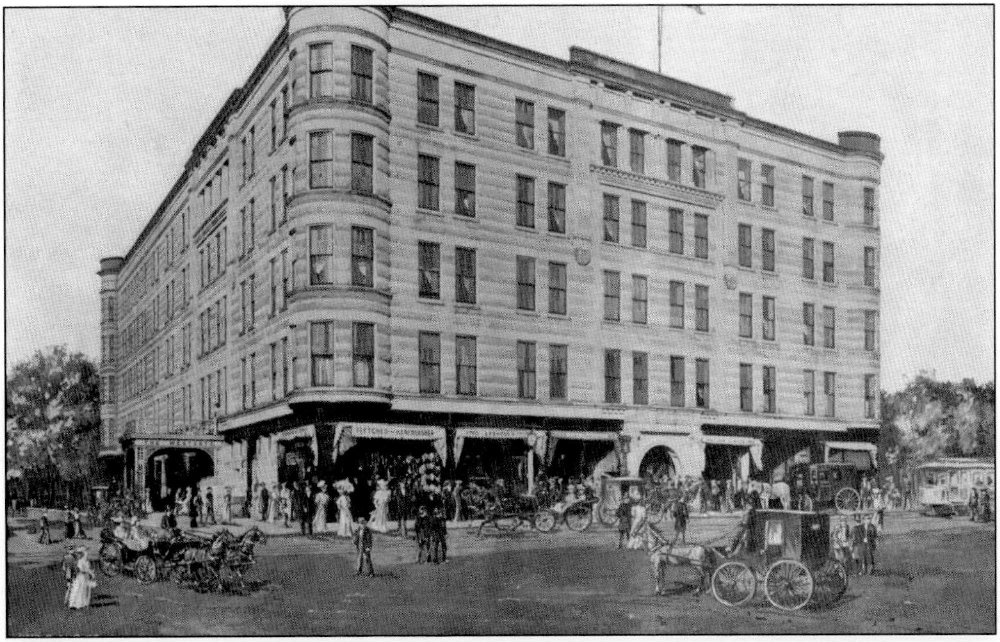

Pictured in 1906, a Dalbey photograph states that this is the "Westcott Hotel Silloway & Gay, Proprietors. Geo. J. Gay, Manager," which stood on the corner of Tenth and Main Streets in Richmond. Designed by W.S. Kauffman, the Westcott was intended to be the premier hotel of Indiana in its heyday. The grand opening was September 10, 1895. J.M. Westcott, an early Richmond business leader, was the man for whom the hotel was named. The Westcott closed in 1976 and was razed in 1977. (Courtesy Morrisson-Reeves Library.)

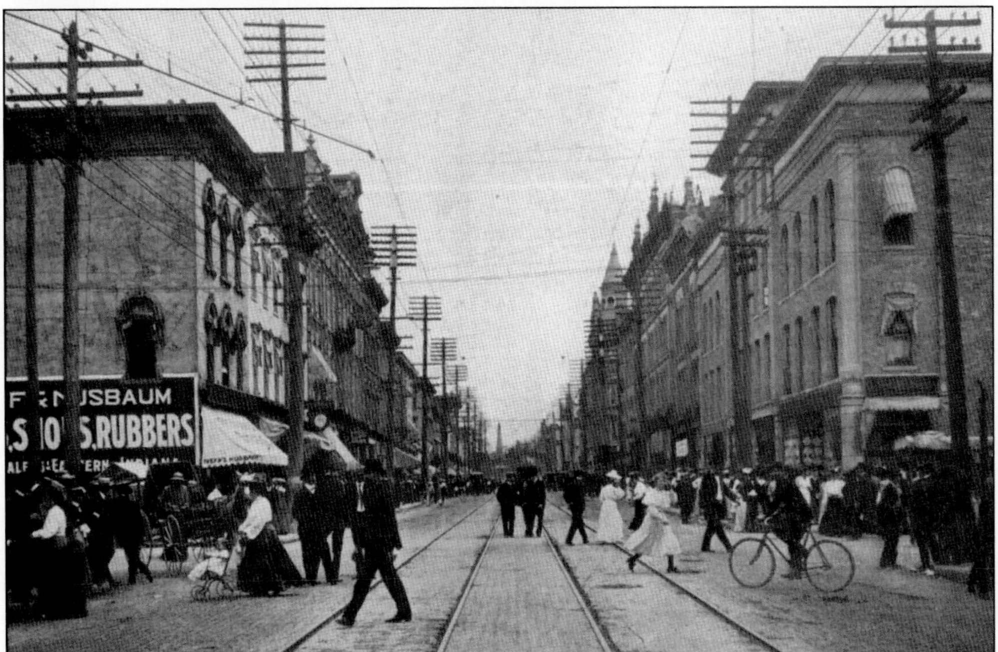

Another 1906 Dalbey photograph depicts Main Street looking east from Seventh Street in Richmond. (Courtesy Morrisson-Reeves Library.)

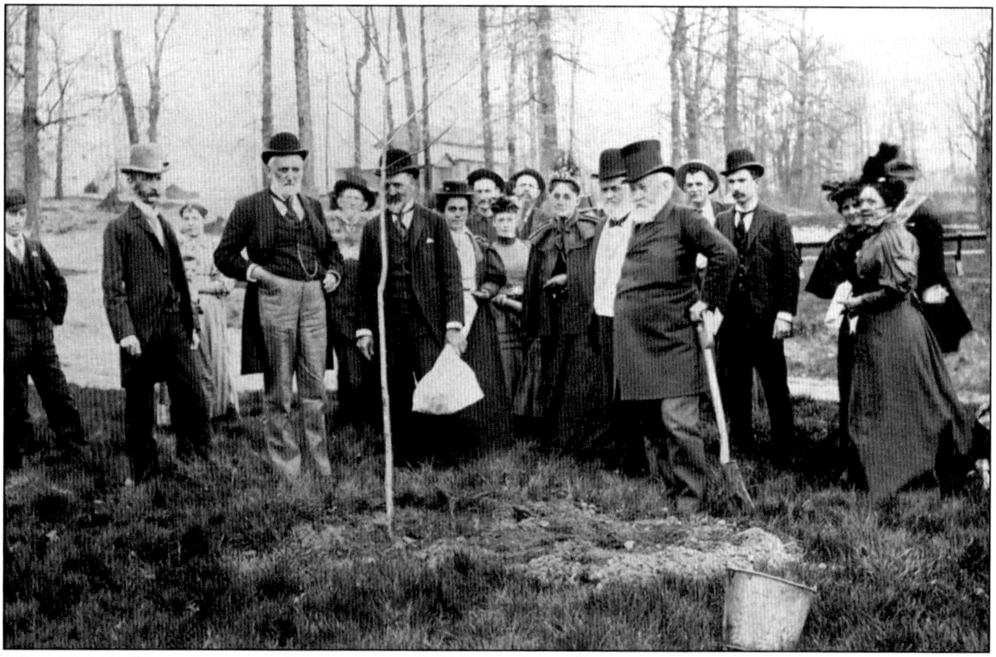

This 906 Dalbey photograph is captioned, "Tree Planted in Glen Miller Park by Benj. Harrison, April 25, 1895." In 1895, Harrison spent four months in Richmond as a lawyer representing the heirs of Richmond banker James L. Morrisson; it was the longest 19th-century jury trial in America. During the trial, Harrison planted a white ash tree near the Glen Miller Park pond on April 25, 1895. For Richmond's bicentennial in 2006, a new plaque was put at the tree and a new tulip poplar planted nearby by Harrison's great-grandson, Dr. Benjamin Harrison Walker. (Courtesy Morrisson-Reeves Library.)

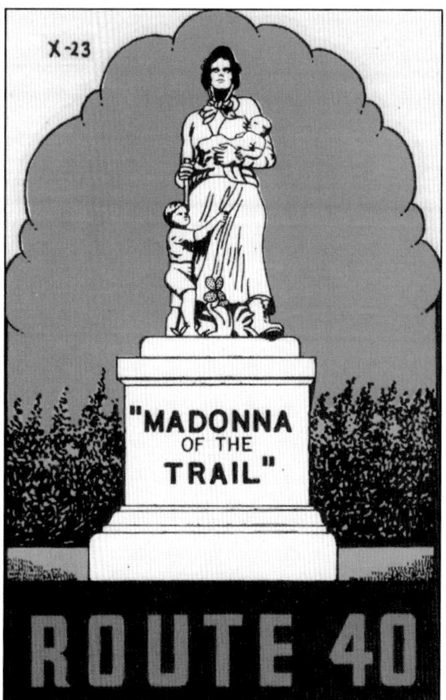

A 1950s decal shows the *Madonna of the Trail* statue that stands at the entrance of Glen Miller Park at the intersection of the National Road and North Twenty-second Street. The memorial was specifically chosen to rest at the site of the National Road's first tollgate, which was erected in about 1850. In commemoration of pioneer mothers of the covered wagon days, this statue is the ninth of 12 links in the Great National Shrine erected by the Daughters of the American Revolution along the National Road Trail (US 40) from Cumberland, Maryland, to Upland, California. (Alan E. Hunter collection.)

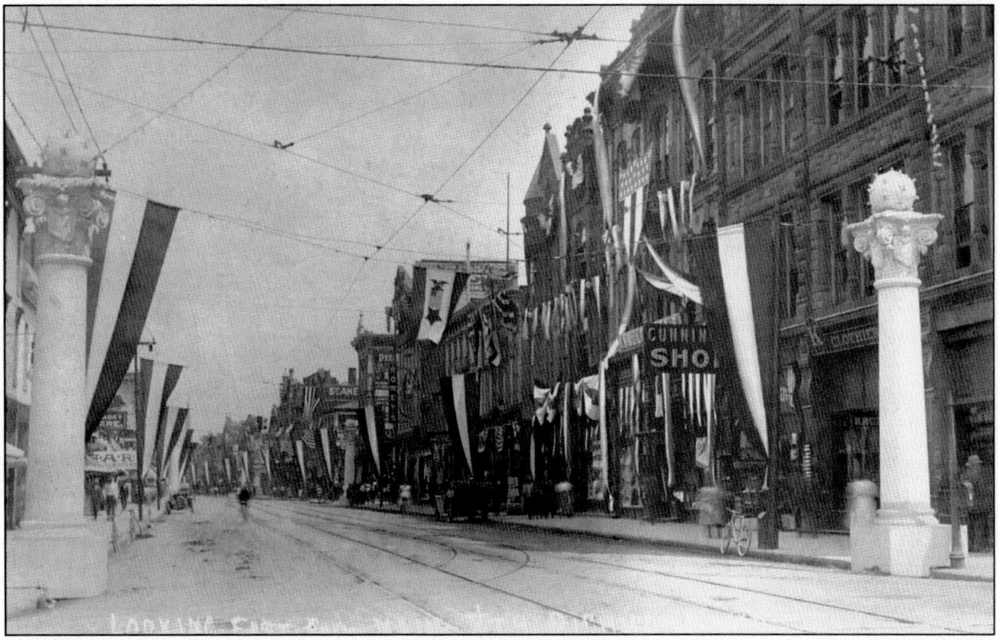

A c. 1911 postcard states, "Looking East from Main & 8th Street Richmond, Ind.," and shows the street decorated for a 1911 Grand Army of the Republic (GAR) Parade of former Civil War soldiers. The interurban tracks can be seen in the center of the road. (Courtesy Morrisson-Reeves Library.)

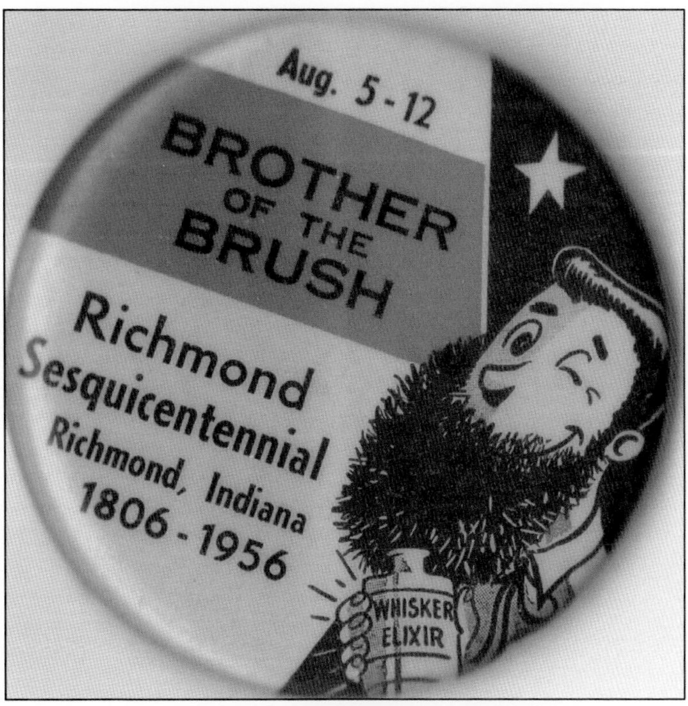

This is a 1956 Richmond, Indiana, sesquicentennial celebration pin. (Alan E. Hunter collection.)

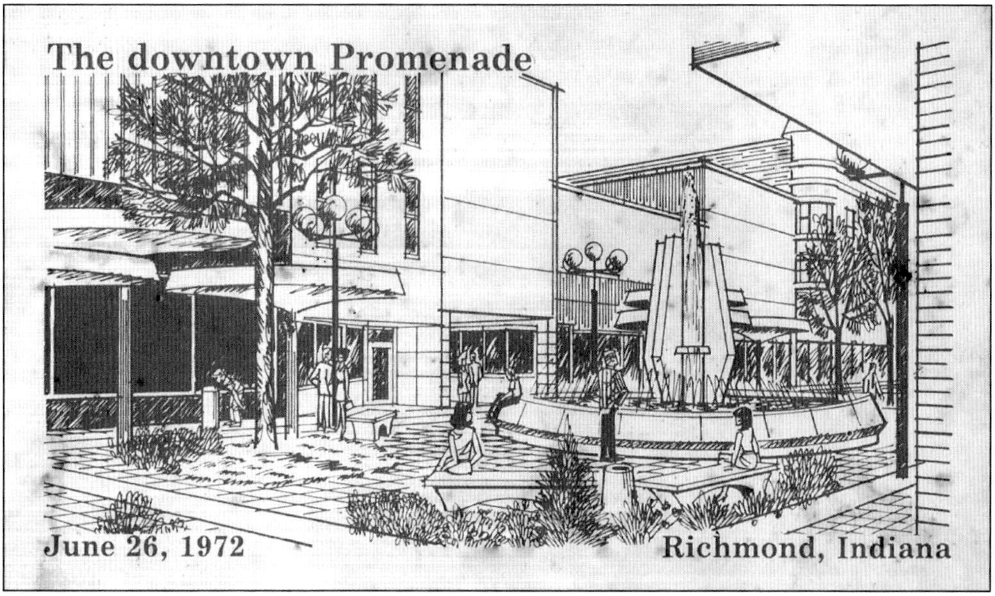

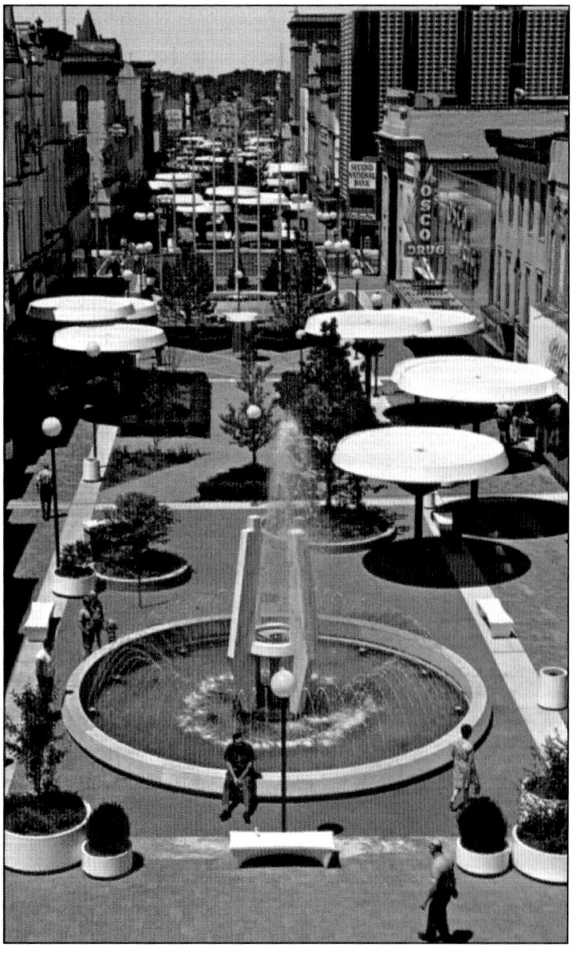

Shown here is a souvenir playing card from the official grand-opening celebration of the promenade in Richmond, Indiana, on June 26, 1972. On Saturday, April 6, 1968, in downtown Richmond, a double explosion occurred at 1:47 p.m., killing 41 people and injured more than 150. The first explosion was due to natural gas leaking from one or more faulty transmission lines under the Marting Arms Sporting Goods store, located at the intersection of Sixth and Main Streets. A secondary explosion was caused by gunpowder stored inside the building. (Alan E. Hunter collection.)

This postcard depicts the promenade in Richmond, Indiana, with Osco Drugs and Richmond's Second National Bank visible in the upper right corner. (Alan E. Hunter collection.)

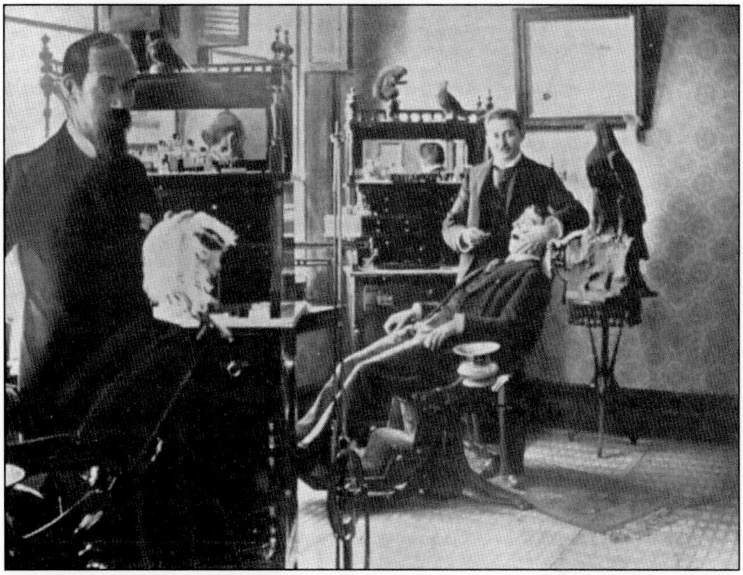

The interior of Wilson & Pierce dentist office, located over 830 Main Street in Richmond, is seen in this 1896 Dalbey photograph. (Courtesy Morrisson-Reeves Library.)

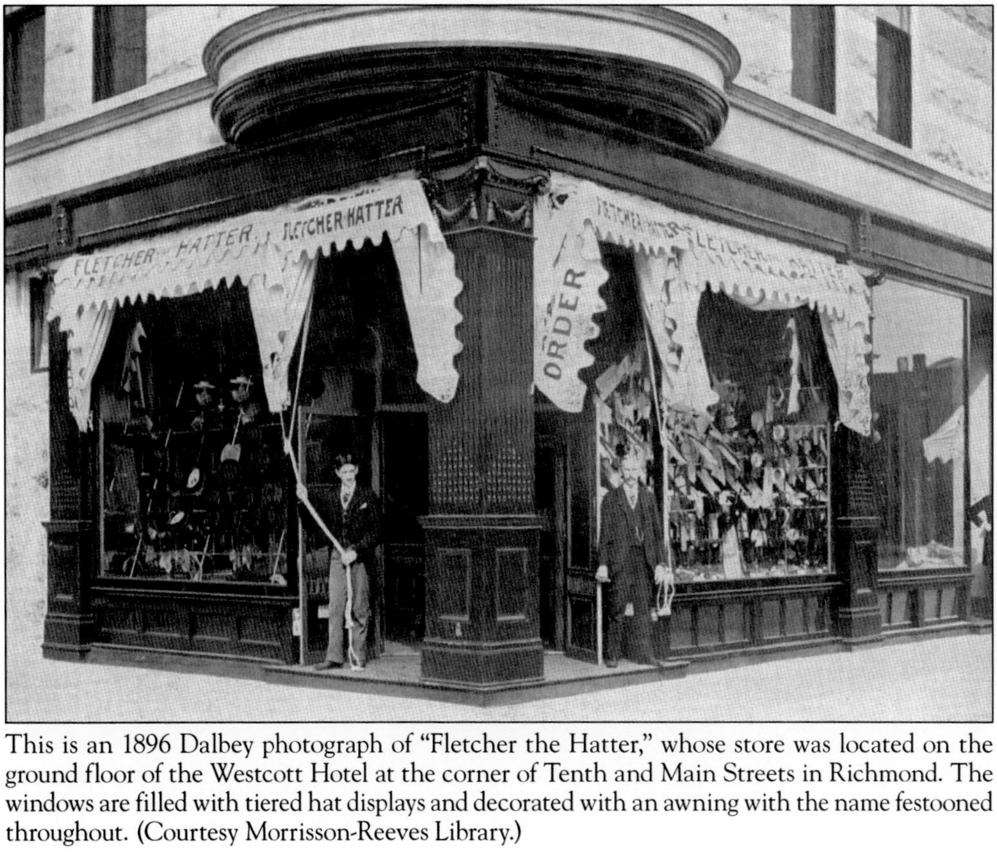

This is an 1896 Dalbey photograph of "Fletcher the Hatter," whose store was located on the ground floor of the Westcott Hotel at the corner of Tenth and Main Streets in Richmond. The windows are filled with tiered hat displays and decorated with an awning with the name festooned throughout. (Courtesy Morrisson-Reeves Library.)

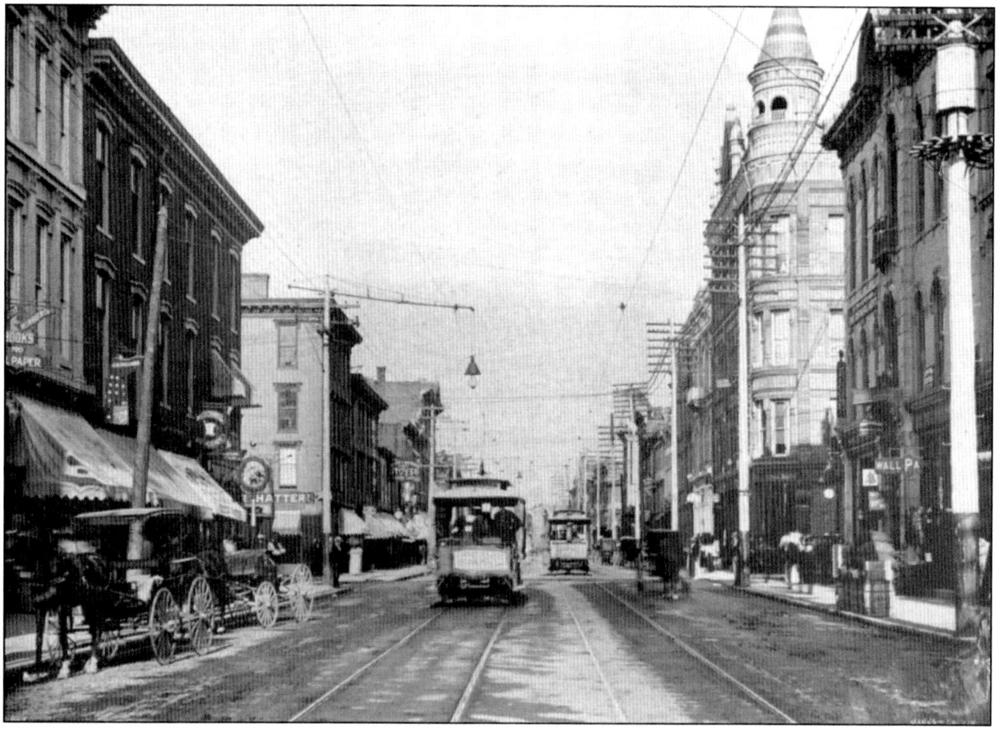

An 1896 Dalbey photograph captures the Main Street Trolley chugging down the National Road viewed looking east from Eighth Street in Richmond. The sides of the buildings have many great 3-D occupational signs for boot makers, pharmacists, and watchmakers. (Courtesy Morrisson-Reeves Library.)

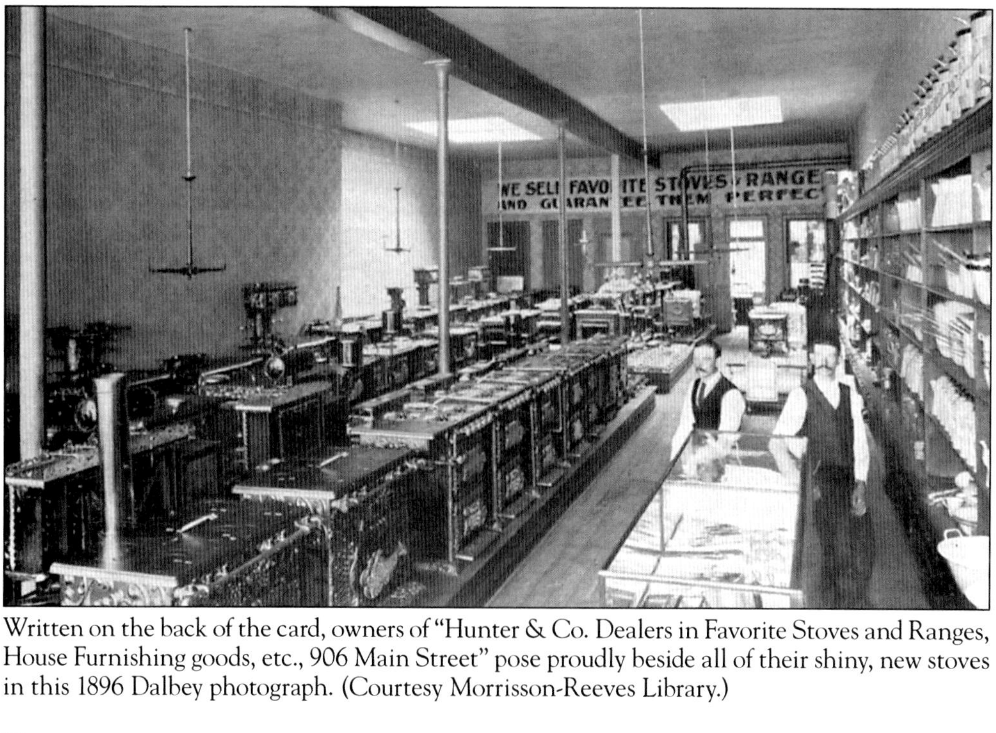

Written on the back of the card, owners of "Hunter & Co. Dealers in Favorite Stoves and Ranges, House Furnishing goods, etc., 906 Main Street" pose proudly beside all of their shiny, new stoves in this 1896 Dalbey photograph. (Courtesy Morrisson-Reeves Library.)

In this 1896 Dalbey photograph, the owner of W.L. Morgan's Daily Market, at 929 Main Street, poses outside beside his apron-clad employees. (Courtesy Morrisson-Reeves Library.)

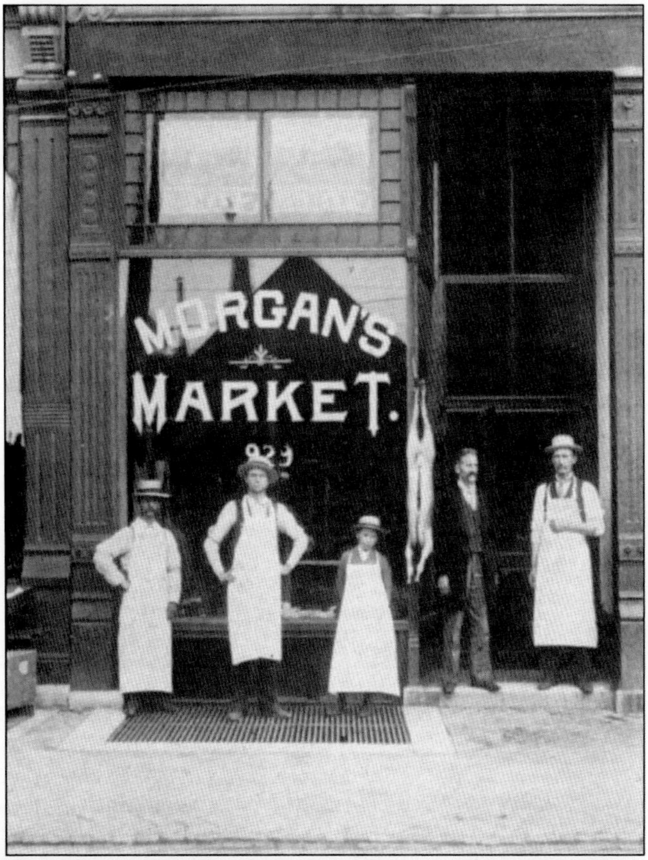

The sign above the door of grocer Van D. Brown, located at 931 Main Street, reads "Bee Hive Grocery," and five men are posing outside, each holding a large, unwrapped turkey carcass in this 1896 Dalbey photograph. (Courtesy Morrisson-Reeves Library.)

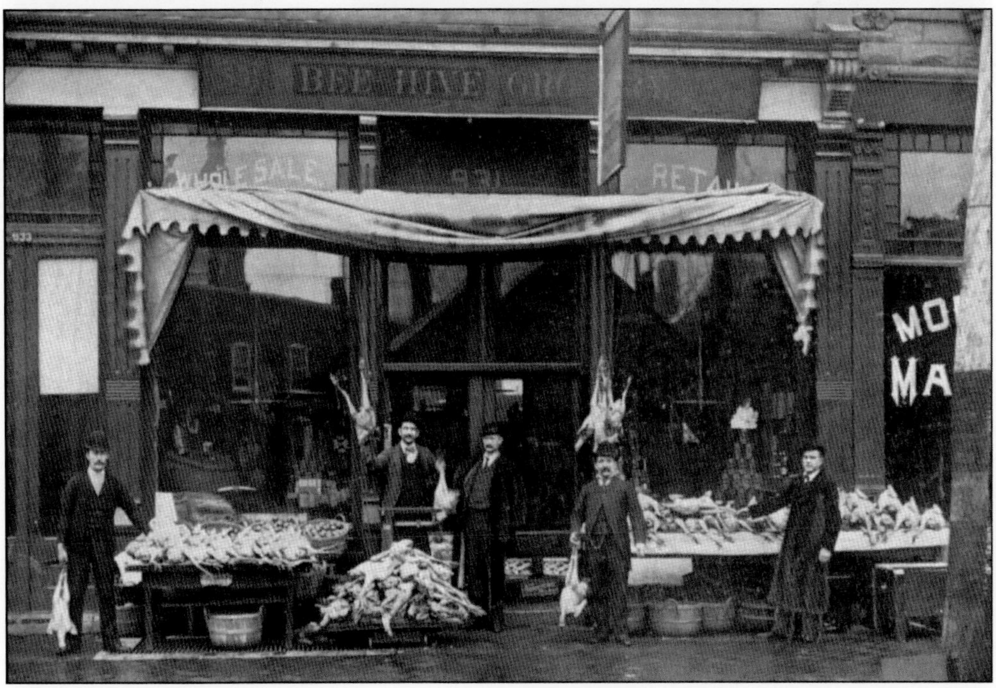

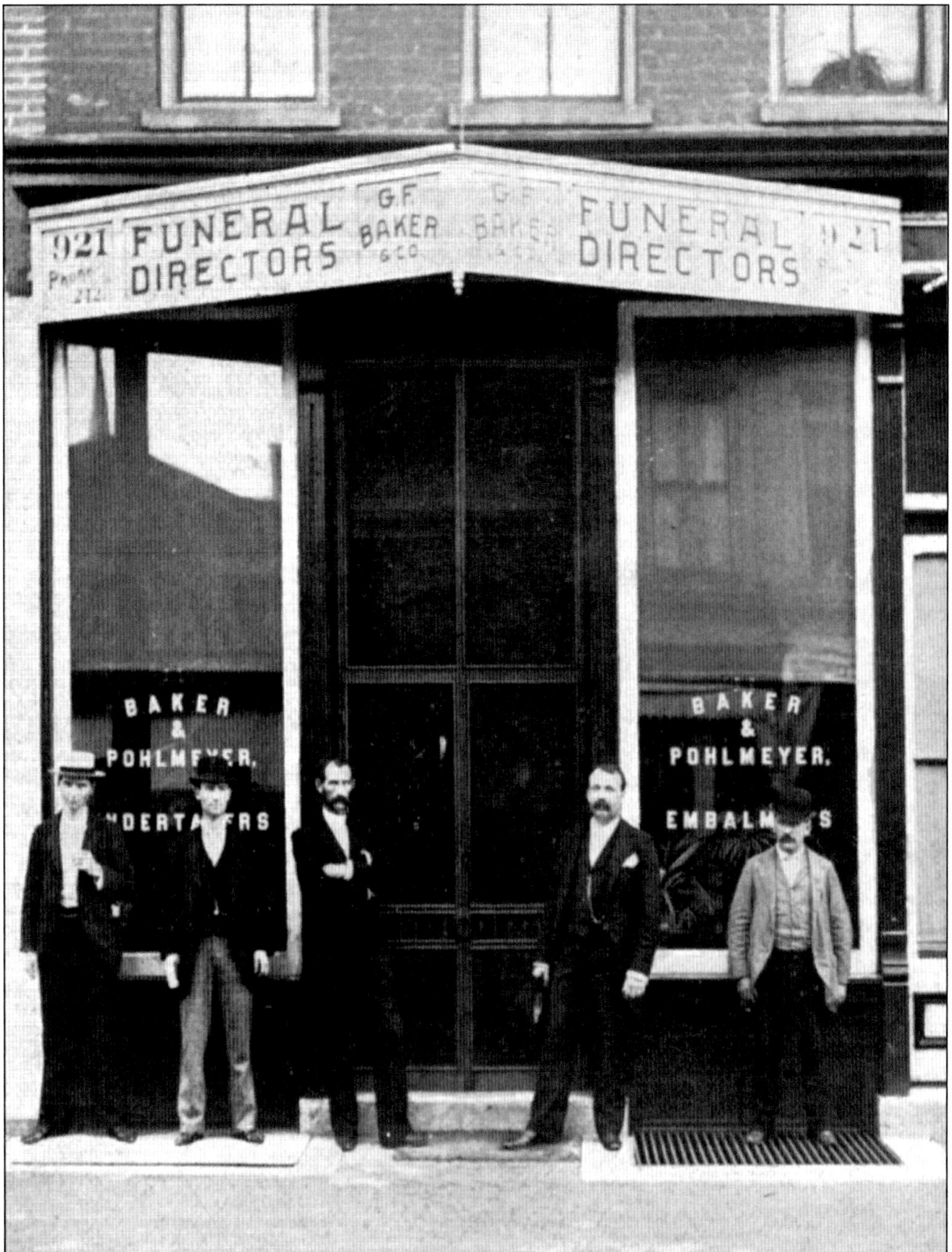

Pictured is Baker & Pohlmeyer, run by funeral directors G.F. Baker and H.J. Pohlmeyer, at 921 Main Street. Five sober-faced men stand outside looking more like an outlaw gang than morticians in this 1896 Dalbey photograph. (Courtesy Morrisson-Reeves Library.)

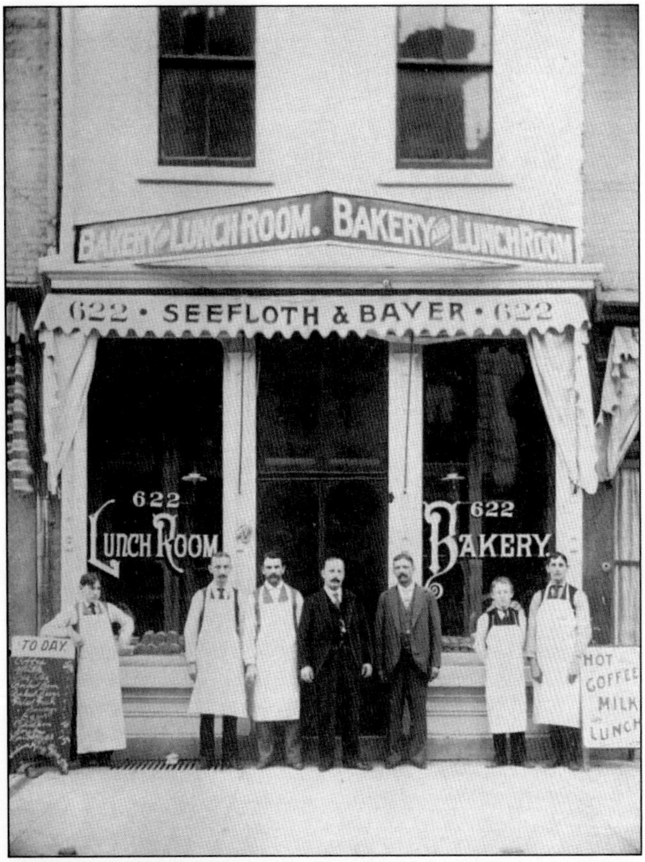

The reverse of this 1896 Dalbey photograph states, "Seefoth & Bayer Retail Store, Cake Bakery and Lunch Room, 622 Main Street. Established 1882 J.H. Seefloth—John C. Bayer." (Courtesy Morrisson-Reeves Library.)

The back of this 1896 Dalbey photograph states, "Seefoth & Bayer Wholesale Bread Bakery Capacity 4000 loaves a day. The finest machine bakery in Eastern Indiana." (Courtesy Morrisson-Reeves Library.)

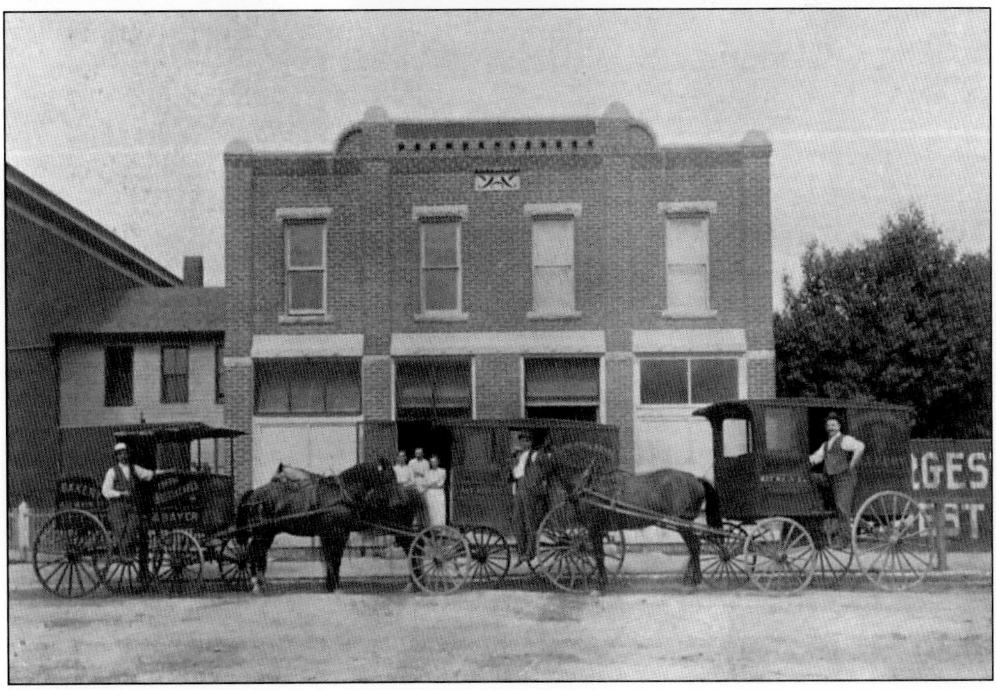

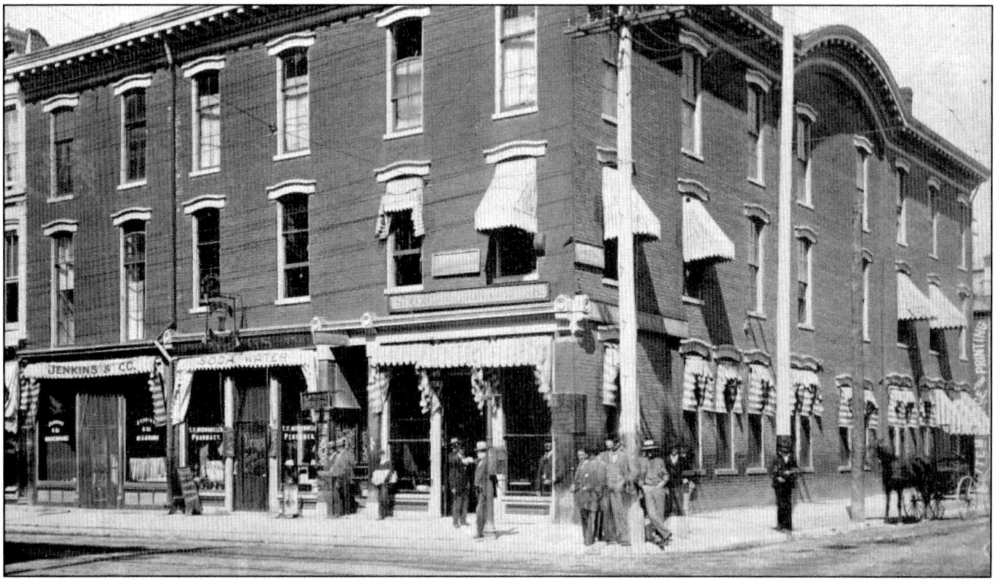

Pictured is the Second National Bank in 1896. The Dalbey photograph states that the capital for the bank was $150,000, and it had a surplus fund of $135,000. The officers of the bank are listed as president W.G. Scott, vice president John M. Garr, second vice president D.G. Reid, cashier John M. Dougan, and assistant cashier Samuel W. Gaar. The photograph also shows the neighboring businesses of jewelers Jenkins & Co. (left), established in 1853, and druggist and pharmacist T.F. McDonnell (right). (Courtesy Morrisson-Reeves Library.)

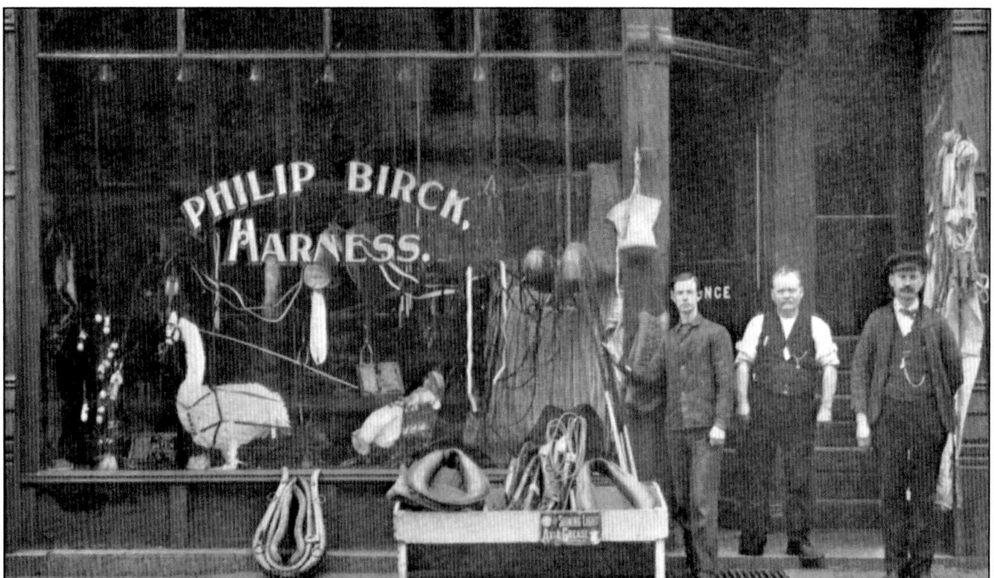

This 1906 Dalbey photograph pictures "Philip Birck, Manufacturer of Harness and Collars, And Dealer in all kinds of horse goods. No. 509 Main St., The Wiggins Stand," located on the corner of 10th and Main Street in Richmond. Designed by W. S. Kauffman, the Westcott Hotel was intended to be the "premier hotel of Indiana" in its heyday. The grand opening was September 10, 1895. J. M. Westcott, early Richmond business leader, was the man for whom the hotel was named. The Westcott closed in 1976 and was razed in 1977. (Courtesy Morrisson-Reeves Library.)

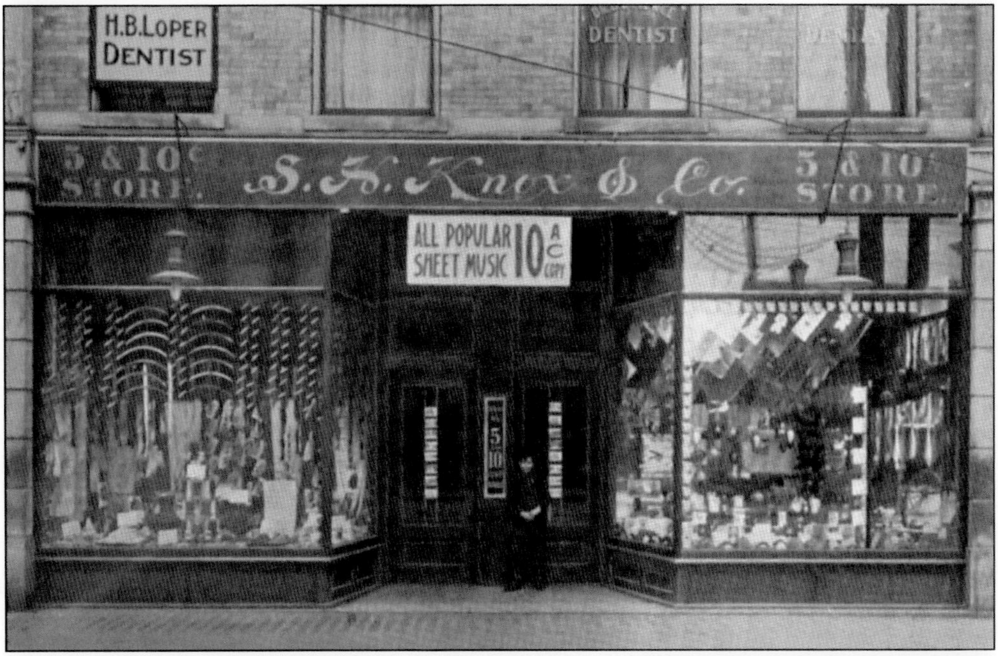

The sign out front of S.H. Knox & Co., a five-and-dime store at Main and Seventh Streets in Richmond, reads, "All Popular Sheet Music 10 Cents a copy" in this 1906 Dalbey photograph. H.P. Loper, a dentist, had an office above. (Courtesy Morrisson-Reeves Library.)

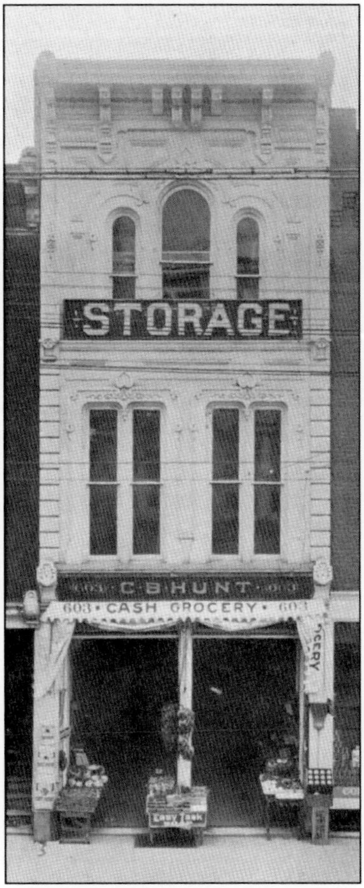

This is a 1906 Dalbey photograph, and the caption states, "Hunt's Grocery, Established 1860. 603 Main Street. Clayton Hunt, Sr. 1860–1864, C. Hunt & Sons, 1864–1868, Hunt Bros. 1868–1872, Clayton B. Hunt 1872– " in Richmond. (Courtesy Morrisson-Reeves Library.)

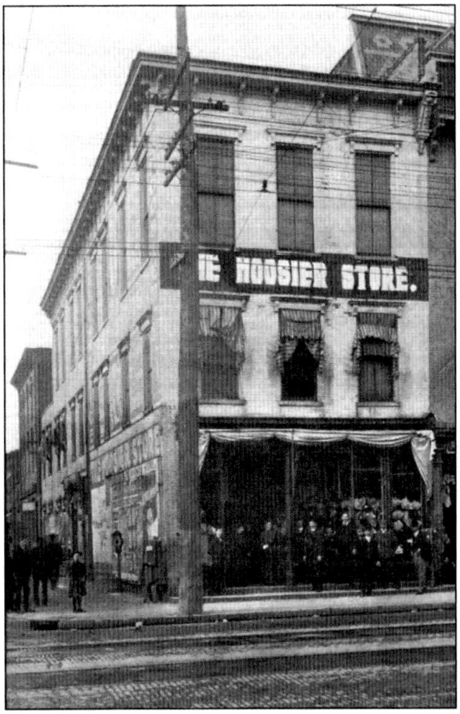

The exterior of the Hoosier Store at the corner of Sixth and Main Streets in Richmond is seen in this 1906 Dalbey photograph. Albert W. Gregg and John F. Ackerman opened the store in 1901 next to the Phillips Theatre, which had been there since before the Civil War. In 1910, John F. Bartel bought into the Hoosier Store. That same year the partners bought part of the theater, which had closed in 1908, and expanded the business into that building. (Courtesy Morrisson-Reeves Library.)

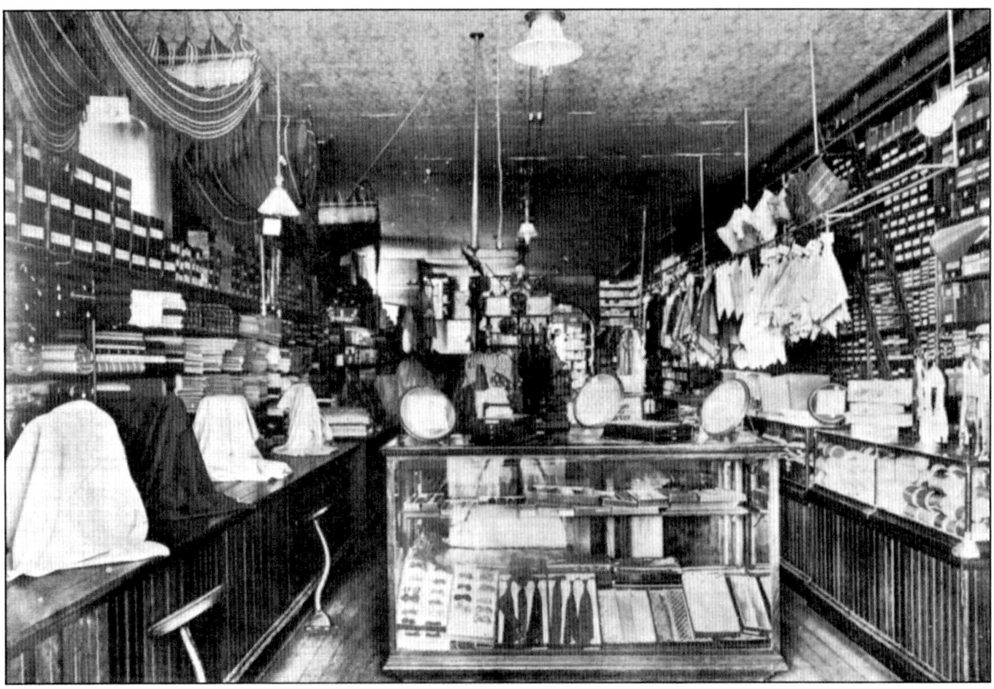

This 1906 Dalbey photograph captures the interior of the Hoosier Store at Sixth and Main Streets in Richmond. The store was located directly across the street from the massive 1968 explosion and sustained considerable damage. In 1973, it was renovated into an office building and renamed the 600 Building with a new exterior of white onyx and green marble columns. (Courtesy Morrisson-Reeves Library.)

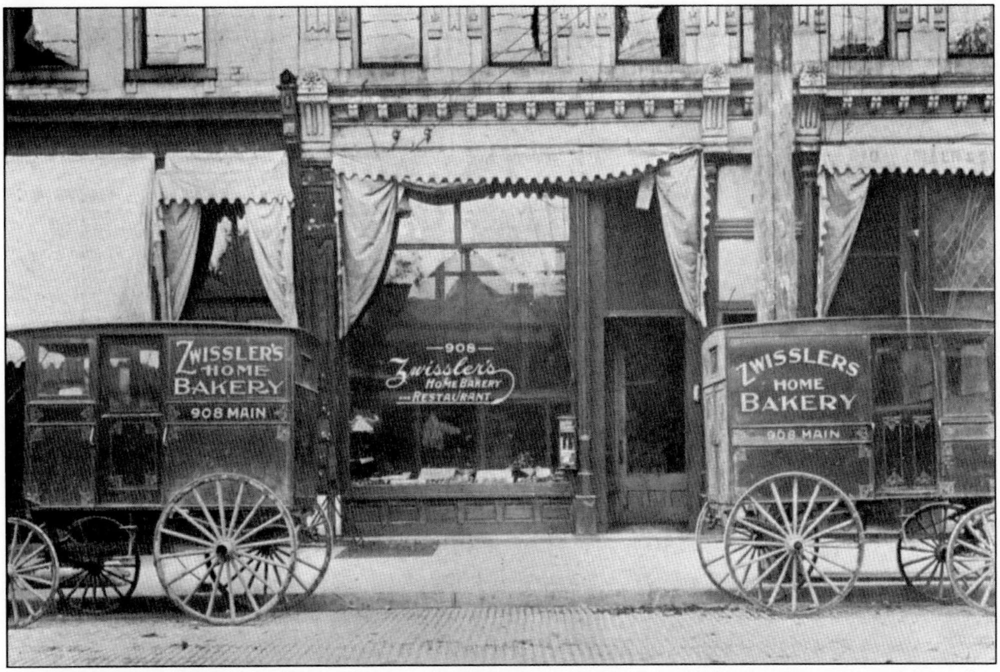

Zwissler's Home Bakery and Restaurant, at 908 Main Street in Richmond, is captured in this 1906 Dalbey photograph. (Courtesy Morrisson-Reeves Library.)

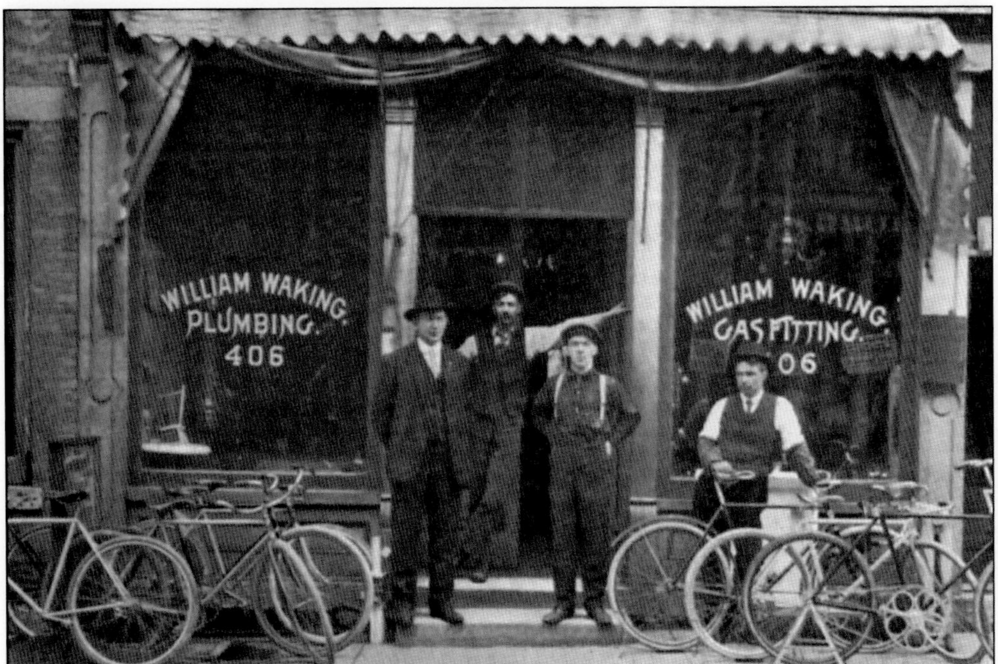

Seen in a 1906 Dalbey photograph is William Waking's plumbing, heating, and sporting goods store at 406 Main Street in Richmond. (Courtesy Morrisson-Reeves Library.)

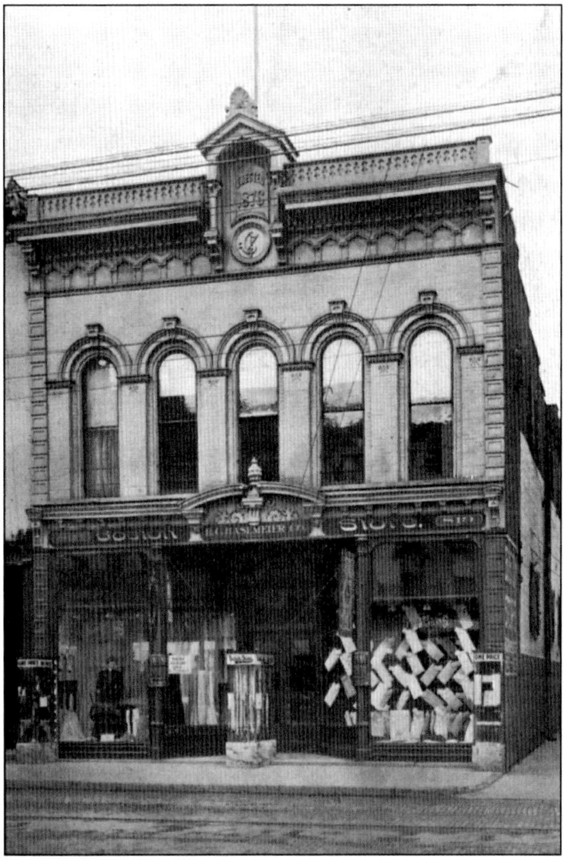

This 1906 Dalbey image has the caption, "Boston Store, H.C. Hasemeier Co. Dry Goods, Ladies Ready-Made Garments, Rugs, Mattings, Linoleums, Oil Cloths and Window Shades, 819 and 821 Main Street," referring to Richmond. (Courtesy Morrisson-Reeves Library.)

Here is an interior view of the Boston Store in Richmond. The 30-foot-by-165-foot first floor is the subject of another 1906 Dalbey photograph. (Courtesy Morrisson-Reeves Library.)

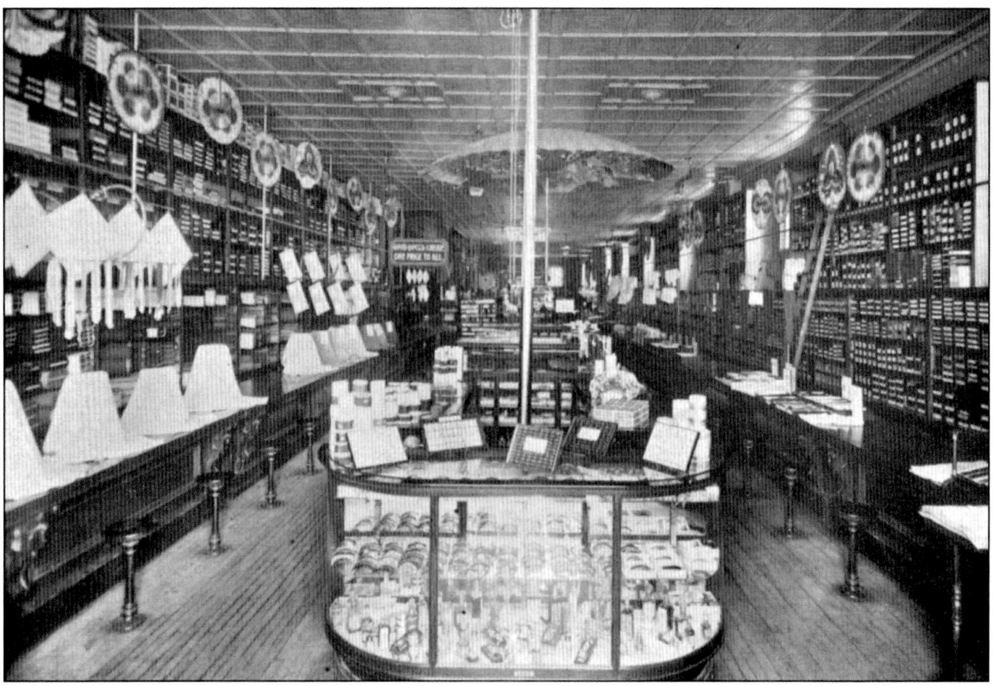

The back of this 1906 Dalbey photograph states, "W.N. Johnson, Slate and Tin Roofing, Copper and Galvanized Iron Cornice, Metal Ceiling, Plumbing, Steam, Hot Water and Hot Heating, 533 Main Street." The store did business in Richmond. (Courtesy Morrisson-Reeves Library.)

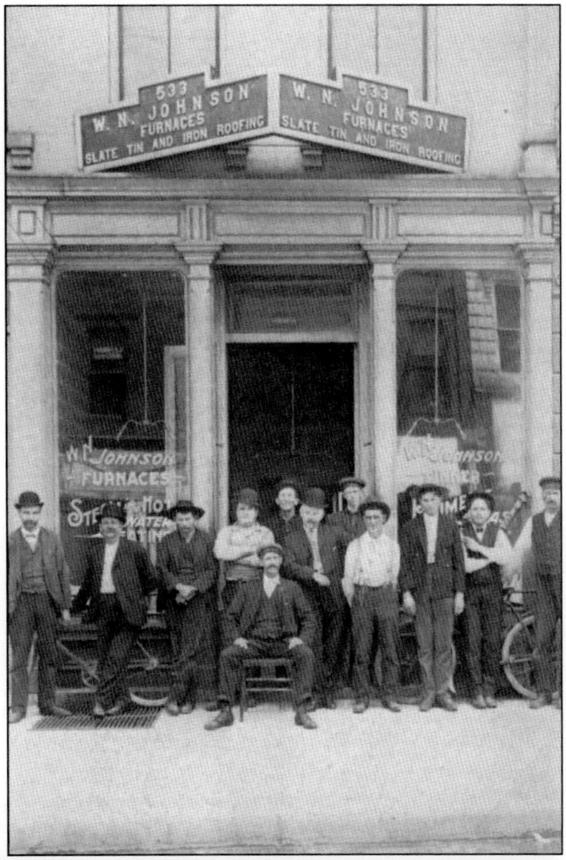

The caption of this 1906 Dalbey photograph reads, "Interior View of W.N. Johnson's Store, 533 Main Street," which was located in Richmond. (Courtesy Morrisson-Reeves Library.)

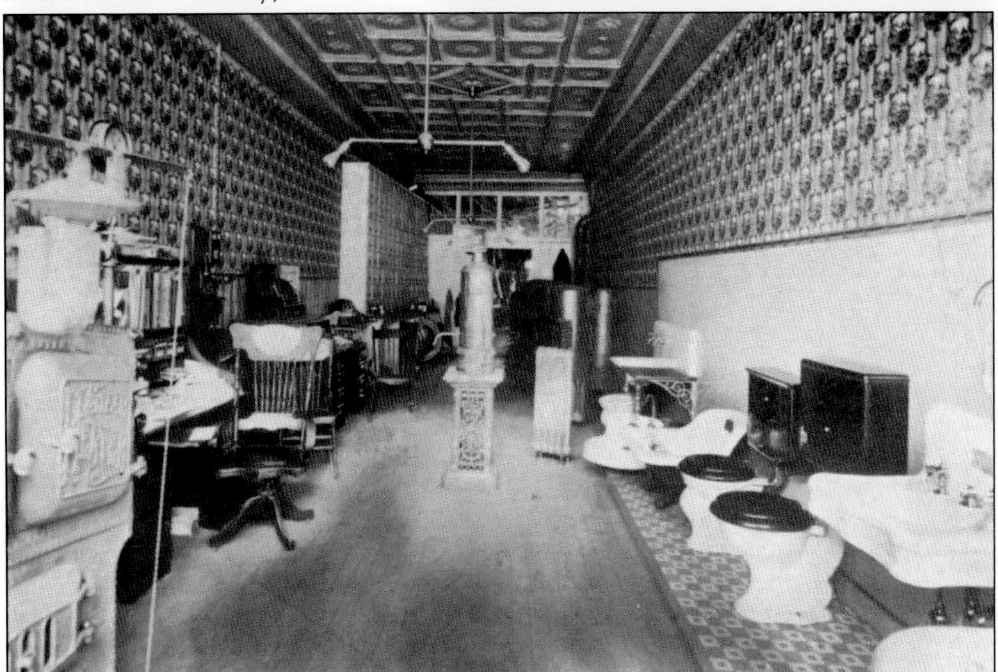

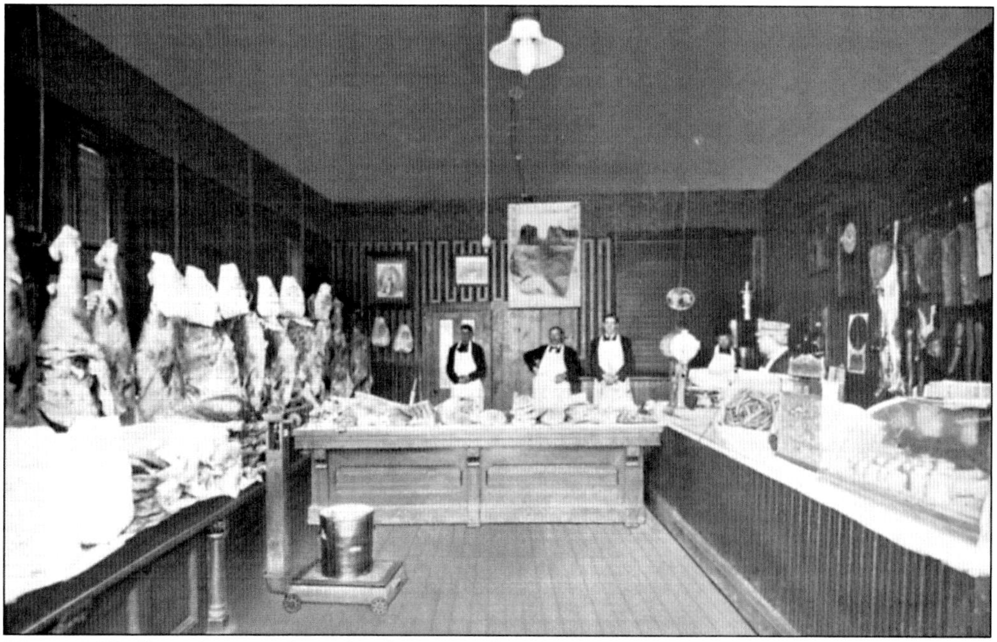

This 1906 Dalbey photograph is of Maher & Hadley, dealers in all kinds of fresh and smoked meat, sausage, and other items. The business was found at 1037 Main Street in Richmond. (Courtesy Morrisson-Reeves Library.)

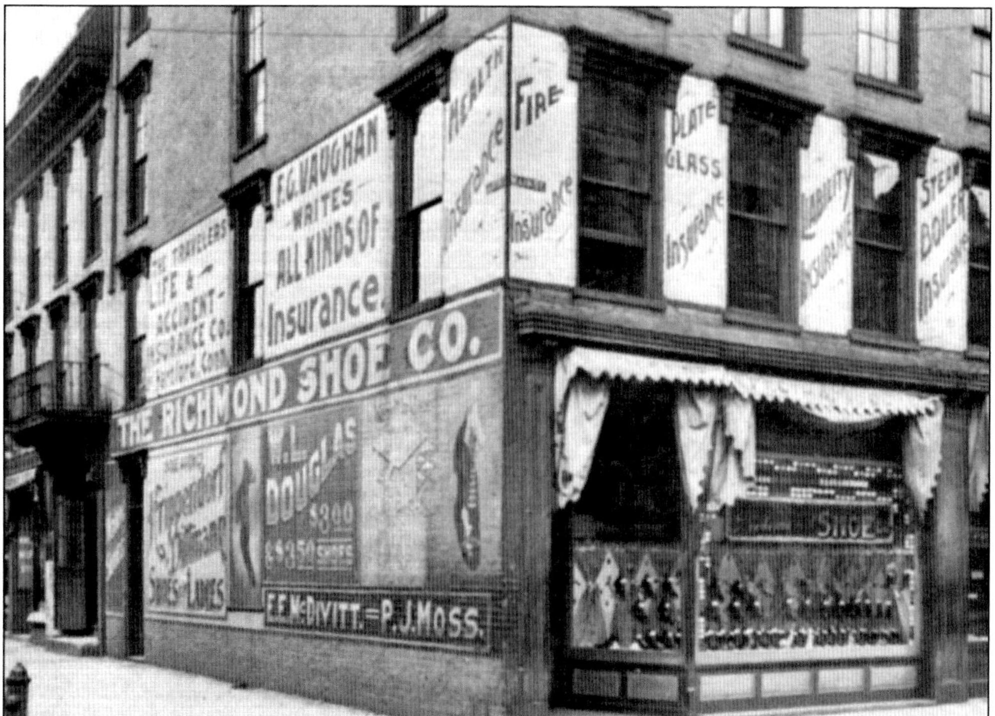

Pictured in 1906 is the Richmond Shoe Company, which sold fine footwear at the corner of Eighth and Main Streets in Richmond. (Courtesy Morrisson-Reeves Library.)

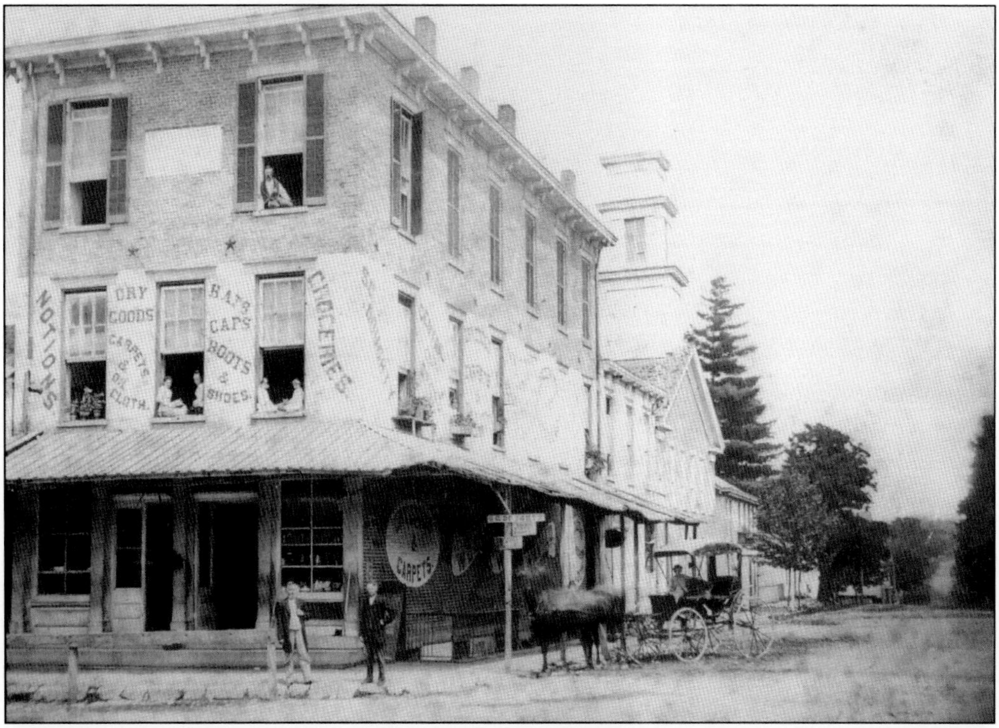

Pictured in the 1880s is the three-story Centerville Odd Fellows lodge located at the northwest corner of Main and Cross Streets. The building was dedicated in 1860 with the lodge on the third floor, rooming house on the second floor, and S.C. Doughty dry goods store on the bottom floor. The store featured several large painted signs on the front and side that read, "Dry Goods Carpets & Oil Cloth-Notions-Hats, Caps, Boots and Saddles-Groceries-S.C. Doughty-Central Cash Store." Several people are posing for the camera, and a man sits on the upper lodge windowsill proudly wearing his Odd Fellows vestment over his shoulders. Two men stand on the corner as a horse and buggy prepares to drive past on the dirt road. (Courtesy Ron Moore.)

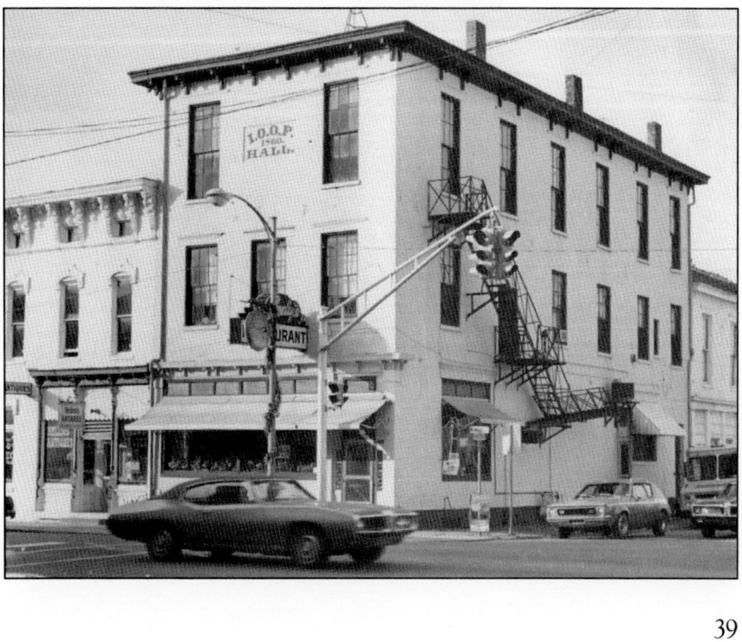

The Odd Fellows Lodge appears here in the early 1970s with the addition of a fire escape and Jody's Restaurant on the lower level. Notice streetlights decorated for the Christmas season. (Courtesy Ron Moore.)

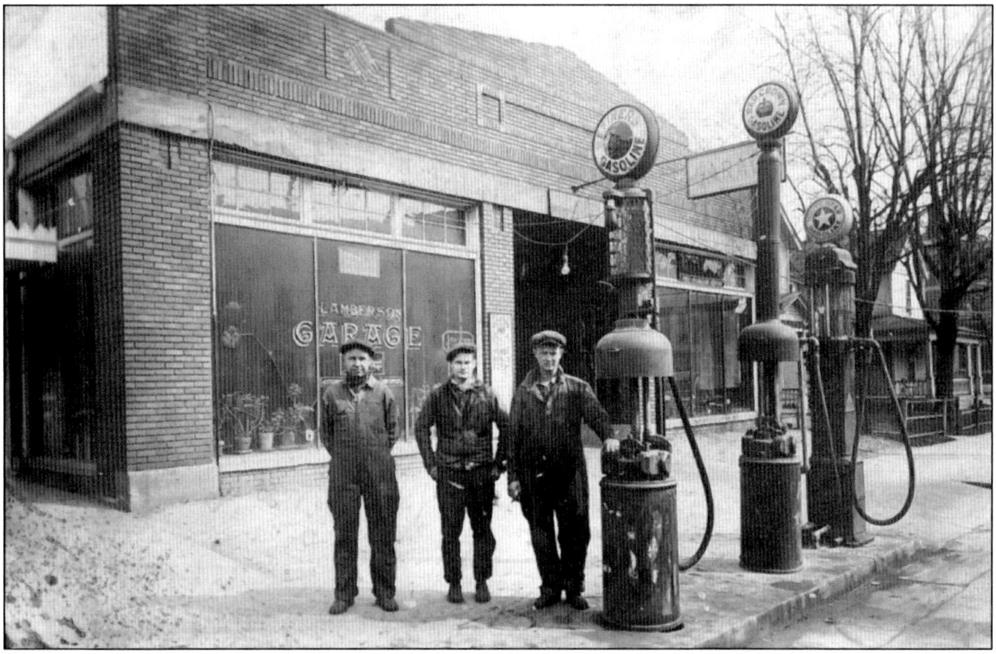

Here is the Lamberson Garage on the north side of the National Road in Centerville. This 1920s photograph shows the mechanics posing proudly against the old-fashioned gravity pumps that offered the Standard Oil Red Crown brand of gasoline. (Courtesy Verlon Webb-Webb's Antique Mall.)

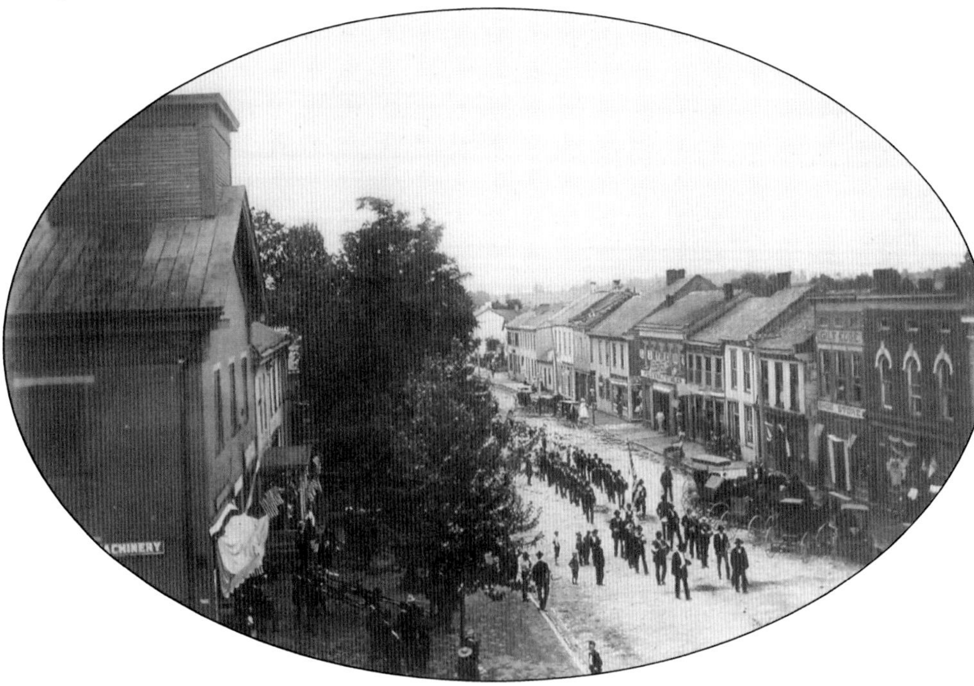

Pictured is the National Road looking west as a GAR parade of old Civil War soldiers marches down the center of the dirt road. The photograph appears to be from the 1880s, as there are no interurban tracks. (Courtesy Ron Moore.)

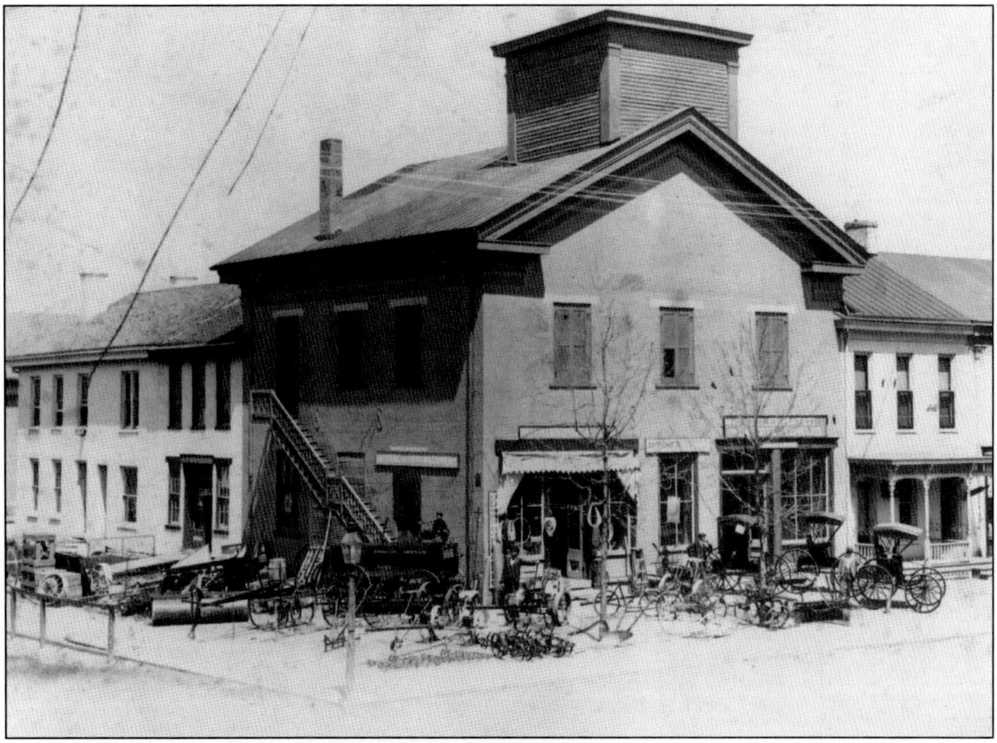

The Dunbar & Sons Hardware store, located on the southeast corner of the National Road and South Morton Avenue/South Centerville Road, is pictured here. The photograph appears to be from the 1880s, and the building features large signs for Deering machinery, LaPorte vehicles, and Hoosier stoves. The employees and members of their families can be seen leaning against bicycles, wagons, and plows out front. (Courtesy Ron Moore.)

This photograph of the Wayne County Courthouse on the National Road in Centerville was taken in the 1890s after the county seat was relocated to Richmond. The building is shown housing a paint and hardware store with paint signs visible and rolls of unused wire fencing piled at the side. The structure is no longer standing. (Courtesy Ron Moore.)

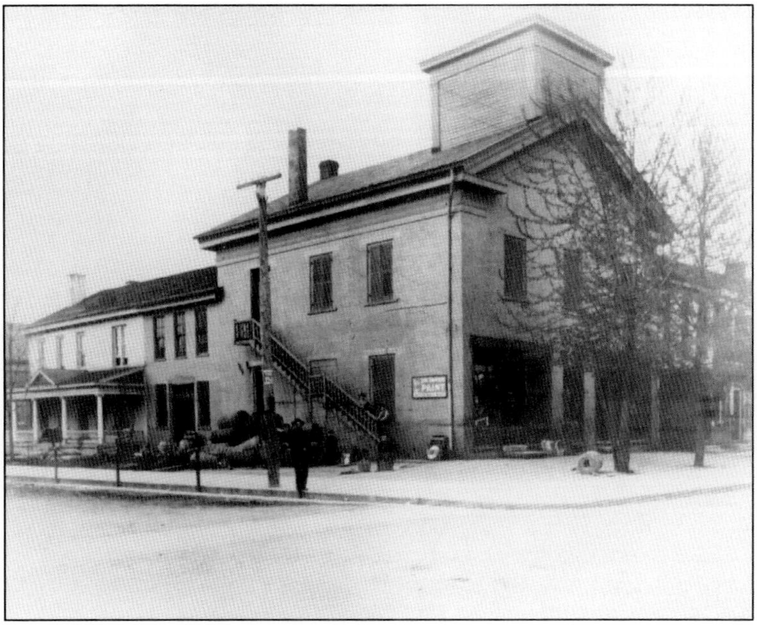

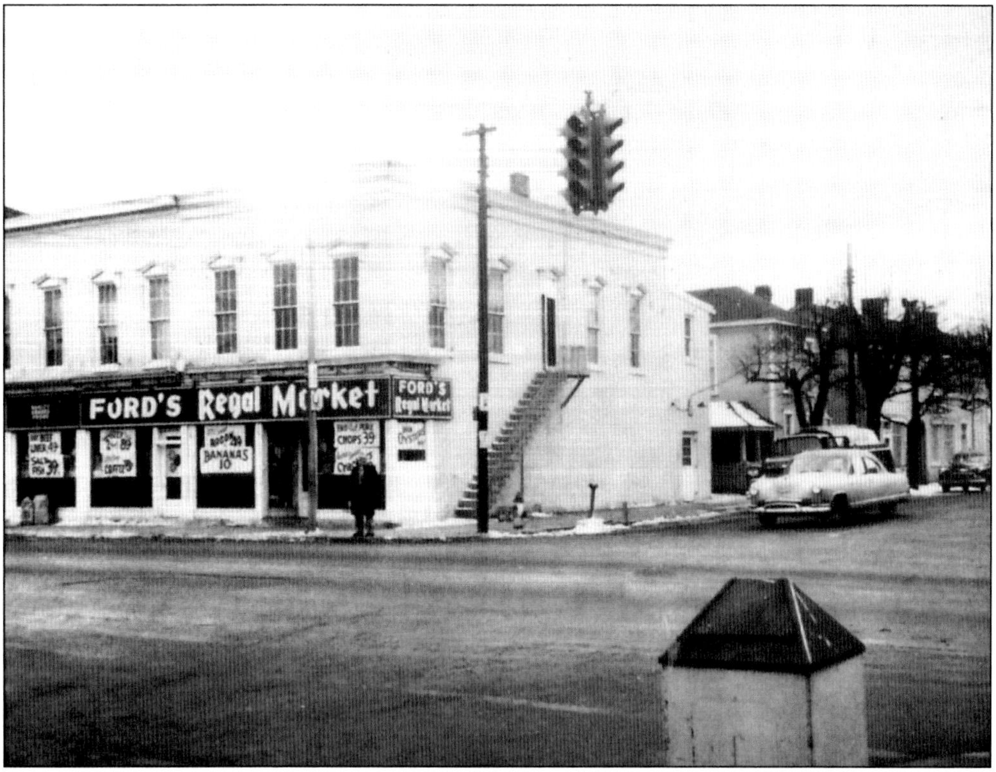

This is the National Road at 101 East Main Street looking southeast at Ford's Regal Food Market. The photograph appears to be from the 1950s. (Courtesy Ron Moore.)

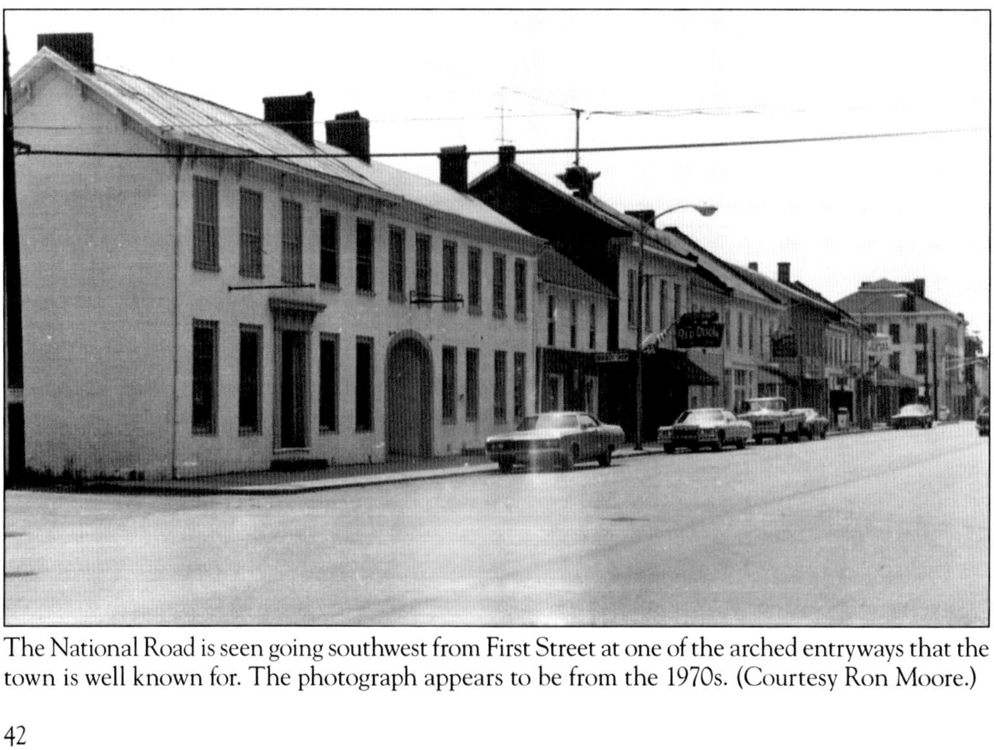
The National Road is seen going southwest from First Street at one of the arched entryways that the town is well known for. The photograph appears to be from the 1970s. (Courtesy Ron Moore.)

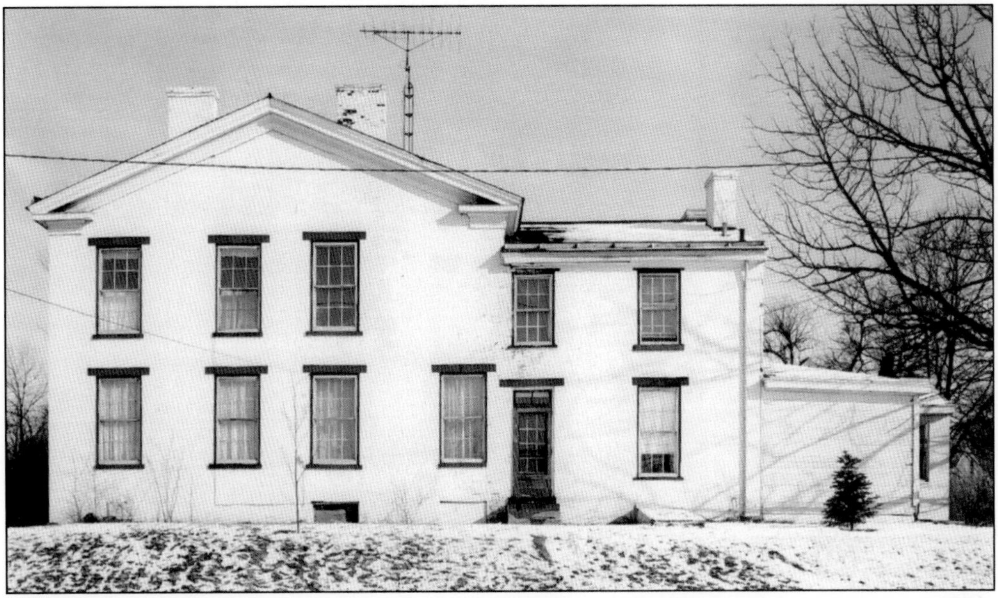

The Oliver P. Morton home is perhaps the most famous house in Centerville. Newspaper publisher Jacob Julian built the stately home near the railroad and called it Eden Spot. He later sold the home to future Indiana governor Oliver P. Morton. While living in this house, Morton was elected lieutenant governor on the ticket with Henry S. Lane. Judge William A. Peelle bought the Morton mansion after his term as secretary of state expired. Judge Peelle died there on July 1, 1902. This 1970s image shows the west side of the house from the National Road. (Alan E. Hunter collection.)

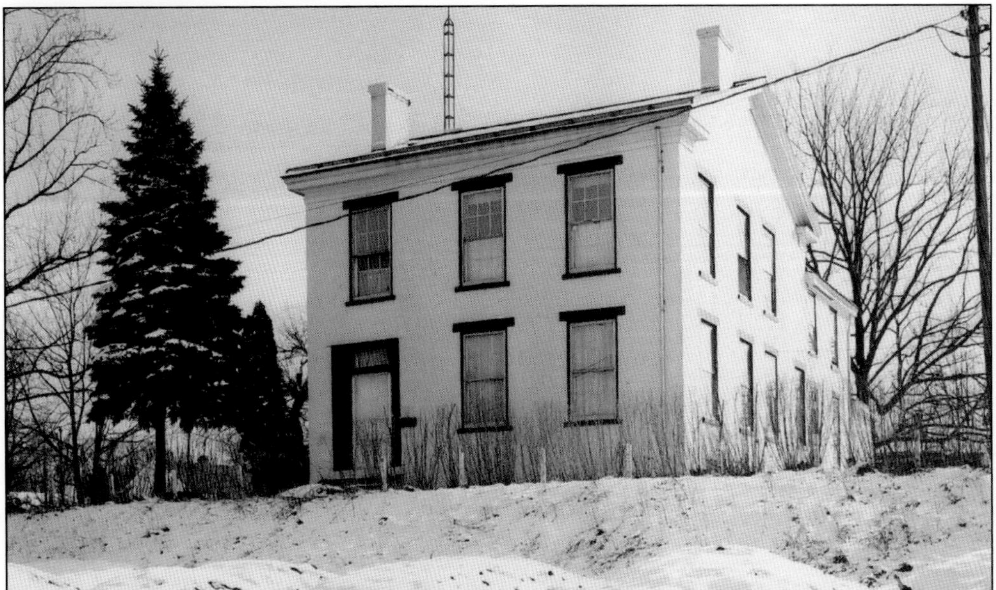

This southwest view of the Oliver P. Morton house in Centerville on the National Road was taken from the spot of the official Indiana historical marker sign that reads, "Residence of Oliver P. Morton, Governor of Indiana during the crucial years of the Civil War, 1861–1865. US Senator 1867–1877. Morton was the first native-born governor of Indiana." (Alan E. Hunter collection.)

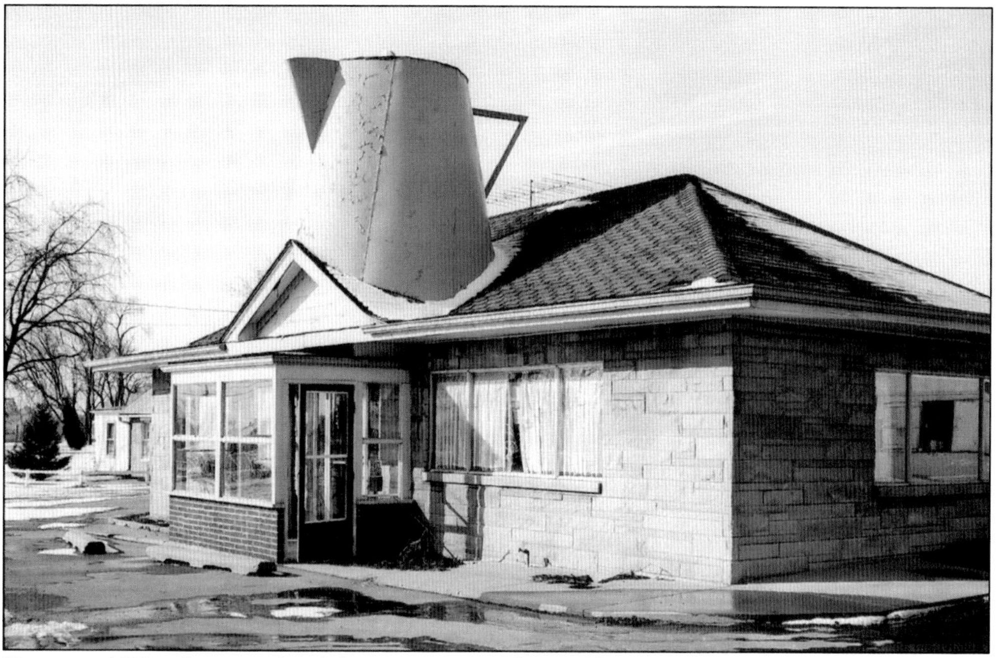

Here is a 1970s photograph of the entrance to the Coffee Pot Restaurant in Pennville (west of Centerville). The building's signature 15-foot-tall metal coffee pot can be seen positioned prominently above the door. The restaurant was one of the most recognizable buildings on the Indiana National Road until the weight of the coffee pot caused the roof to buckle and ultimately cave in. The restaurant was razed in the 1990s. (Alan E. Hunter collection.)

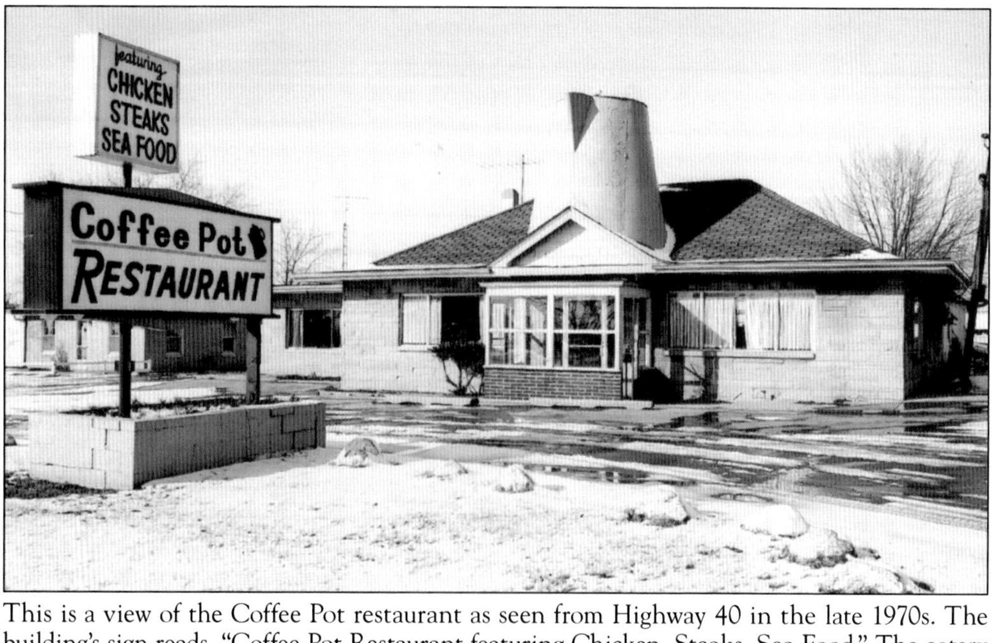

This is a view of the Coffee Pot restaurant as seen from Highway 40 in the late 1970s. The building's sign reads, "Coffee Pot Restaurant featuring Chicken, Steaks, Sea Food." The eatery was one of the first restaurants in the state to serve Colonel Sanders' Kentucky Fried Chicken in the years before it became a nationwide chain. In those days, Colonel Sanders would often deliver his secret-recipe chicken to the restaurant himself. (Alan E. Hunter collection.)

Two

Cambridge City to Dunreith

From the Whitewater Canal to Overbeck Pottery and the Huddleston Farmhouse, Cambridge City has an intact streetscape that again shares the story of the pike towns along the Historic National Road. The Whitewater Canal connected Cambridge City to Lawrenceburg, Indiana, and Cincinnati, Ohio, on the Ohio River, and this became an important transportation route with the National Road for the community. Today, travelers can drive this route along the Whitewater Canal Scenic Byway and learn that story. The Overbeck Sisters, whose home is well preserved in town, were famous for the pottery that they created, and the Huddleston family, which lived just outside of town, operated an inn for travelers along the National Road. All of these sites still remain and contribute to the overall integrity of the byway.

Heading out of Cambridge City and past the Huddleston farmhouse, travelers begin ascending a slight rise on the road heading into Dublin. Many think the name is connected to Irish settlers, but it harkens back to a time when travel was a more difficult task. Today, the rise seems small compared to other hills on the National Road, but in the 1840s it required pioneers to double up on their oxen. This "doublin' up" led to the town's namesake, Dublin.

The next pike town along the route of the road heading westward is Lewisville, which is famous for its Stoplight Festival and two incredible landmarks along the byway. The Houston Brick building was one of the first successful preservation projects along the route, which was led by Rep. Tom Saunders and his wife, Sue. This historic structure now serves as the community building and center for Lewisville. Just across the street in the next block west is the Guyer Opera House. This building was recently restored, but it has been used for performances for years. Visitors may still enjoy a play from the upstairs stage and performance room, which has superb acoustics.

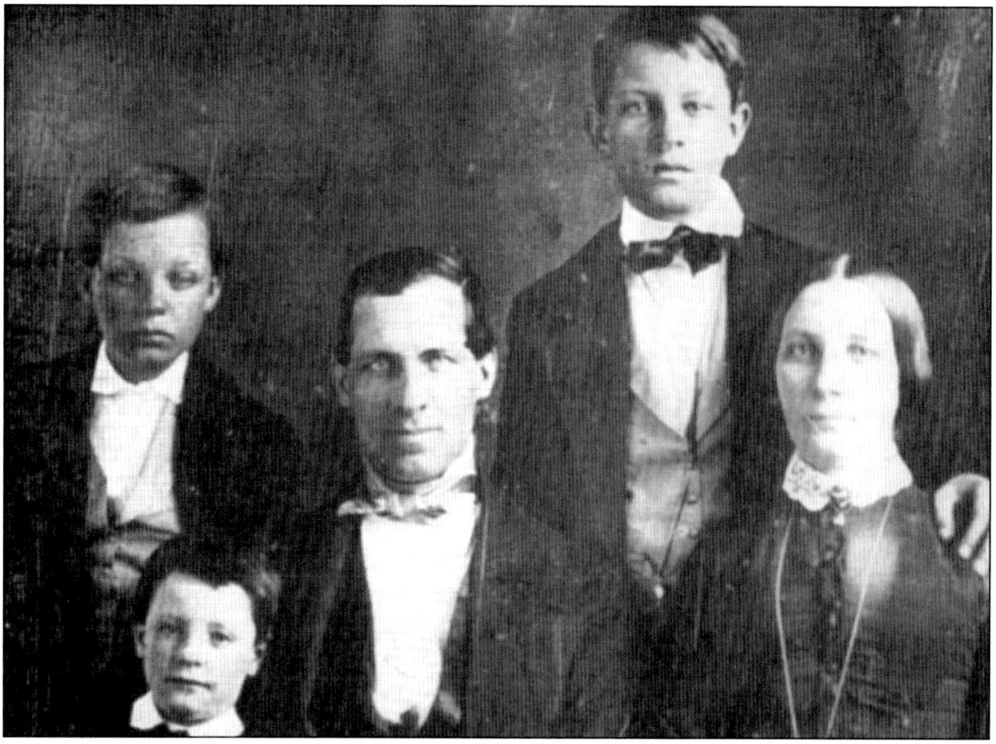

Solomon Meredith, his wife, Anna, and their children are pictured around 1846. Meredith served as sheriff of Wayne County and later went on the fame as the leader in charge of the famed Iron Brigade at Gettysburg. In July, the Iron Brigade carried the honors of Gettysburg, and General Meredith was so severely wounded in the battle that he was never again fit for active duty. Solomon and Anna had four children, three of which are pictured here. The first son, Samuel H., was a first lieutenant in the 19th Indiana Regiment. He was severely wounded at the Battle of Gainesville in 1862, and again at Gettysburg, and his death occurred while he was on a furlough at his father's home in 1862. A second son, David M., was a captain in the 15th United States Infantry and was severely wounded at the Battle of Chickamauga; he died in 1867. The third son, Henry Clay, who died in 1882, achieved prominence in agriculture and in public affairs. The fourth child, Mary, died in infancy. (Courtesy Cambridge City Library-History Room.)

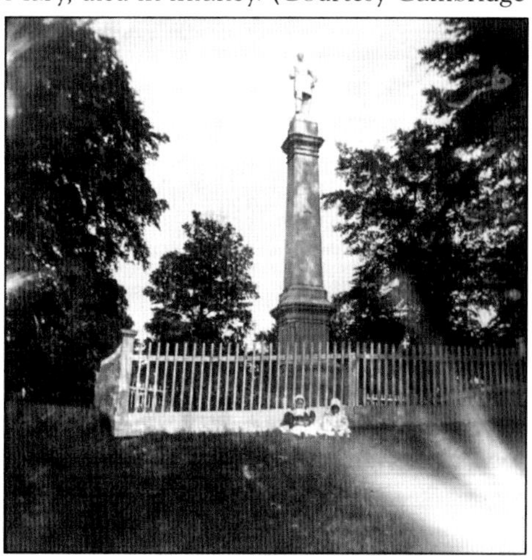

The grave and monument of Gen. Solomon Meredith, hero of the Battle of Gettysburg, appears here in the 1890s. Two small children can be seen seated in front of the white wrought-iron gate that once surrounded the grave when it was located just east of the Meredith farm near Vandalia. When the massive monument was moved to Riverside Cemetery in Cambridge City, it fell over on top of one of the workers, killing him. (Courtesy Cambridge City Library History Room.)

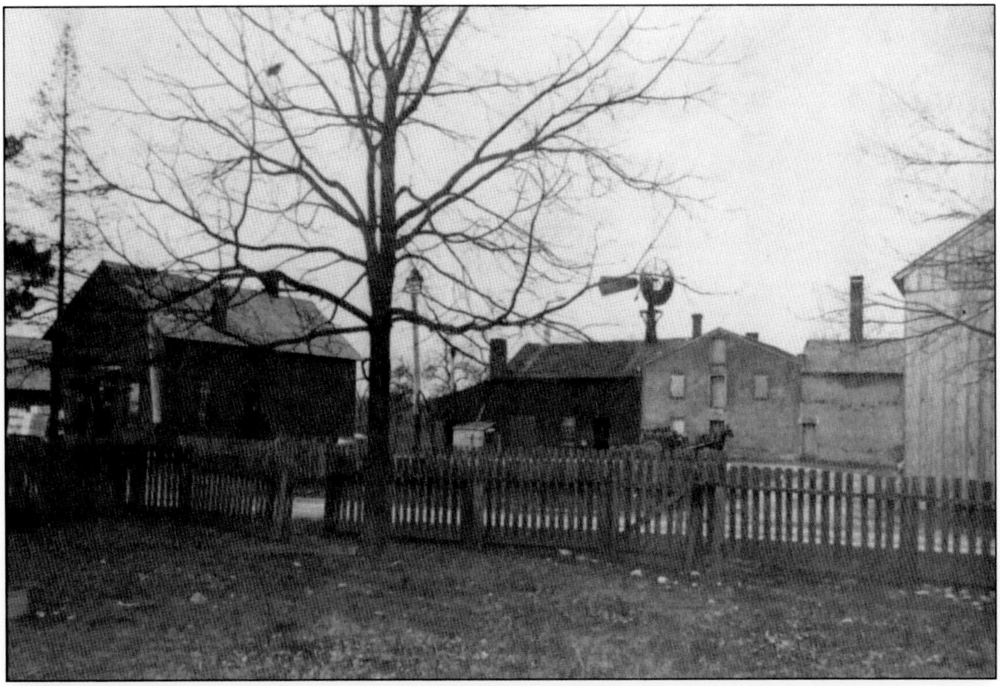

The Ingerman Brewery in Vandalia is pictured around 1900. The brewery produced ale and beer made from choice hops grown in the Cambridge City area. (Courtesy Cambridge City Library History Room.)

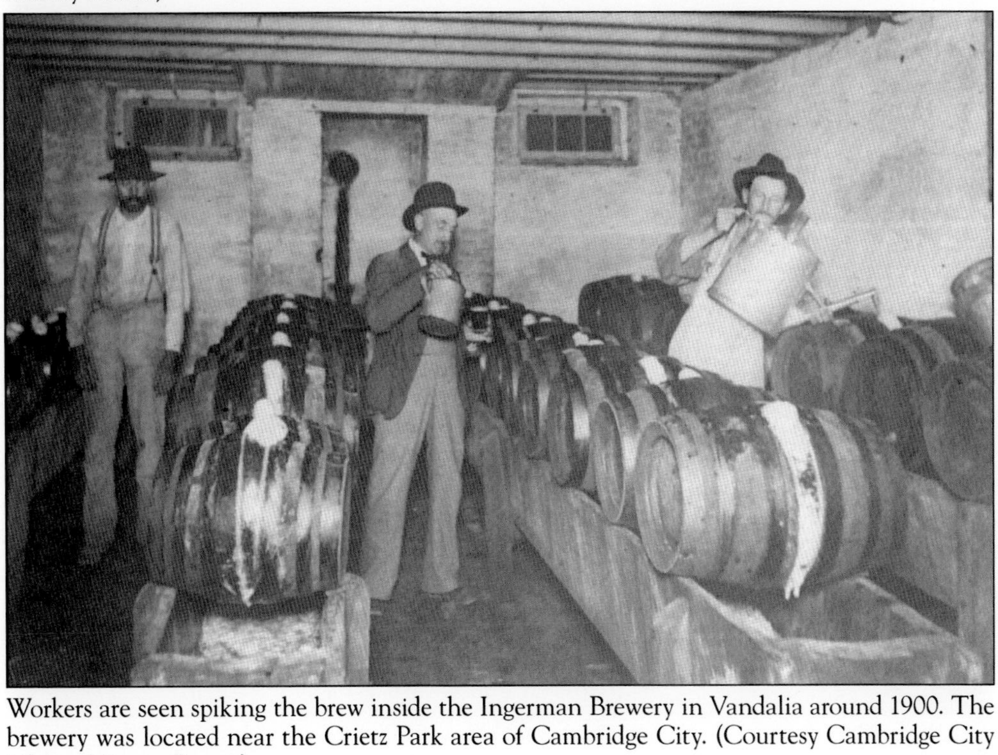

Workers are seen spiking the brew inside the Ingerman Brewery in Vandalia around 1900. The brewery was located near the Crietz Park area of Cambridge City. (Courtesy Cambridge City Library History Room.)

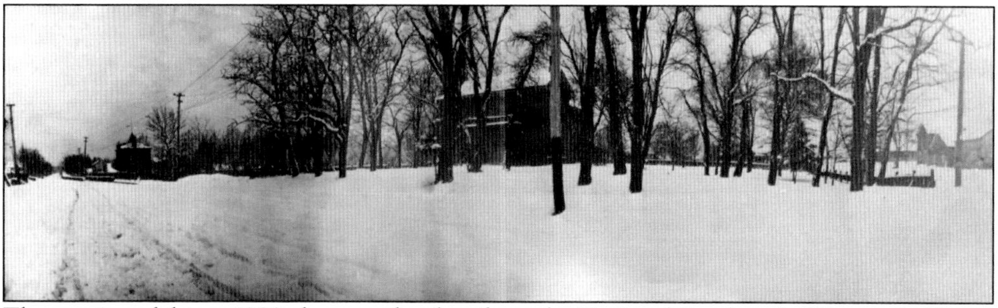

The caption of this c. 1900 photograph taken from the National Road reads, "East end of River Bridge—Mohler residence—Vandalia." The road is covered with snow, which has wagon wheel tracks running through it. (Courtesy Cambridge City Library-History Room.)

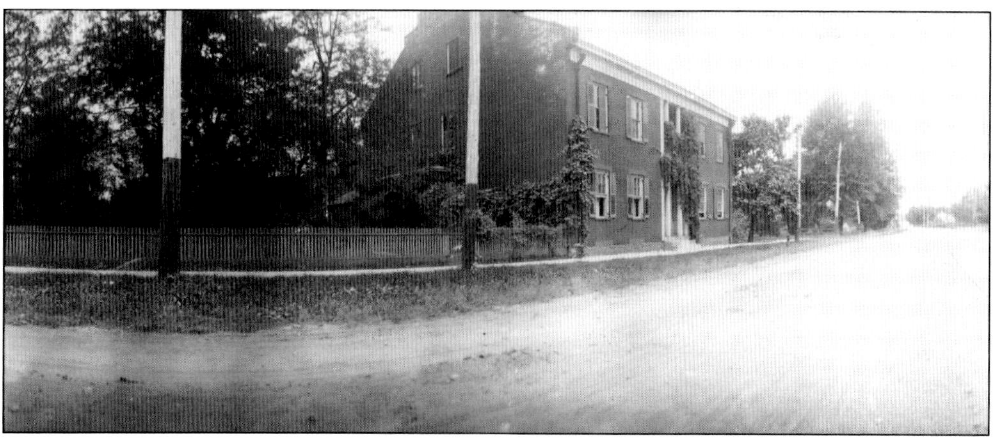

This is a c. 1900 photograph of the old Conklin house taken from the corner of Main Street and Lincoln Drive. (Courtesy Cambridge City Library-History Room.)

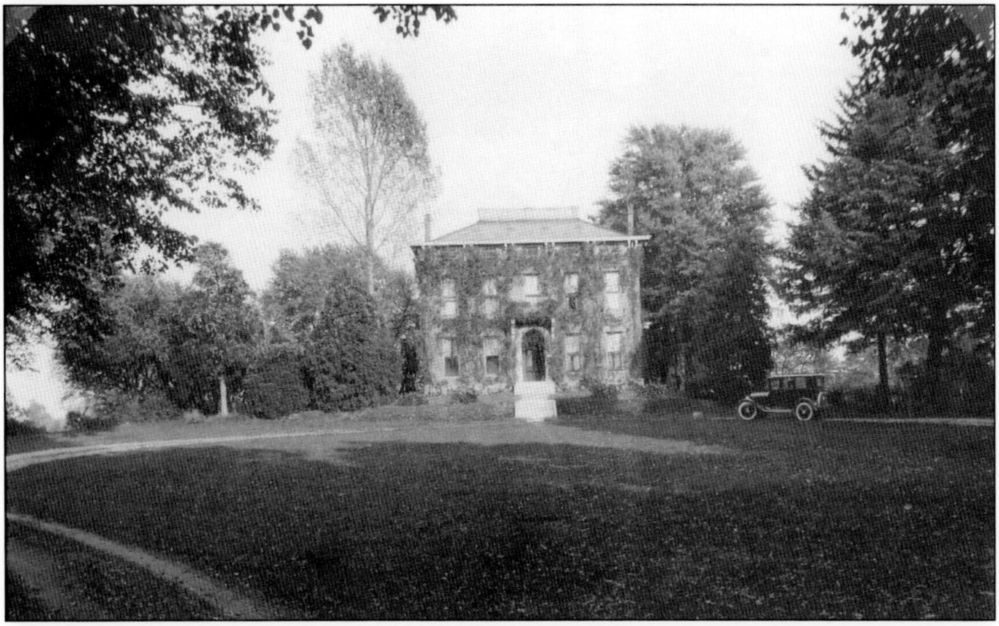

The Kimmel house, pictured here around 1910, became known as Rose Hill Mansion for the hundreds of rose bushes that covered the rise leading up to the home. The massive 15-room redbrick mansion, on seven acres of land, is located on Meredith Street across from the Solomon Meredith home. It is known for its distinctive heart-shaped driveway. (Courtesy Cambridge City Library-History Room.)

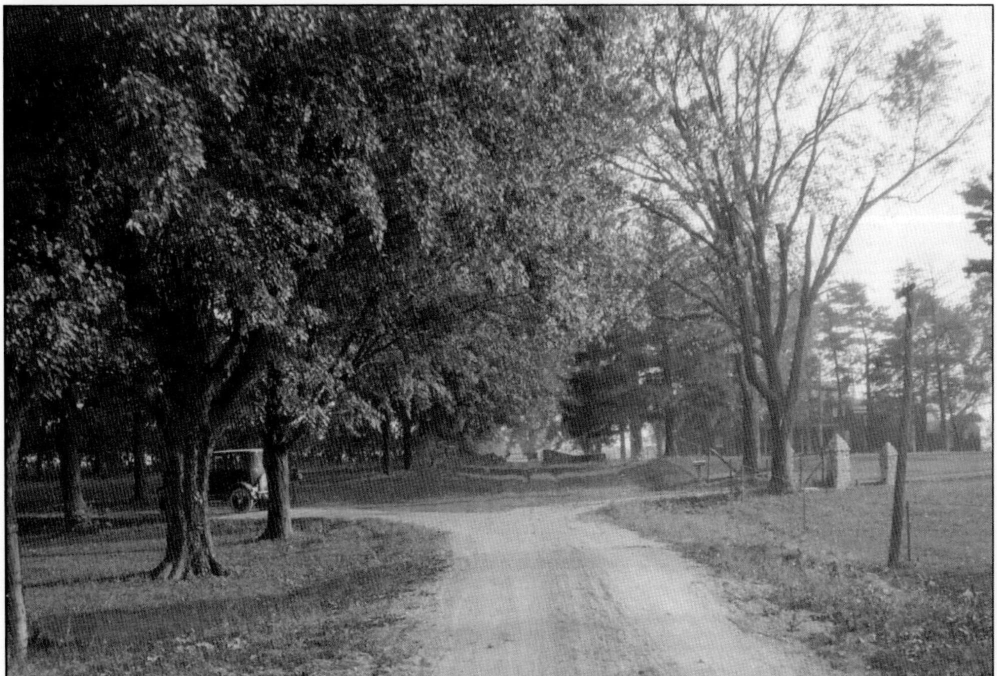

This c. 1910 view of Meredith Street shows the Meredith house on the right and the entrance to Rose Hill Mansion on the left. (Courtesy Cambridge City Library-History Room.)

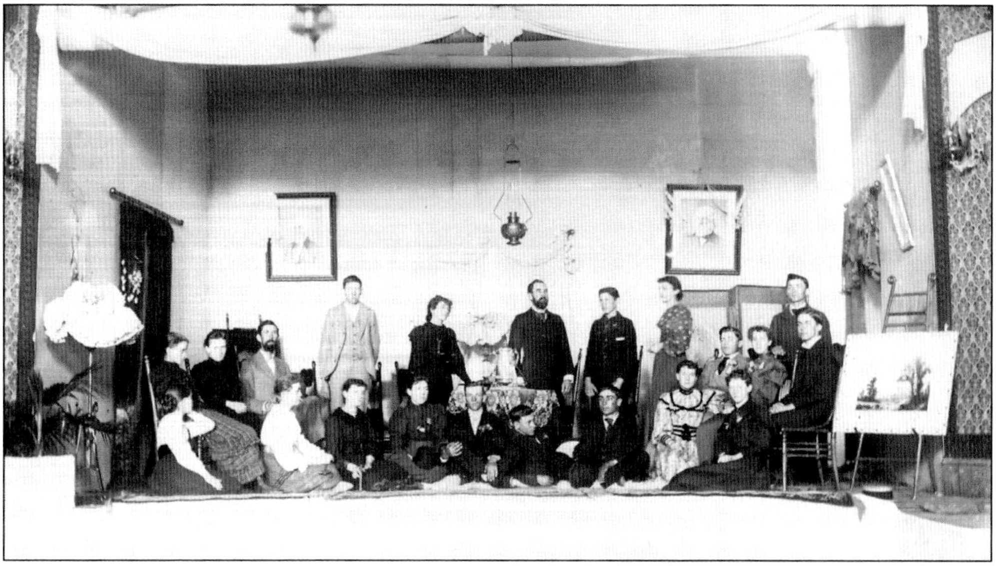

A large, c. 1900 cabinet photograph shows the cast of a long forgotten play at the Cambridge City Opera House. Mary Frances Overbeck, of the famed Overbeck Sisters pottery family, is in the cast and is seated in a chair on the far left. Two of the young ladies seated on the floor are holding hammers in their hands, which were probably used to help decorate the set. (Courtesy Cambridge City Library-History Room.)

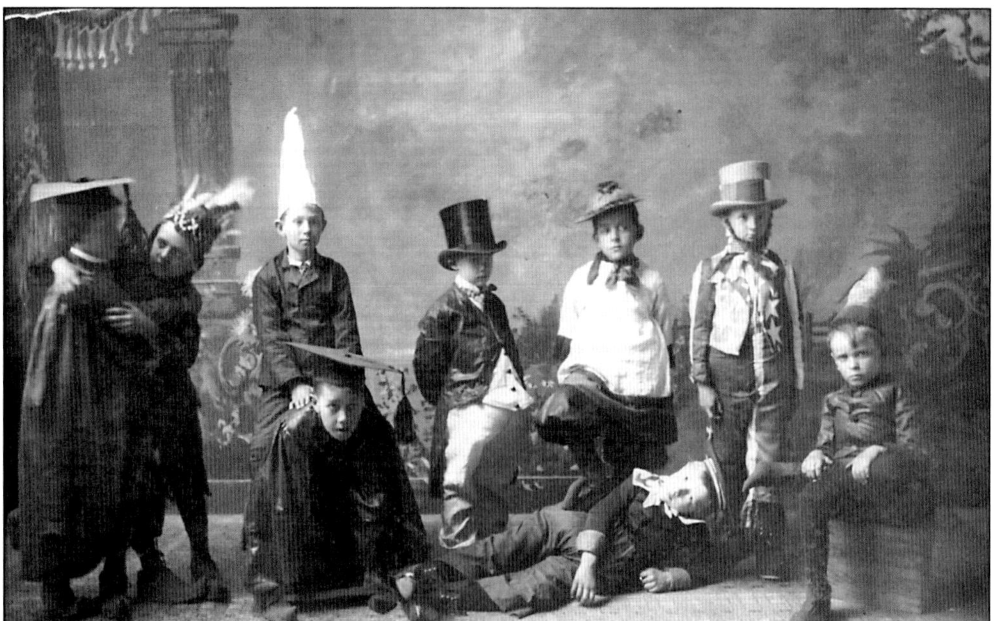

Pictured is a grade-school production at the Cambridge City Opera House, located at 119 West Main Street, sometime in the late 1800s. Although the name of the play is long forgotten, it was obviously historical in theme as the elfin characters are dressed as Uncle Sam, Native Americans, college students, and a man with a potbelly and a silk top hat. Some of the children in the production are identified as, in no particular order, Charles Young, Paul Wright, Harry Kuster, John Marson, Russel Worl, and Harry Barefoot. (Courtesy Cambridge City Library-History Room.)

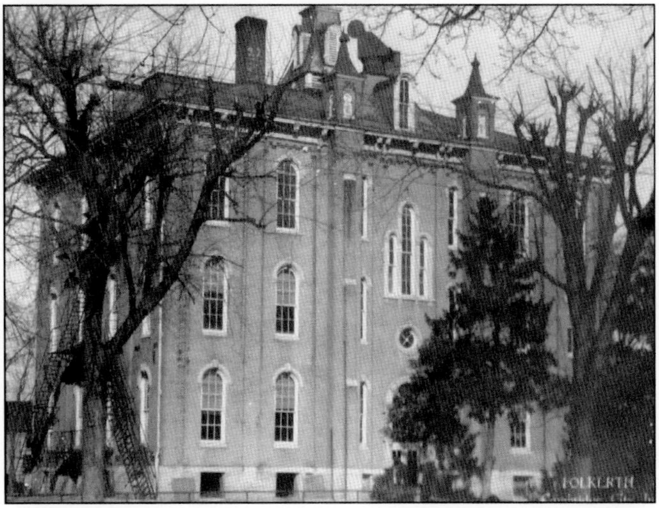

This early-1900s cabinet photograph shows Old Central School on the National Road in Cambridge City. The school opened in 1869 and served as the grade school and high school until 1923, and then only as a grade school until it was condemned in 1933. It was razed, and the New Central School was built on the same location. The photograph was taken by Folkerth Cambridge City. (Courtesy Cambridge City Library-History Room.)

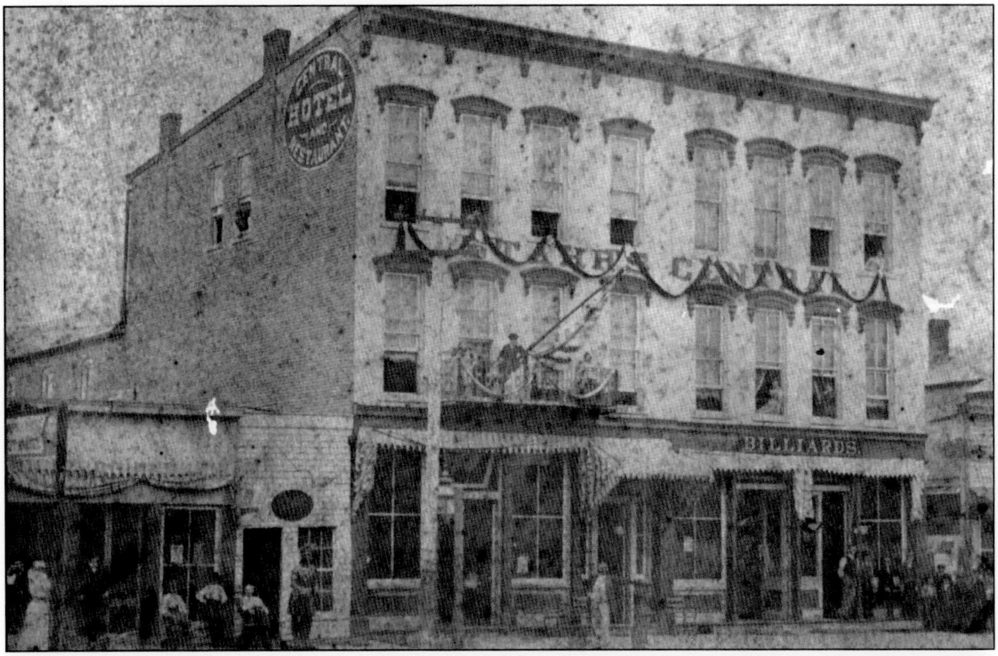

Here is a cabinet photograph of the Stahr Central Hotel on the National Road in Cambridge City taken on September 26, 1881—a week after the assassination of Pres. James A. Garfield. Black mourning cloth is draped below the windows, which almost all contain women and children posing for the camera. The men stand on the wooden sidewalks below with a life-sized wooden Indian on display in front of the cigar store located on the building's first floor. The photograph is actually autographed and dated by hotel owner William Stahr, who can be seen leaning on the beam in front of the building. (Courtesy Rick Newton.)

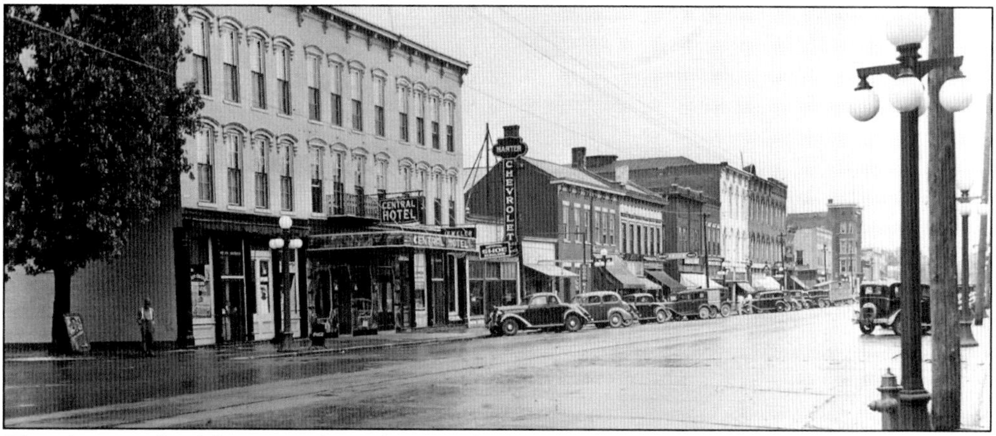

This photograph of the Central Hotel in Cambridge City was taken in the late 1930s. A billiards hall and cigar store are on the ground floor of the hotel. A soda fountain with a Coca-Cola sign out front, a jewelry store, Superior shoe rebuilding shop, Harter Chevrolet car dealership, and Kroger grocery store can also be seen. The Knights of Pythias building is in the distance. The Thompson family purchased the hotel in 1932 and ran it until 1948. The hotel was closed in the early 1960s, and the 92-year-old building was demolished in 1963 after being declared a fire hazard. The Wayne County Bank occupies the spot today. (Courtesy Cambridge City Library-History Room.)

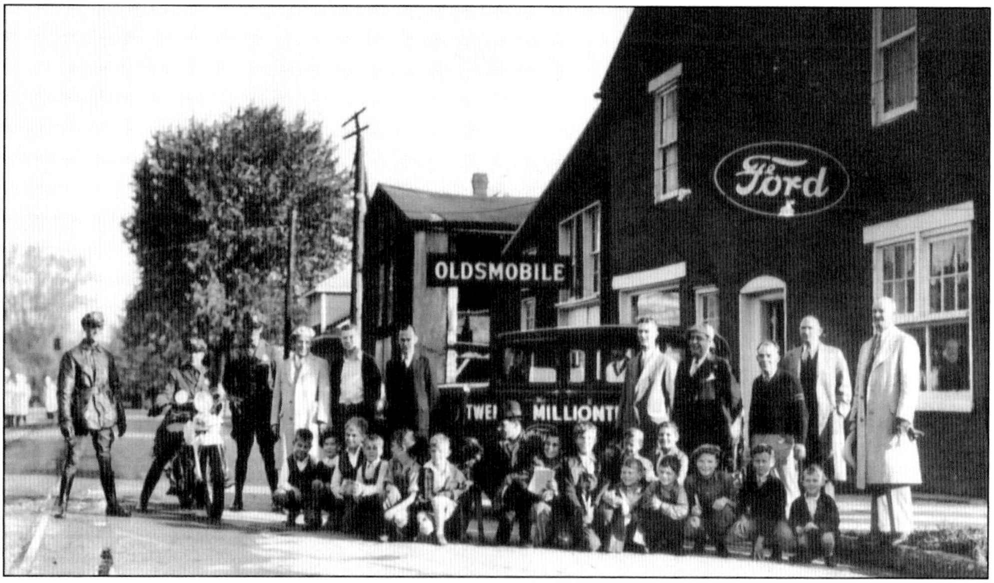

On April 14, 1931, Henry Ford, with his son Edsel in the passenger seat, drove the 20-millionth Ford automobile off the assembly line at the Dearborn, Michigan, plant. The car embarked on a grand tour of the United States with the Ford logo and "Twenty Millionth" emblazoned on its sides and roof. The milestone Ford Model A car bore license plate number 20000000 and was driven from Michigan, to New York, to the West Coast, to Southwest and South, and finally back to Dearborn. A steady stream of dignitaries, including Eleanor Roosevelt, Douglas Fairbanks, and Adm. Richard E. Byrd, drove the car. The vehicle received the checkered flag at the Indianapolis Speedway after making a stop at the local Ford dealership in Cambridge City as part of the tour. The dealership was located at 1 East Church Street in the building currently occupied by the office of Dr. James R. Bertsch, D.O. This shot was taken looking towards the National Road, which is one block north. (Courtesy Jim and Norma Bertsch.)

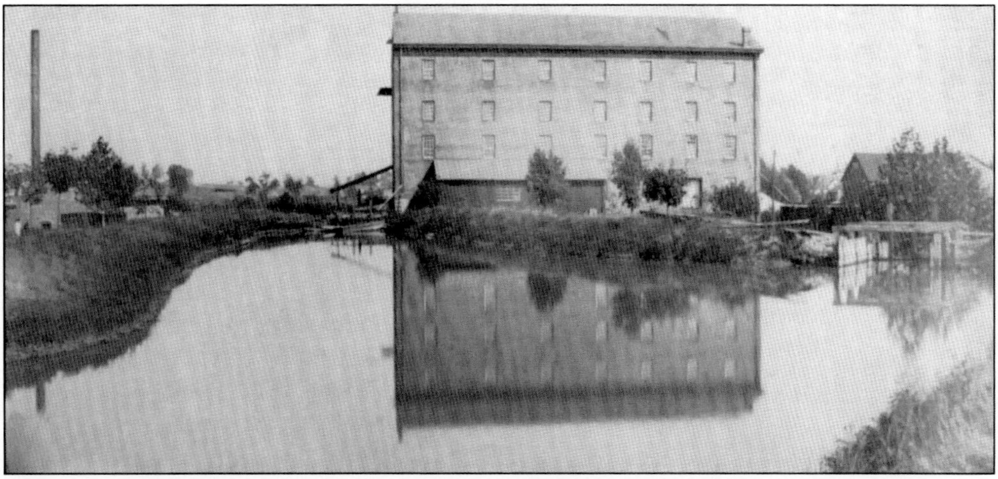

Pictured is the Old Well from the cover of the 1907 Western Wayne business directory provided by the Cambridge City Chamber of Commerce. (Courtesy April and Mark Riggle.)

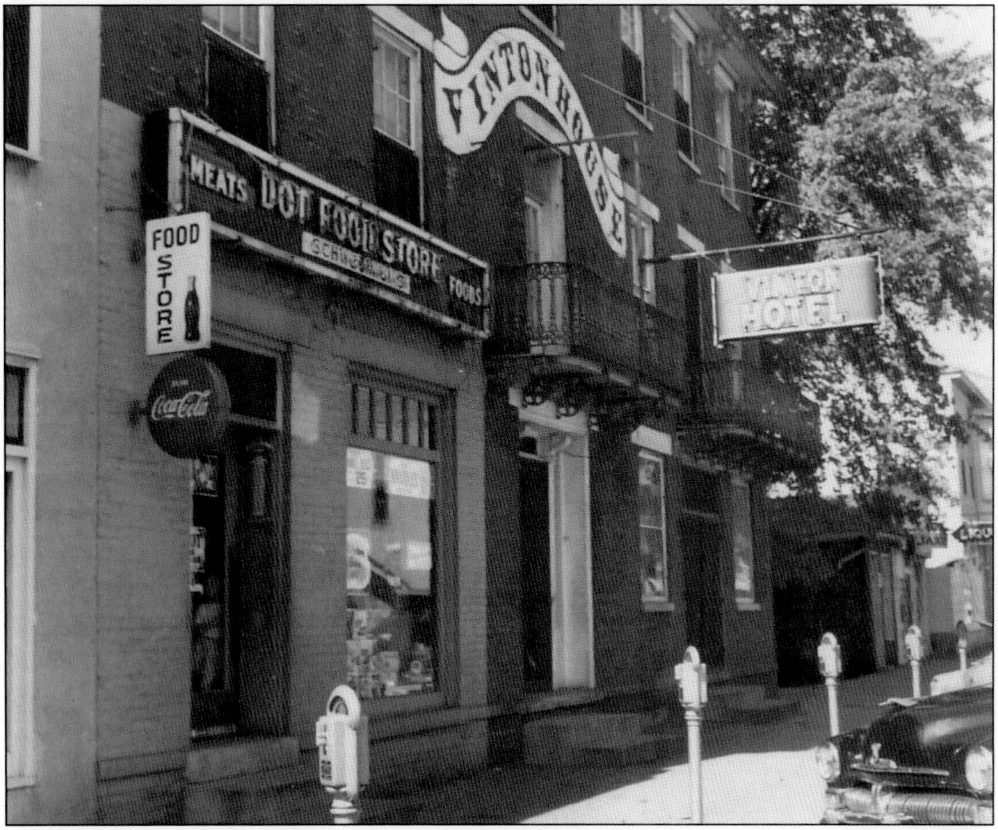

This picture of the Vinton House Hotel was taken sometime in the late 1940s with the Dot Food Store located in the eastern portion of the first floor of the hotel. The old metal "Vinton Hotel" sign hangs over the door, and the food store features a two-piece Coca-Cola sign attached to the front of the building. Notice the parking meters located on the National Road in front of the hotel. Those meters are no longer there, proving that not everything increases in price over time, as parking is free on this spot today. (Courtesy Cambridge City Library-History Room.)

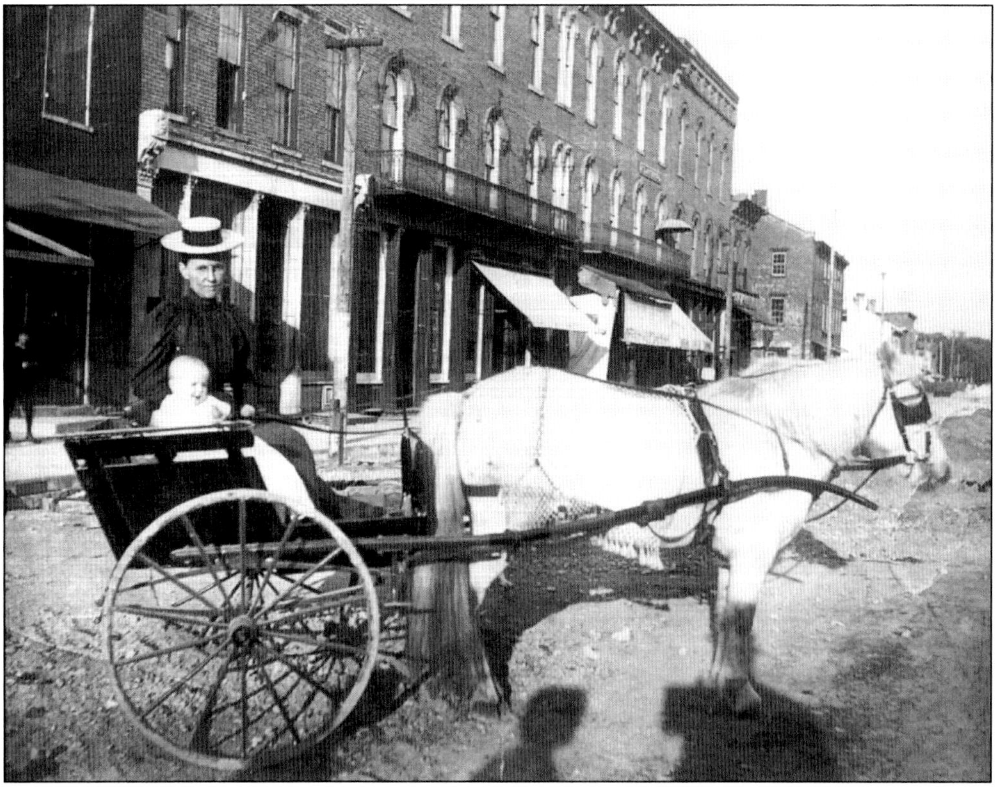

A woman and child in a horse and buggy have stopped for a moment to have their picture taken on the National Road in Cambridge City. The scene is looking north on Main Street sometime in the late 1800s before the arrival of the interurban. The Hurst Building can be seen in the background with its distinctive iron railing, and the Conklin Building occupies the sight of the future Danner's five-and-dime store. Notice the shadow of the photographer and the old-fashioned box camera in the lower portion of the image. Today, the building in the background is home to the Pour House restaurant at 109 West Main Street. (Courtesy Cambridge City Library-History Room.)

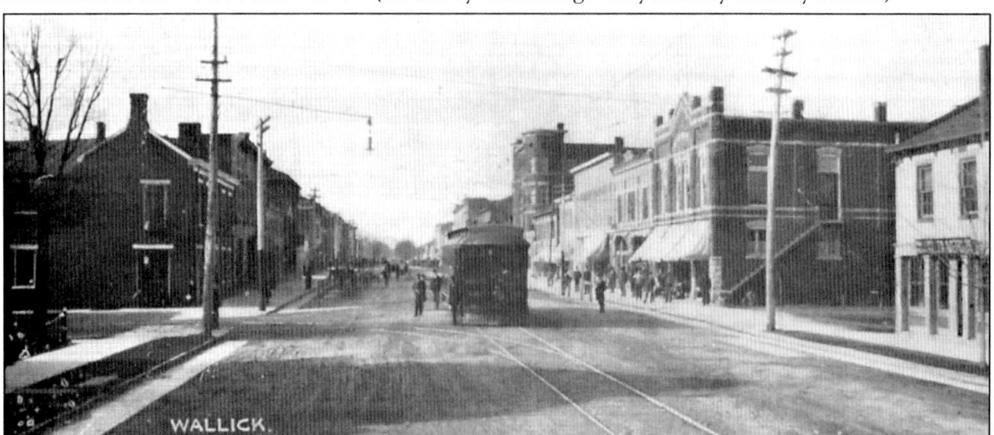

The arrival of the first interurban passenger coach in Cambridge City was on Friday, November 14, 1902. The photographer's mark is from Wallick Cambridge City. (Courtesy April and Mark Riggle.)

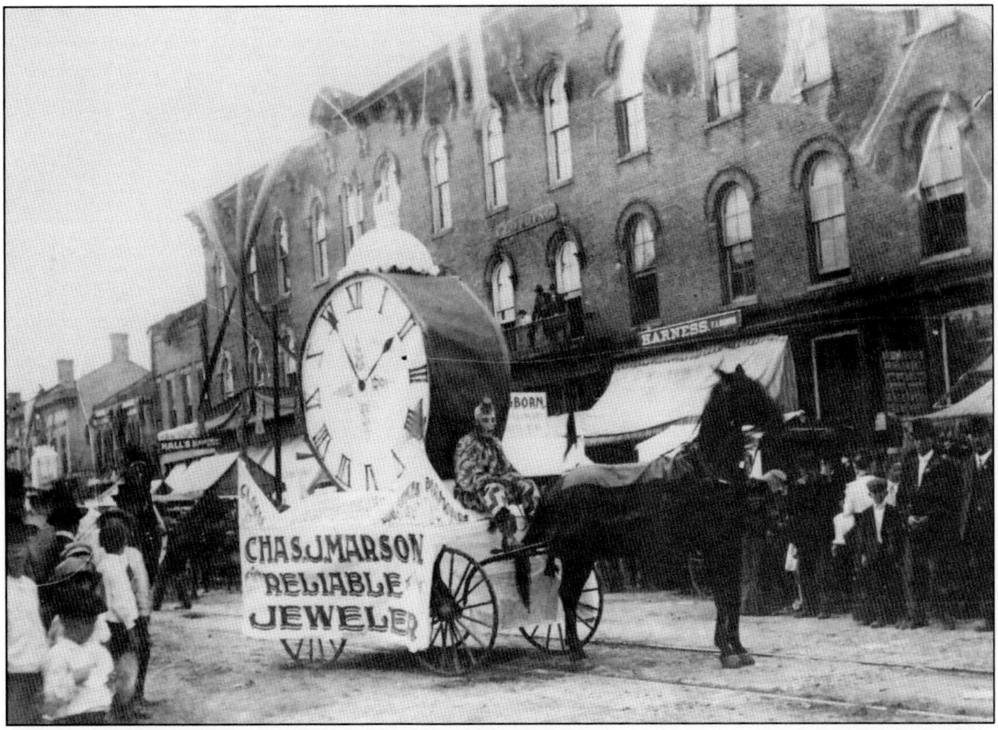

A 1905 photograph of a Cambridge City parade on Main Street depicts a man dressed as a clown driving a large clock-shaped, horse-drawn float sponsored by the Chas. J. Marson Reliable Jeweler store. (Courtesy Cambridge City Library-History Room.)

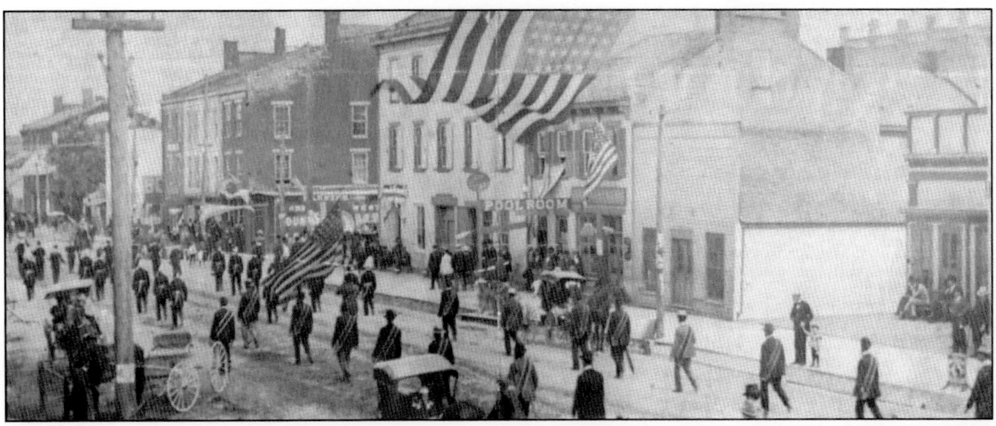

This is West Main Street and South Foote Street as it appeared in 1901. A GAR parade of former Civil War soldiers wearing large sashes marches east on the National Road. The road is lined with American flags waving proudly. (Courtesy April and Mark Riggle.)

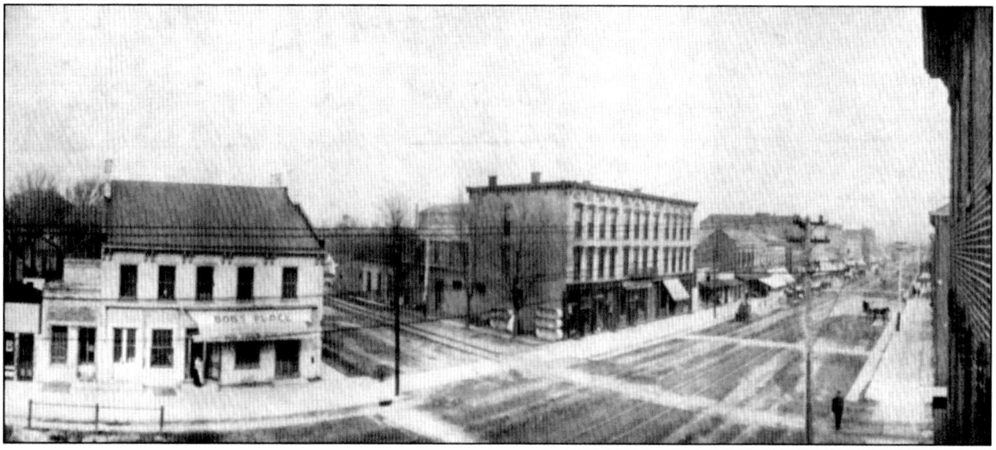

This is the corner of Main and Green Streets in Cambridge as it looked in 1907. The Central Hotel is shown on the right corner, and Bob's Place is on the opposite corner. (Courtesy April and Mark Riggle.)

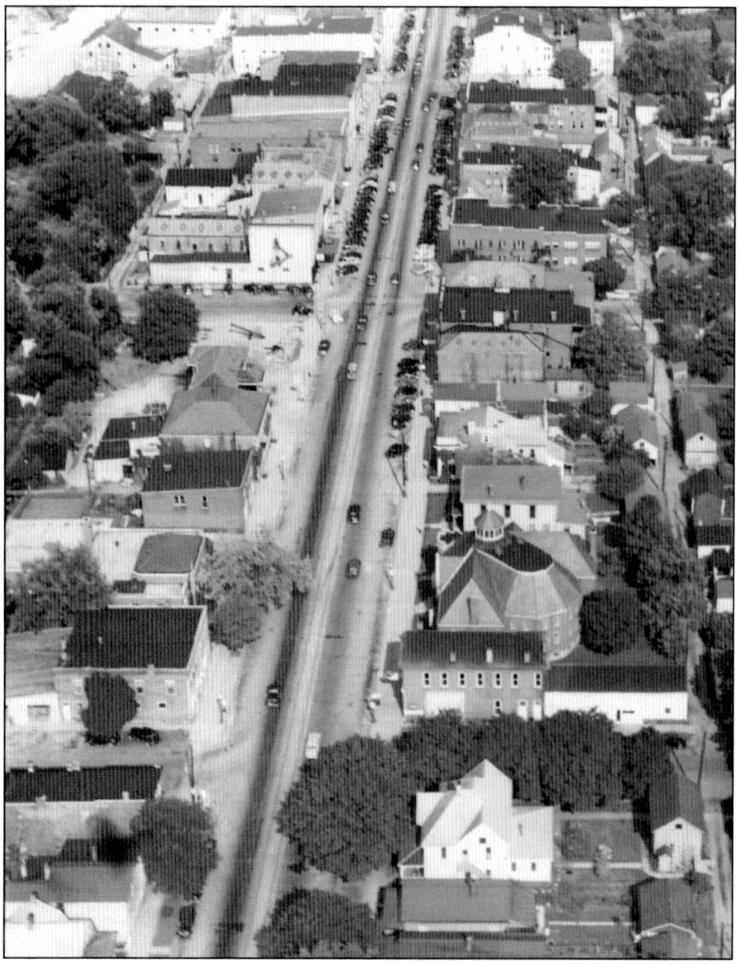

This overhead view is of the National Road as seen from the western edge of Cambridge City looking east. It was taken sometime in the late 1940s. (Courtesy Cambridge City Library-History Room.)

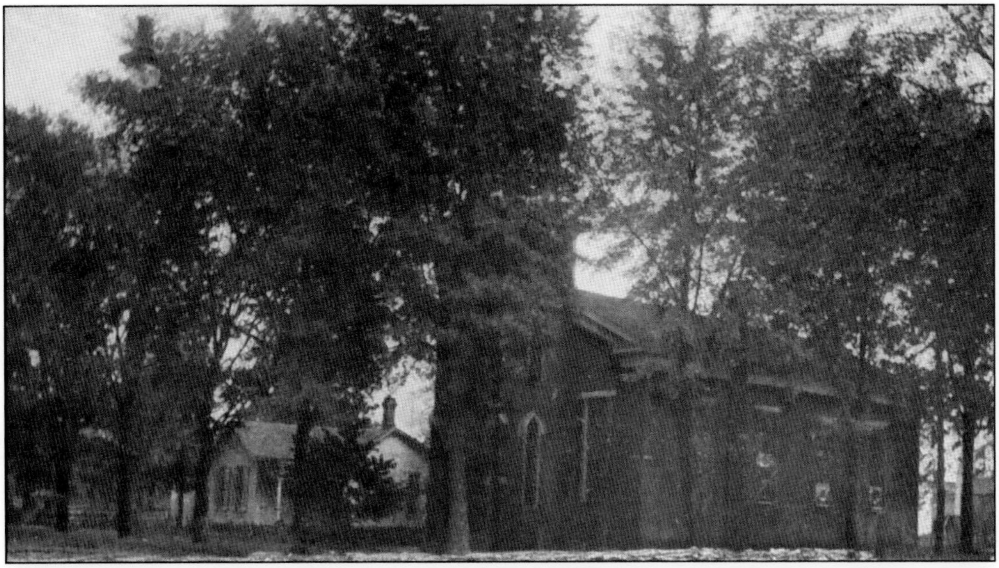

Pictured is Cambridge City Presbyterian Church, at 136 West Church Street, in a c. 1900 postcard. Built in 1857, the church was originally constructed of native redbrick made from materials in the creeks and streams that surrounded it. For the first few years, the church was an open-air building with no roof. During the opening months of the Civil War, the ladies of the church raised money to put a new roof on the building by selling three meals a day to the many units of soldiers being formed in town. One of these units included members of Cambridge City's famous 19th Indiana—Solomon Meredith's Iron Brigade. (Alan E. Hunter collection.)

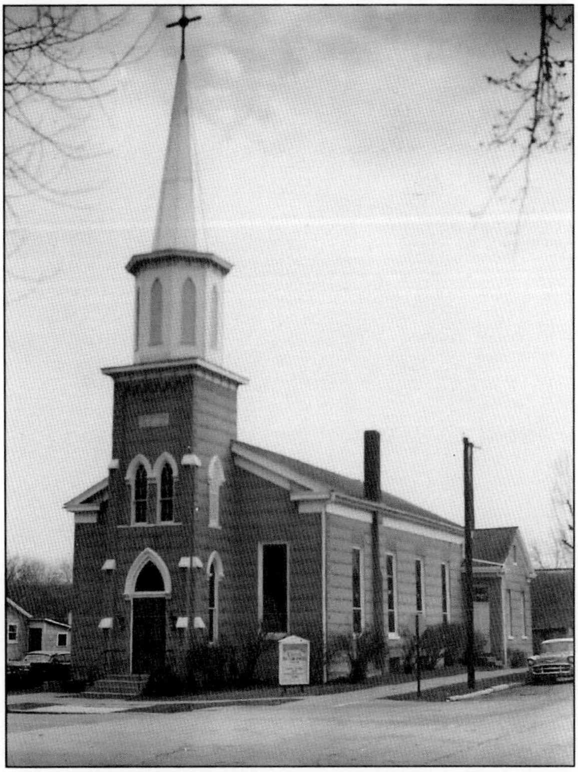

Sometime around 1910, the church's redbrick exterior was covered with a more regal-looking composite material that gave it a limestone hue. In 1935, the church was raised up on jacks, and a basement was dug out for use as a congregational meeting room. The church was carefully lowered back down, and classrooms and offices were added to the back. This picture was taken in 1961 during the 125th anniversary of the church. (Alan E. Hunter collection.)

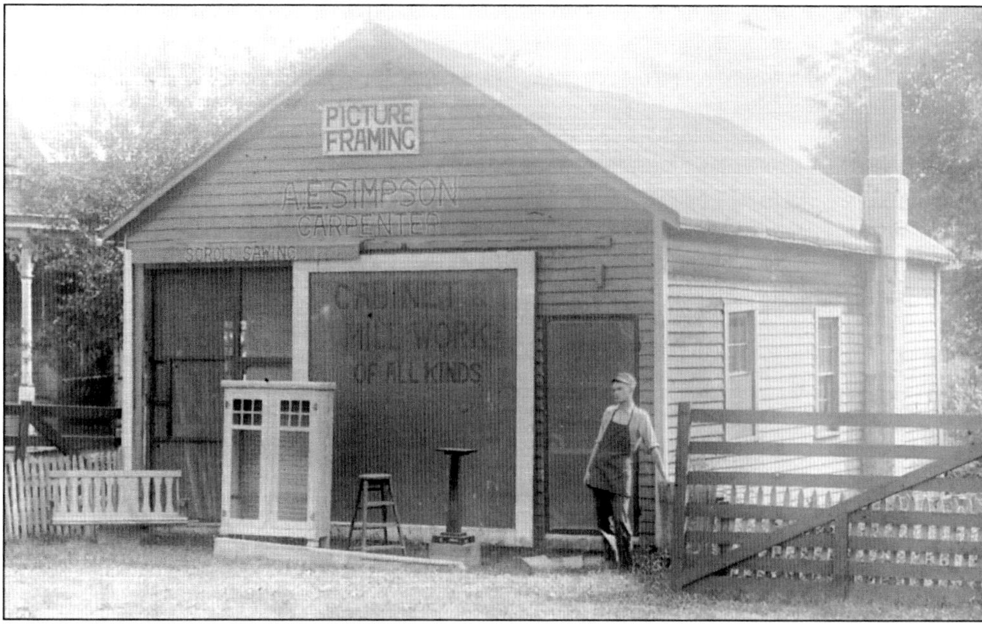

This photograph of a typical Hoosier carpenter's shop on the National Road was taken in 1903. A.E. Simpson is posing outside with some of his handiwork, including a pedestal, fence section, ladder, and kitchen cabinet. The caption on the back reads, "No job to small or to large for the Besy Service. Exterior of A.E. Simpson's Carpenter shop at Dublin, Indiana and a few of the pieces of work produced in it." (Courtesy Patricia H. McDaniel.)

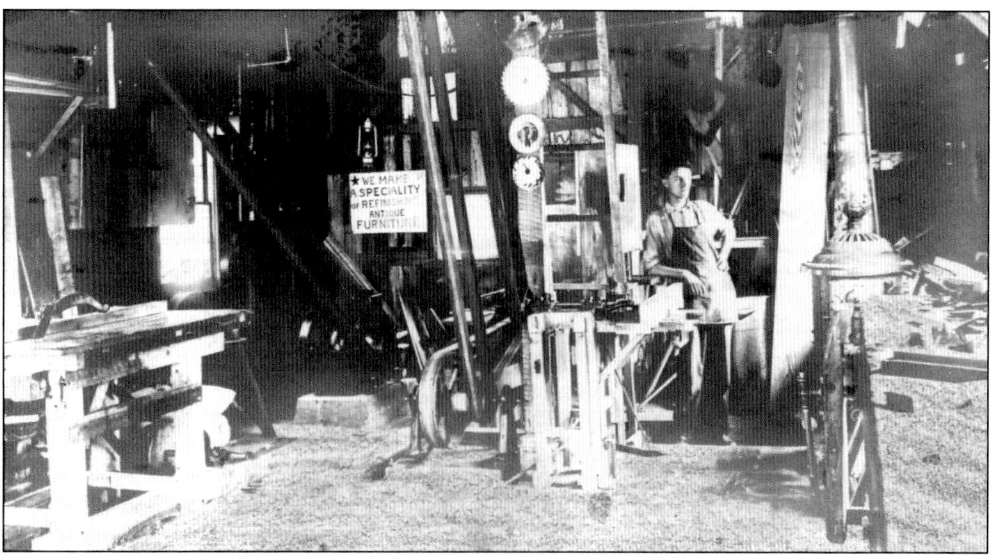

A 1903 interior photograph of A.E. Simpson's carpentry shop captures some of the machines and an unidentified young carpenter in overalls. A handwritten caption on the reverse reads, "We do all kinds of Cabinet and Millwork. Door and window frames, sash, and screens any size desired made on orders. We make a speciality [*sic*] on Enterior [*sic*] finish, such as built in cabinets and refinishing antique furniture." The sign in the photograph states, "We make a speciality [*sic*] of refinishing antique furniture." (Courtesy Patricia H. McDaniel.)

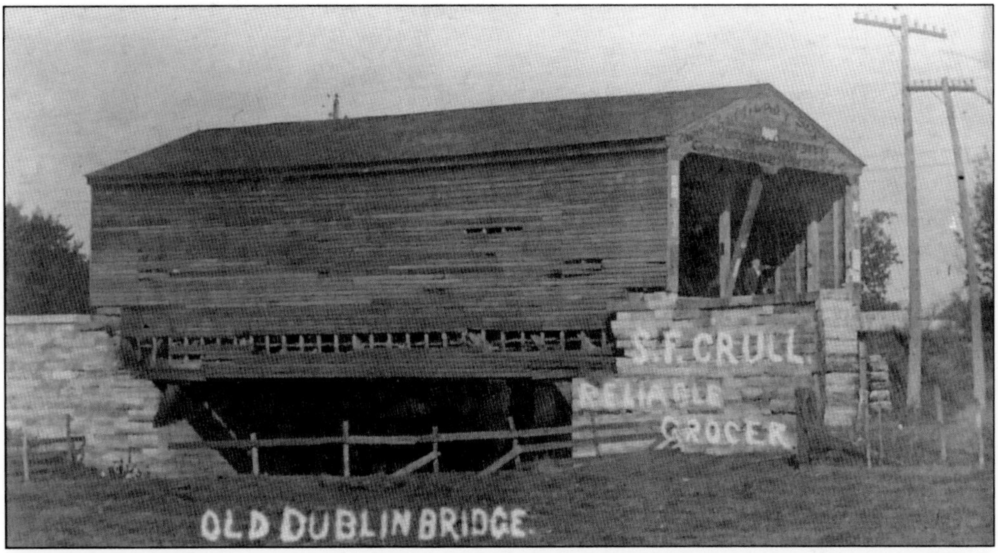

The Old Dublin Bridge, west of Dublin on the National Road, was the first covered bridge on the route of the famed Hoosier Road. It was built in 1834 and demolished in 1921. The bridge features a hand-painted sign on its side that reads, "S.F. Crull Reliable Grocer." Several smaller signs and broadsides are nailed to the front of the bridge with the name "Milroy" on the eaves under the roof. A man wearing a derby hat poses proudly in the opening. Judging by the electric lines and the dilapidated condition of the bridge, this photograph must have been taken shortly before it was demolished. (Courtesy Cambridge City Library-History Room.)

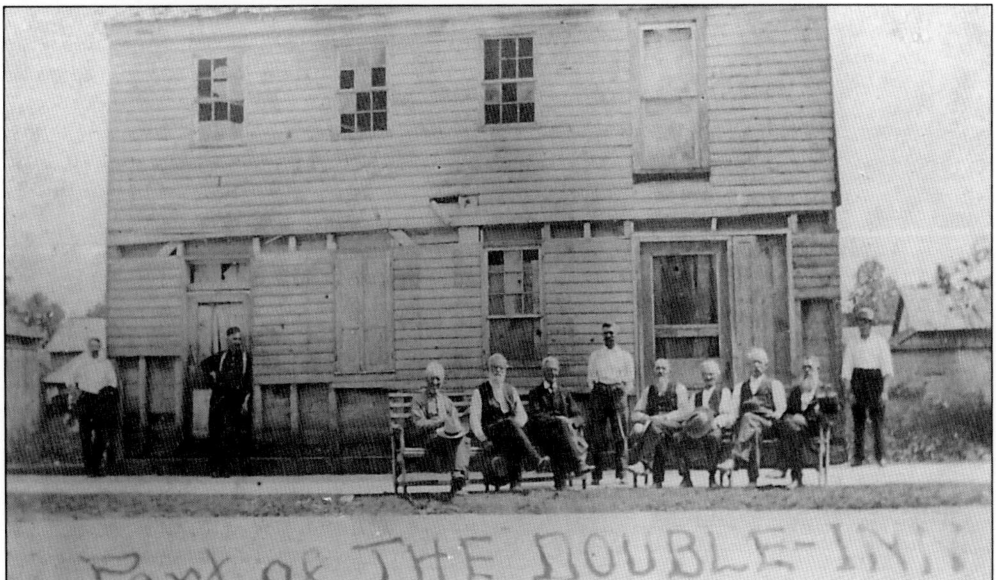

Capitalizing on the equivocality of the town's name, the Double-Inn Hotel, located on the National Road in Dublin, was a popular stop for travelers for over a century. The photograph is captioned, "Part of the Double-Inn" at the bottom. The men posing for the camera are identified as, from left to right, Cass Greene, Clarence Reede, unidentified, Silas Huddleston, Bishop Floyd, Frank Hoffman, Isaac Huddleston, Matt Garthwaite, unidentified, Jacob Huffman, and Paul or Ray Carter. (Courtesy Cambridge City Library-History Room.)

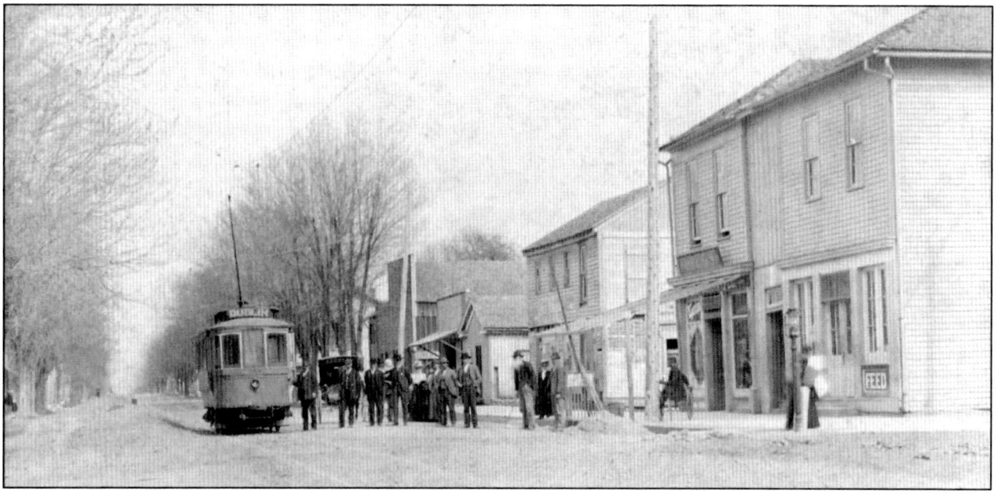

The interurban arrived in Dublin, Indiana, on April 30, 1903. The destination sign over the first-generation electric train reads, "Dublin," as both uniformed trainmen stand proudly beside the car, and townspeople get their first look at the new conveyance. Ironically, the crowd includes a man in a horse and buggy that would soon become obsolete by the interurban system. The Dublin livery, drugstore, and general store are visible at right; Bull Durham tobacco signs cover the general store's exterior. Note the man in the wheelchair on the wood planked sidewalk and the man with the flowing white beard standing cautiously at a distance—he seems very unsure of the modern contraption. (Courtesy Cambridge City Library-History Room.)

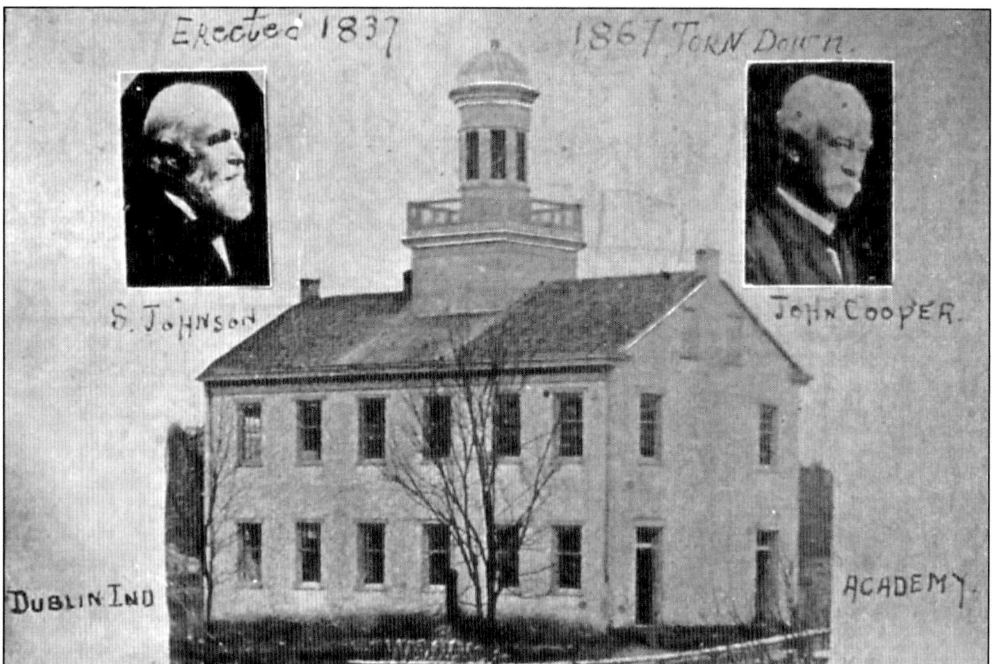

A joint stock company established the Dublin Academy in 1837. The building was later occupied as a public schoolhouse. In 1867, it was torn down and replaced by another schoolhouse that was dedicated on New Year's Day 1868 at a cost of $5,000, with an enrollment of 450 students. The school's two administrators are pictured at the top. (Courtesy Cambridge City Library-History Room.)

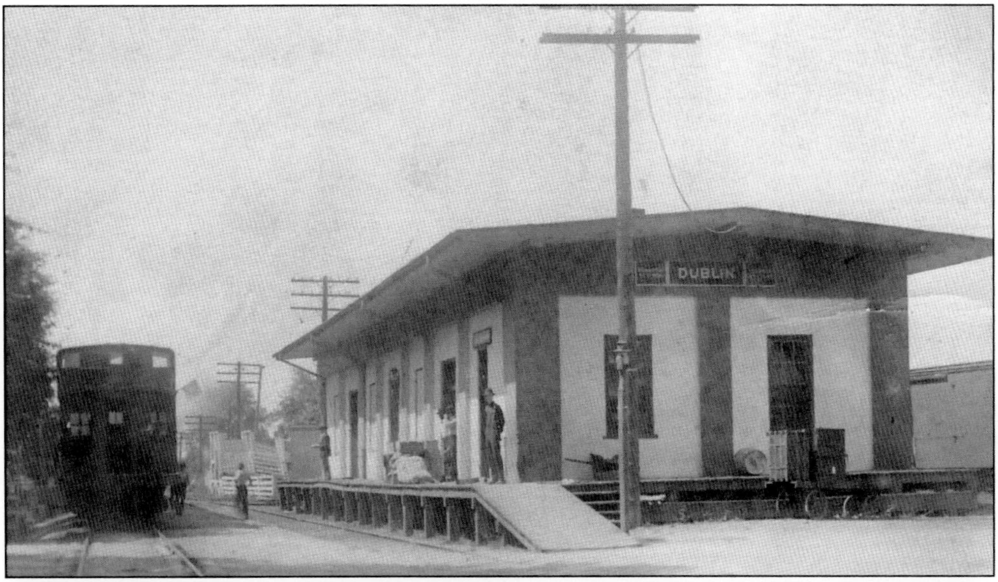

Here is a 1912 photograph postcard of the Dublin Railroad Depot. The sign on the top of the building lists the Dublin name and the miles to Indianapolis and to Richmond. (Courtesy Bill Raney.)

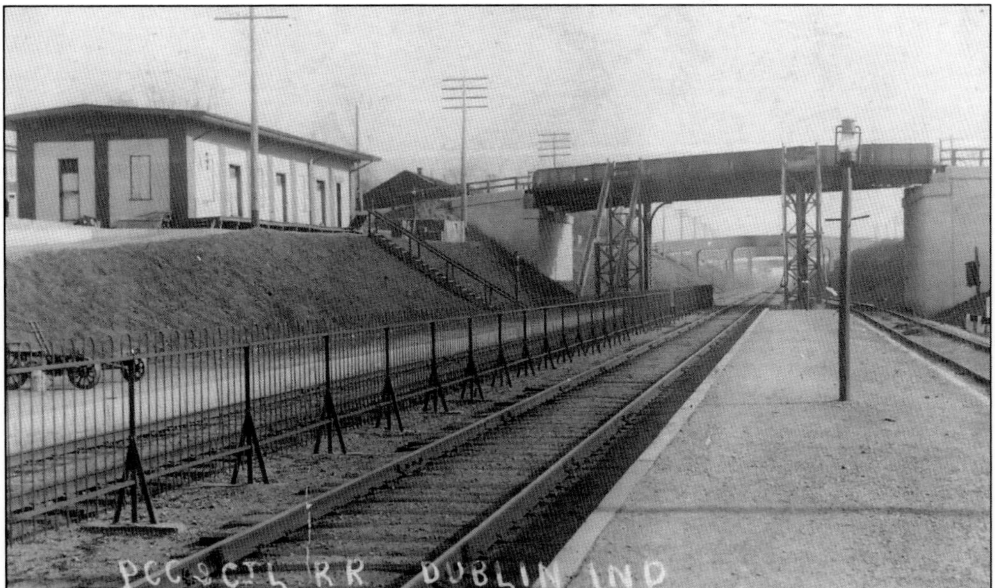

Here is another 1912 photo postcard of the Dublin Railroad Depot. This view shows the stairway descending to the tracks below the depot where passengers arrived and departed. (Courtesy Bill Raney.)

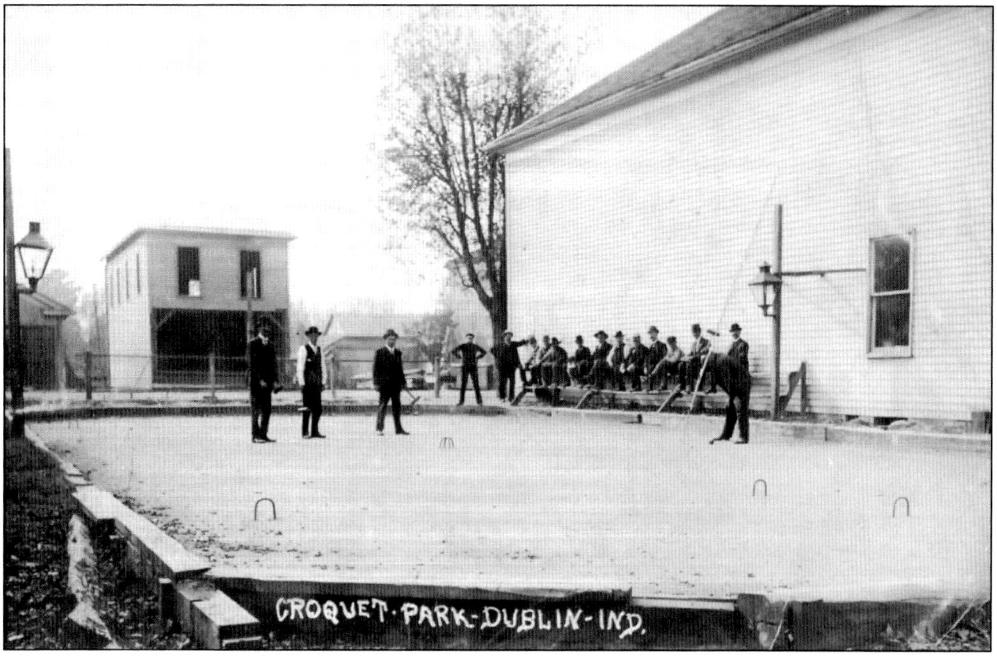

This intriguing c. 1910 photograph postcard, captioned, "Croquet Park Dublin, Ind," depicts a group of men playing and observing croquet on a well-made court that features lighting on the sides and wooden stands for spectators. (Courtesy Cambridge City Library-History Room.)

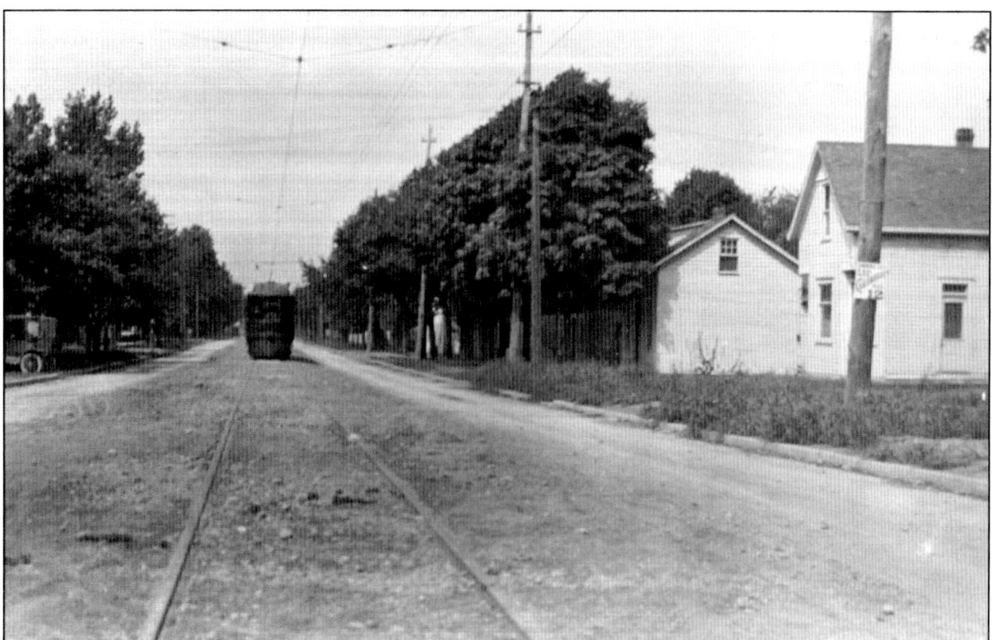

The Dublin interurban is seen chugging right down the center of the National Road around 1918. The sign on the pole on the right announces the upcoming August 12 Chautauqua meeting in nearby Cambridge City, which likely means that this view is facing east. (Courtesy Cambridge City Library-History Room.)

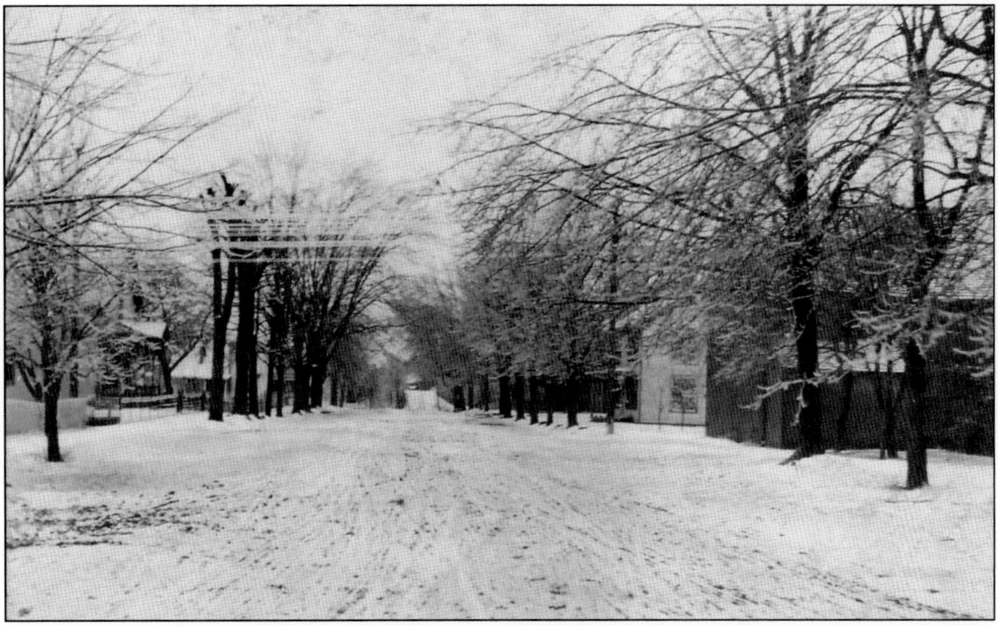

The message on this c. 1918 photograph postcard of the snow-covered National Road in Dublin reads, "Aunt Ann, I thought you might like to see a little bit of Dublin as it looked one morning with sleet on the trees. Norton has a kodak + made the picture. Dublin goes along in the same old way. Wish we could see you, yours, Margaret B. Wilson." She has added "south from Swann's Grocery" on the side. (Courtesy Cambridge City Library-History Room.)

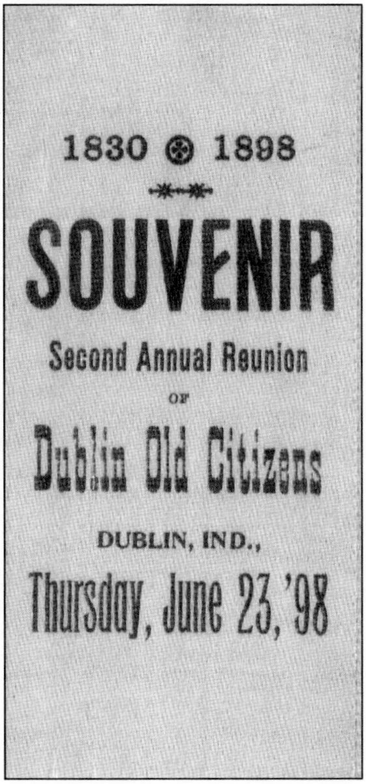

This is an 1898 ribbon from the second gathering of Dublin, Indiana, pioneers and Old Settlers. (Courtesy Bill Raney.)

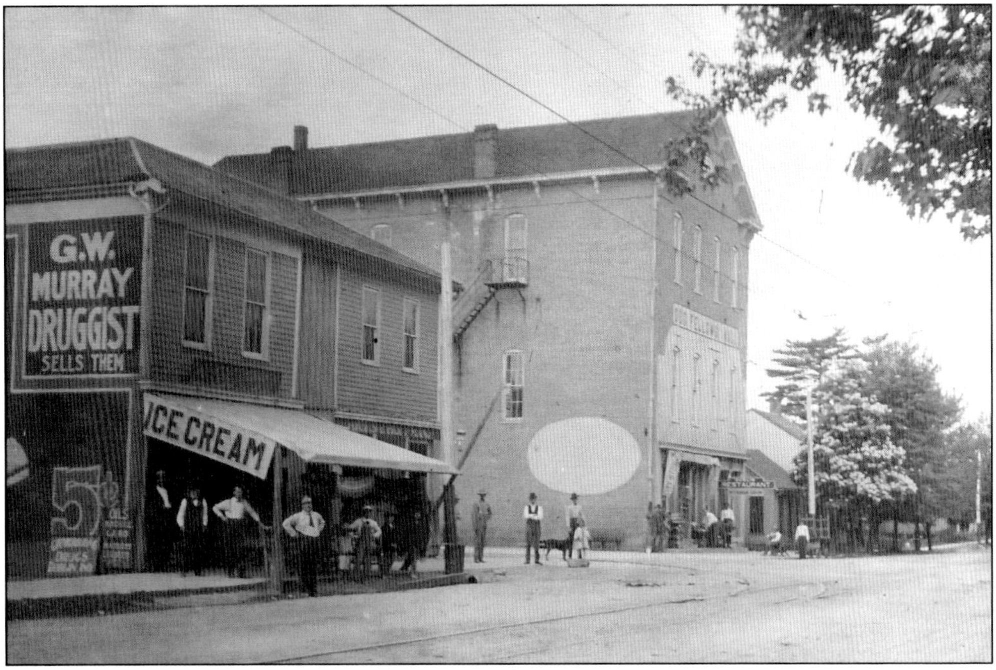

The Dublin Restaurant is seen on the ground floor of the Odd Fellows building in the 1910s. The Odd Fellows Hall painted sign can still be seen on front of the brick building. The Hicks & Hoffman Dry Goods store and G.W. Murray Drug Store are on the opposite corner. These stores would be razed and a gas station would take their place. (Courtesy Cambridge City Library-History Room.)

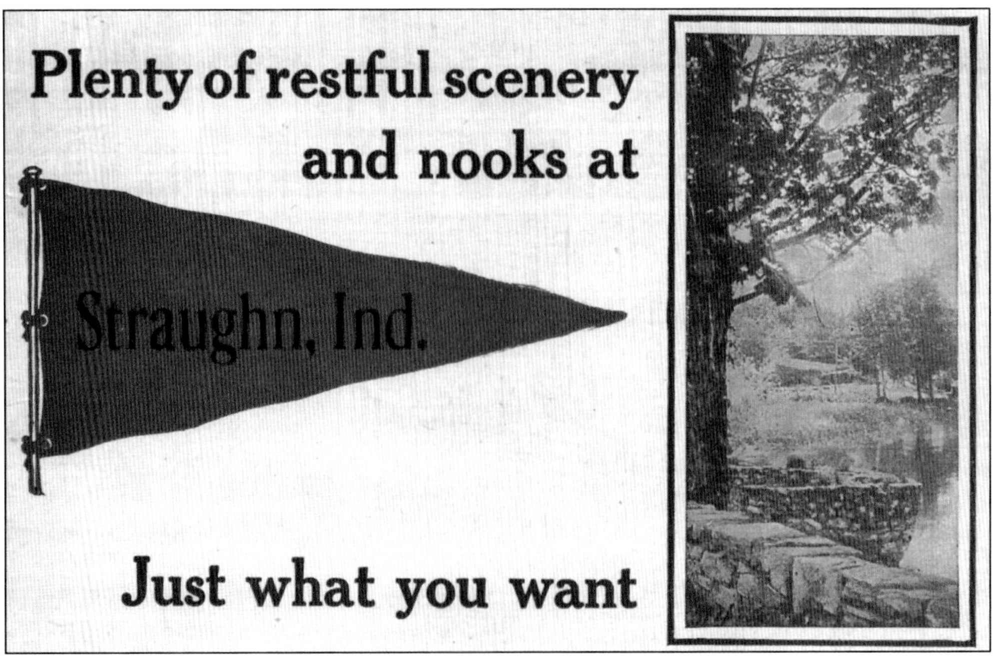

This is a c. 1910 Straughn, Indiana, postcard. (Courtesy Kathy Miller.)

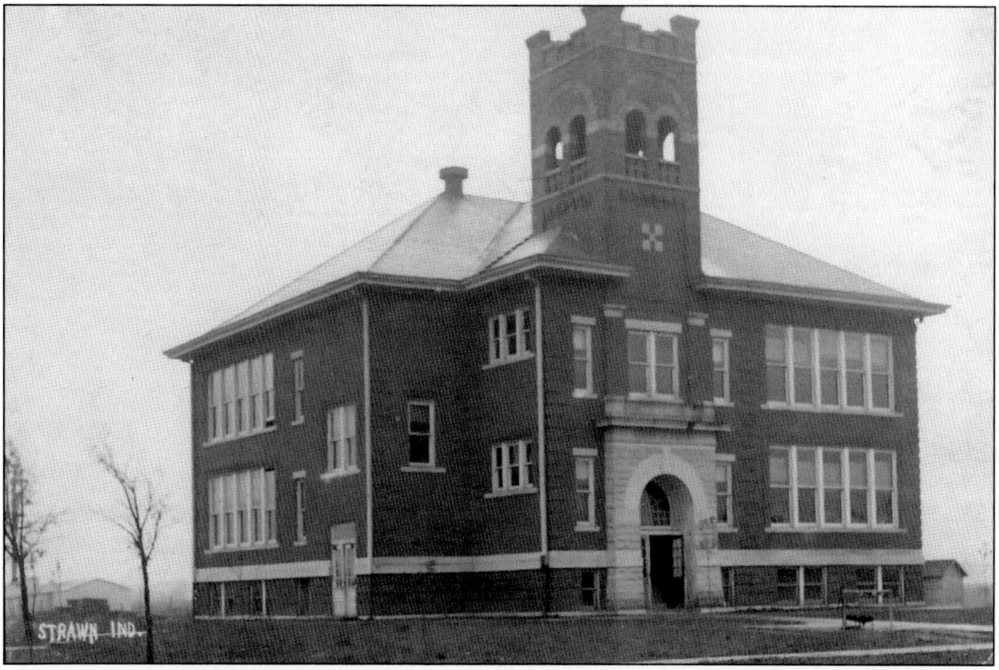

Note the misspelled name at the bottom as "Strawn, Ind." on this c. 1900 Straughn School postcard. (Courtesy Kathy Miller.)

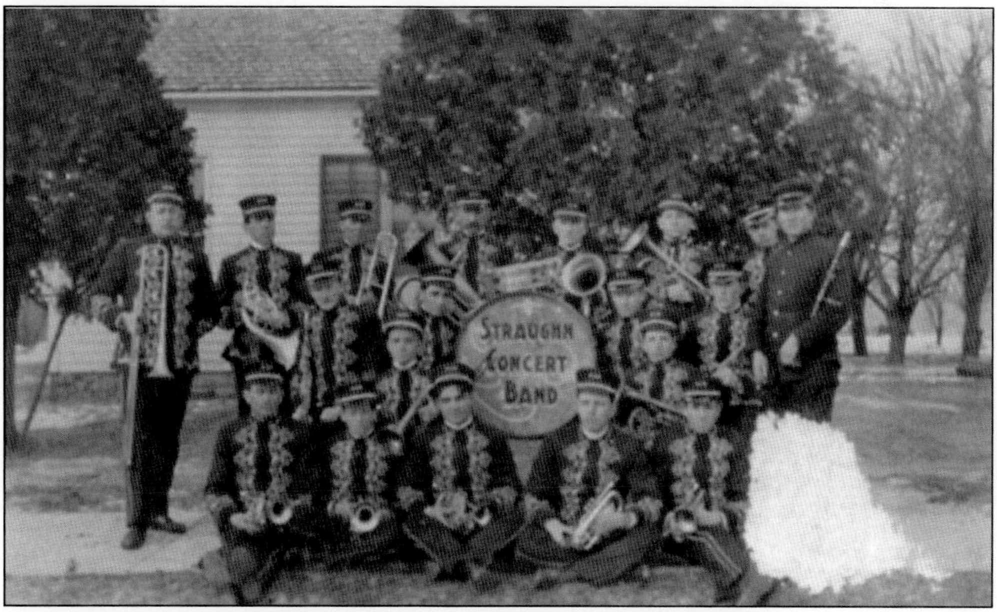

The Straughn Concert Band is pictured in 1908. (Courtesy Kathy Miller.)

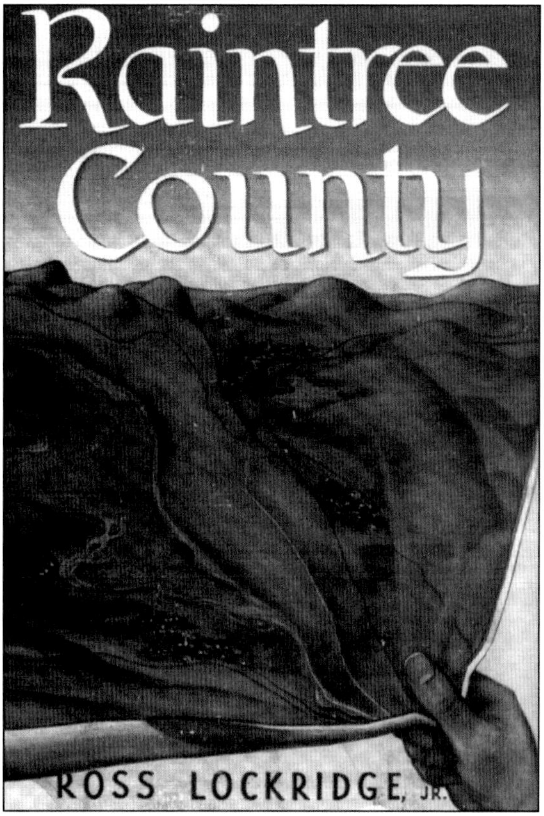

This is the cover of the novel *Raintree County*, by Ross Lockridge Jr., which was published in 1948. The setting for the story is based on Henry County, and the fictional town of Waycross was based on Straughn, Indiana, which is on the National Road. (Alan E. Hunter collection.)

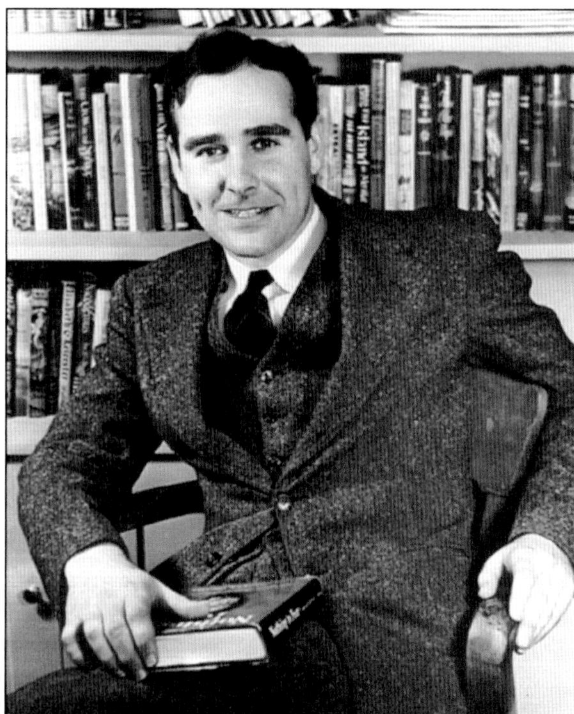

Ross Lockridge Jr. was the author of the novel *Raintree County*. He graduated from Indiana University in 1935 with the highest academic average ever accumulated in the history of the university. Lockridge's novel was received with great critical acclaim. The book takes a look back at the 19th-century history of a fictional Midwestern county through the reminiscences of its protagonist, John Wickliff Shawnessy. Two months after publication and one day before his novel was announced the no. 1 national best seller, Lockridge, suffering from severe depression, took his own life by carbon monoxide poisoning. His grave is in Rose Hill Cemetery in Bloomington. (Alan E. Hunter collection.)

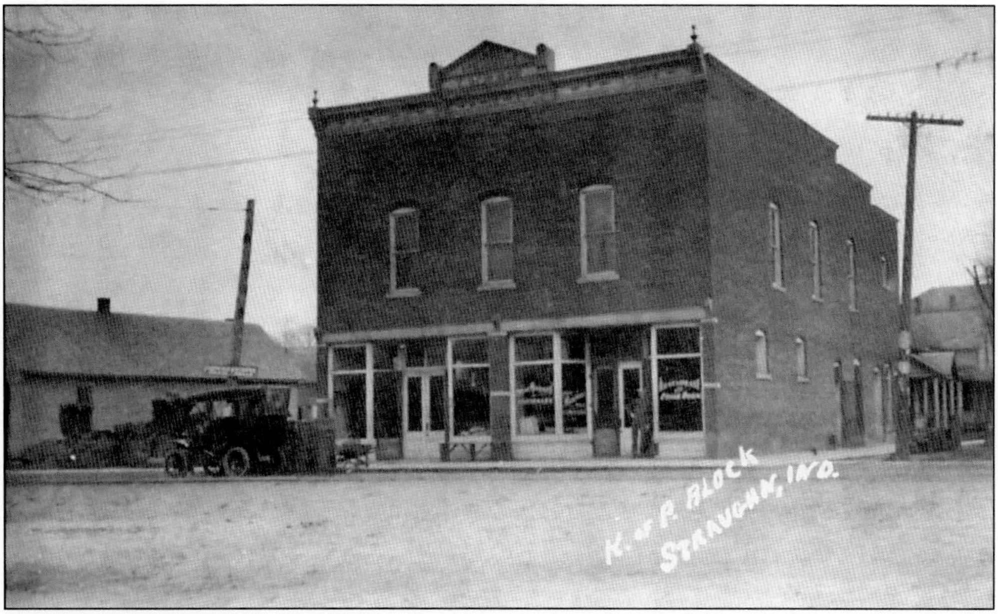

The store window in this c. 1910 photograph of the Straughn Knights of Pythias Building reads, "Meat Market and Stationary" on one side and "Restaurant and Lunch Room" on the other. A man leans against the door jam out front. (Courtesy Kathy Miller.)

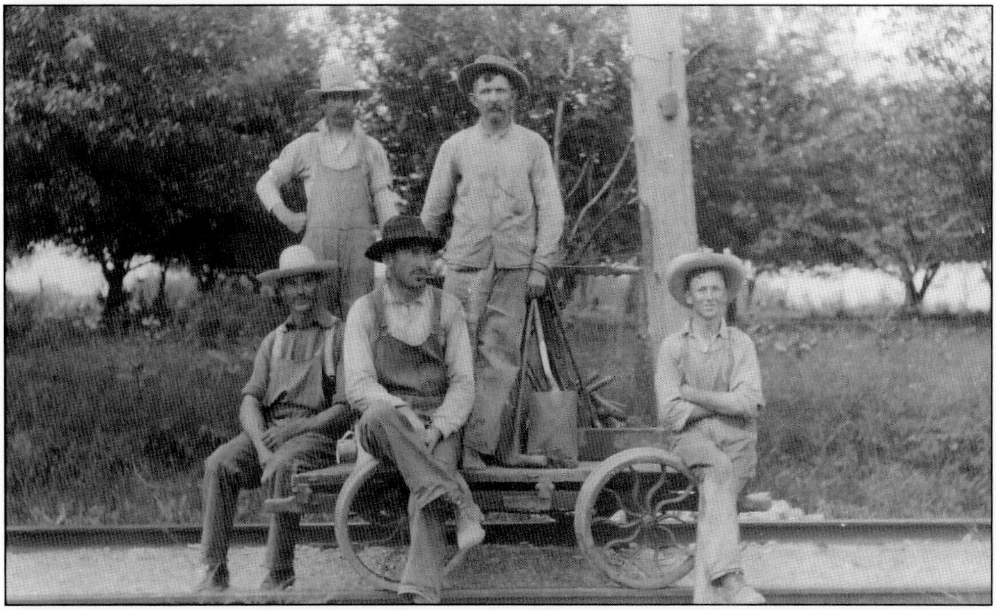

Workers pose while on break from working on the interurban tracks through Lewisville in June of 1909. The men are identified as, from left to right, Steve Robins, Arthur Judd, Clint Borris, Will Kimball, and Harry Davitt. The real-photo postcard is captioned, "Section Foreman & hands." (Courtesy Kathy Miller.)

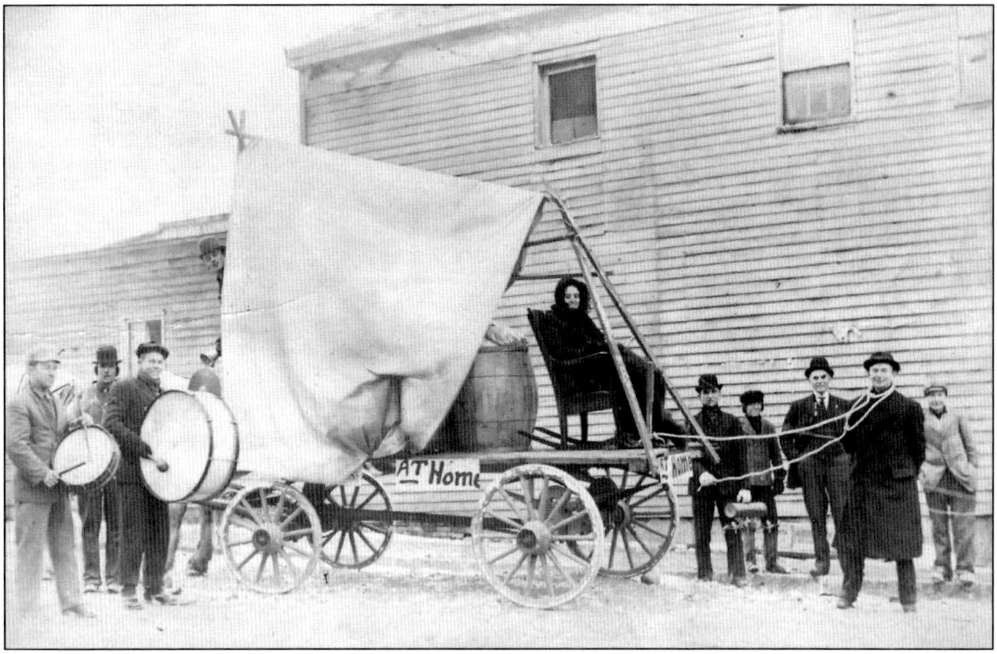

This charming real-photo postcard of an old-fashioned Lewisville wedding parade is captioned, "When Billie Helms Got Married" and features the bride seated in a rocking chair aboard a buckboard wagon (with "At Home" written on the front and sides) pulled by her new husband, who has an ominous-looking noose wrapped around his neck. Two friends follow behind the wagon beating huge drums, and another cigar-chomping friend peeks out from behind the curtain in the rear of the wagon while ringing a school bell. (Courtesy Kathy Miller.)

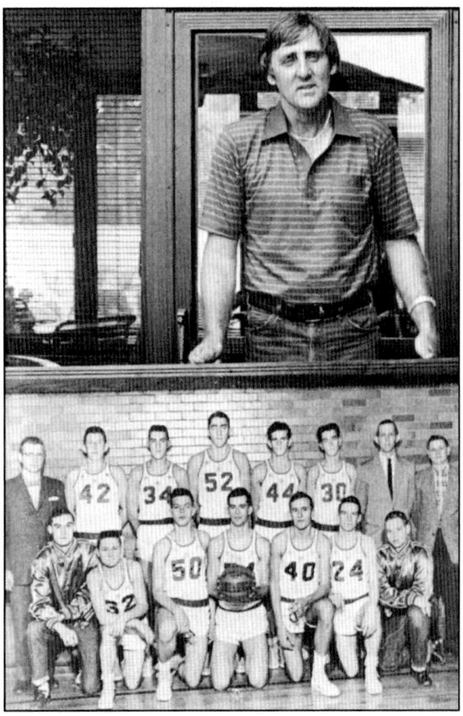

Marion Pierce displays a picture of the Lewisville team he played for. At that time in 1961, Lewisville High School only had 81 students. Pierce held the all-time scoring record for an Indiana high school basketball player for 29 years until Damon Bailey broke it in 1990. His 32.4 points-per-game scoring average is still unbroken. Pierce is wearing uniform number 52 in the team picture; he is holding the framed image outside the offices of his family-owned G.W. Pierce Wrecking Yard located on the National Road in Spiceland. (Courtesy of Susan Hanafee.)

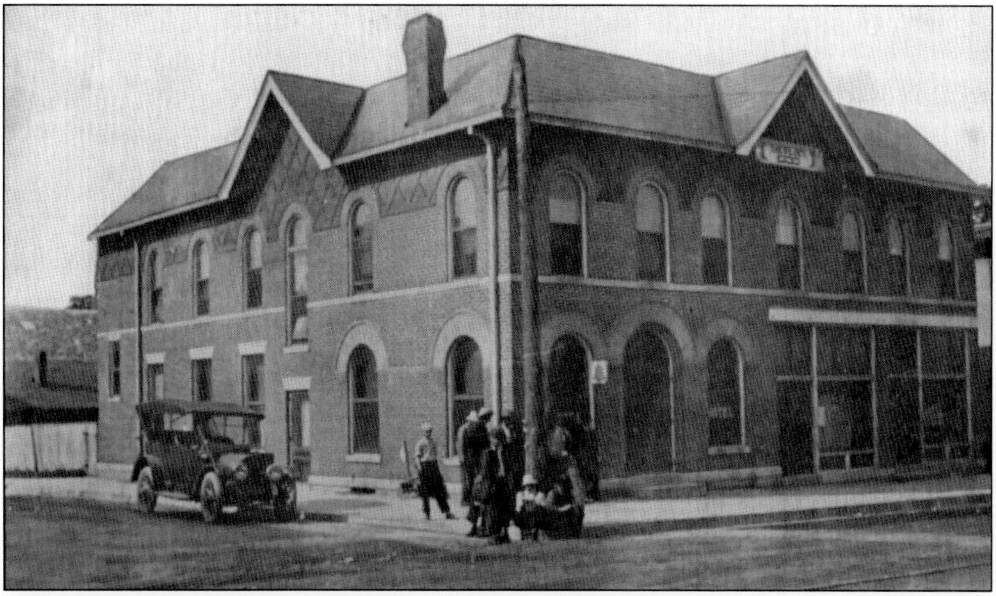

Here is the Wildey Hotel in Lewisville around 1920. A group of people can be seen waiting on the corner for the interurban trolley to arrive. One man is seated on the ground reading the paper, as two of the others read over his shoulder. (Courtesy Kathy Miller.)

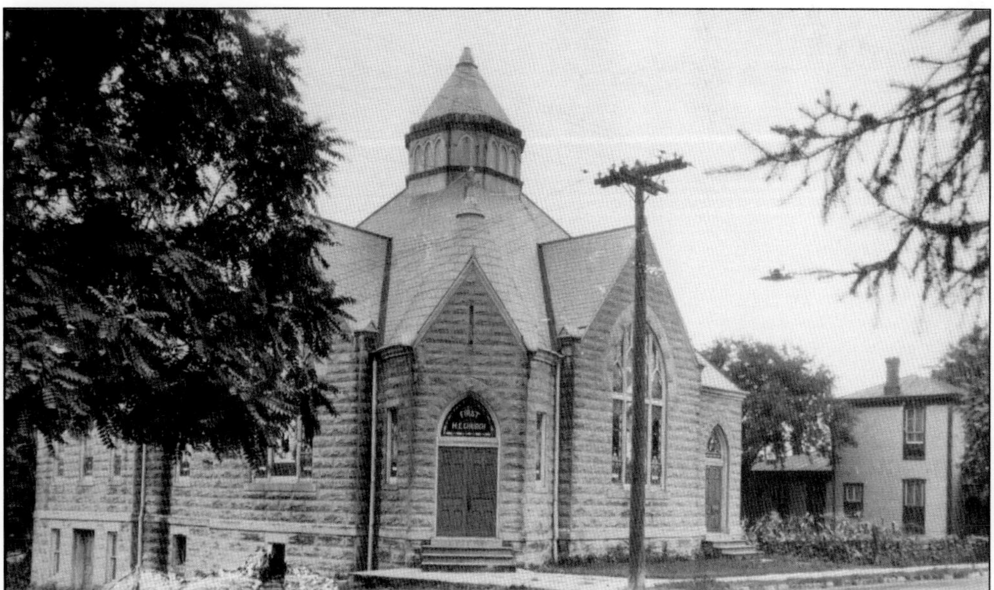

This c. 1915 photograph postcard view is of the First M.E. Church in Lewisville. (Courtesy Rep. Tom Saunders.)

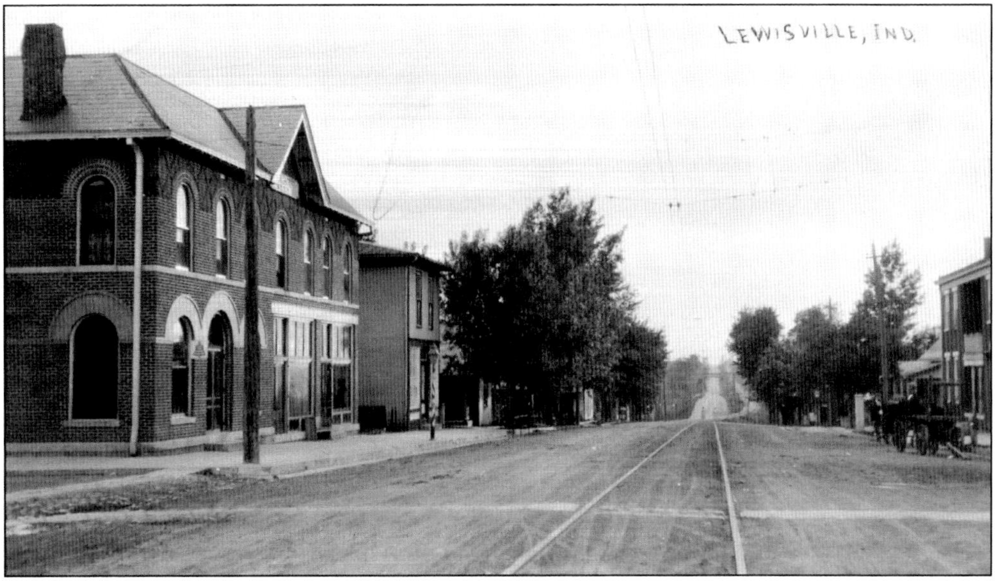

A c. 1915 photograph postcard depicts the National Road in Lewisville. A man poses cross-legged on a wagon on the right, and the ghostly figures of two little girls can be seen in the background, standing on either side of the interurban railroad tracks. The iron bridge can be seen over the road in the far distance as the railroad tracks veer off to the right. (Courtesy Rep. Tom Saunders.)

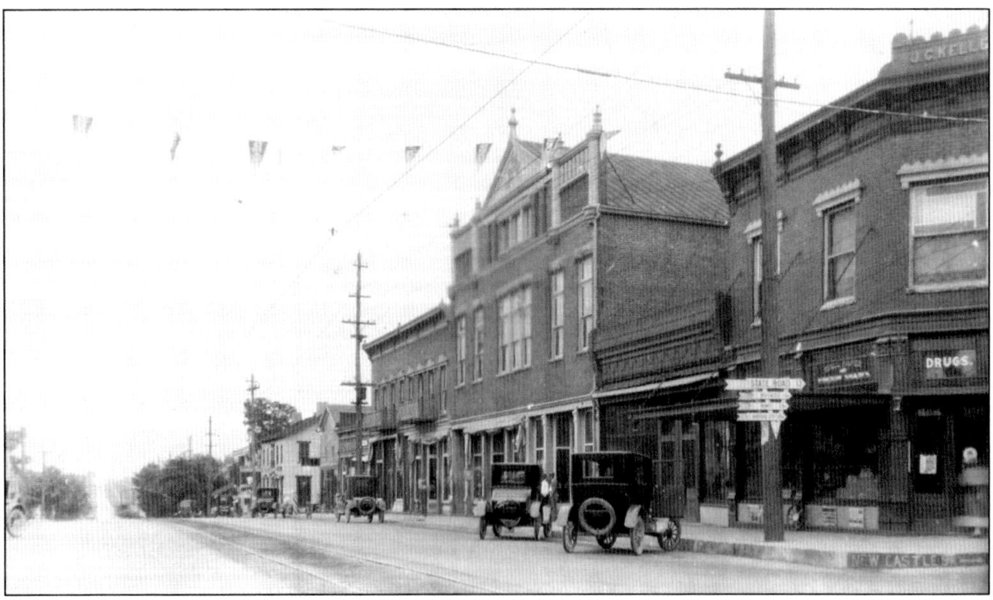

This c. 1915 photograph postcard is titled, "Business Section Lewisville, Ind." and features a view of the National Road in Lewisville looking west. The curb in front of the drugstore located inside the J.C. Keller building on the right side reads, "New Castle 9 Mi." with an arrow pointing north. Curiously, the wooden arrow sign affixed to the pole above reads, "State Road 13 New Castle 8 MI. Munice 25 MI. Hartford City 47 MI." The Guyer Opera House is in the center of the block on the right. (Courtesy Rep. Tom Saunders.)

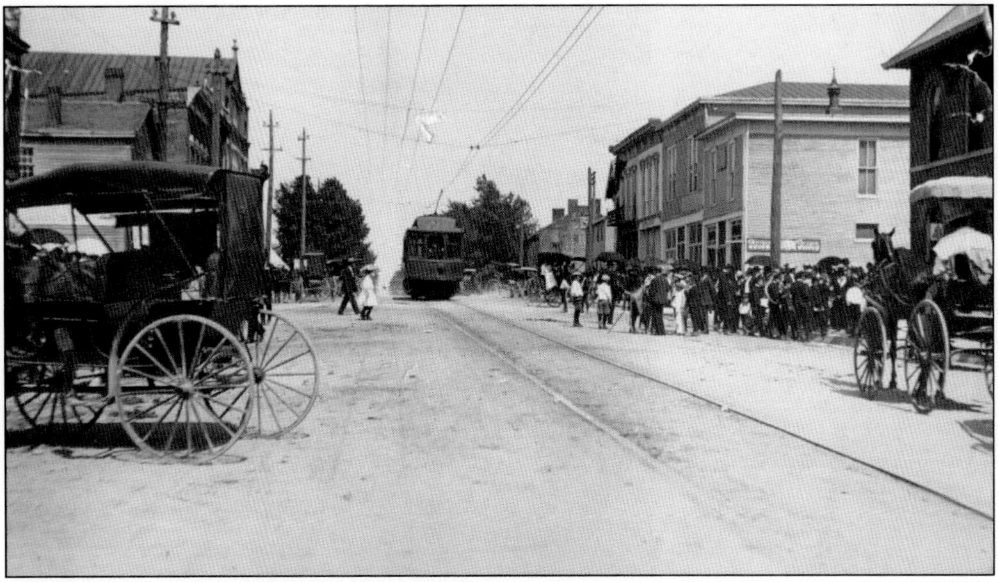

Pictured is the National Road in Lewisville with the interurban train arriving as a parade is breaking up on the right. The band members are seen with their instruments walking towards the alleyway in this c. 1910 picture postcard. (Courtesy Rep. Tom Saunders.)

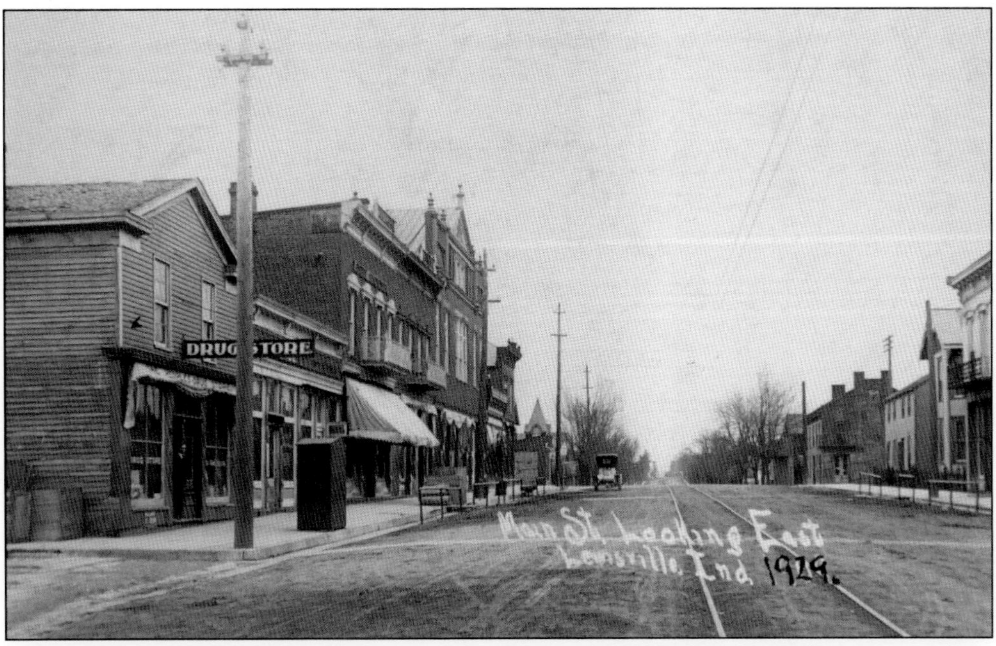

A real-photo postcard captures the National Road in Lewisville and the interurban train tracks in the center. The postcard reads, "Main St. Looking East Lewisville, Ind. 1909." The owner of the postcard has written "1929" in ink over the 1909 date. The interurban tracks are plainly visible, and the hitching posts still line the side of the road on both sides. The druggist has come out of the People's Drug Store and is looking towards the camera. (Courtesy Rep. Tom Saunders.)

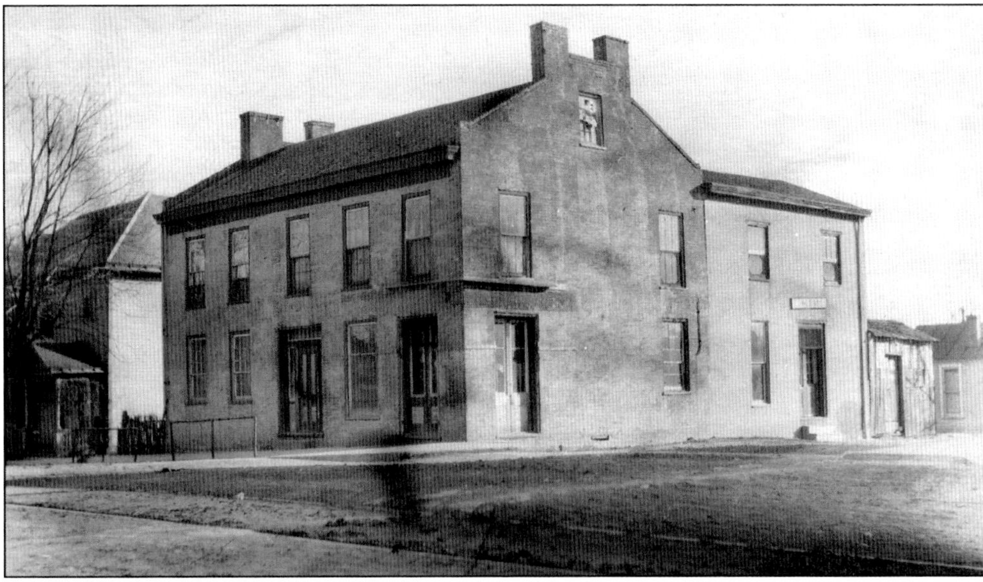

This c. 1910 photograph is of the Houston Brick Building in Lewisville. The William and Fannie Lybrook Houston home was constructed in 1845 and was the first brick building in town. William was a cousin of Texas's Sam Houston and was appointed postmaster in 1837. After many years of serving as a home, inn, vulcanizing shop, restaurant, merchant shops, and finally a vacant eyesore, the Town of Lewisville, under the leadership of Rep. Tom and Sue Saunders, purchased the Houston Brick Building in 1995. The town applied for and received a grant to preserve this place of history. First Lady of Indiana Judy O'Bannon dedicated the Houston Brick Building on February 10, 2000, after a restoration project that took nearly five years to complete. The Houston Brick Building now houses the Lewisville Community Center. (Courtesy Rep. Tom Saunders.)

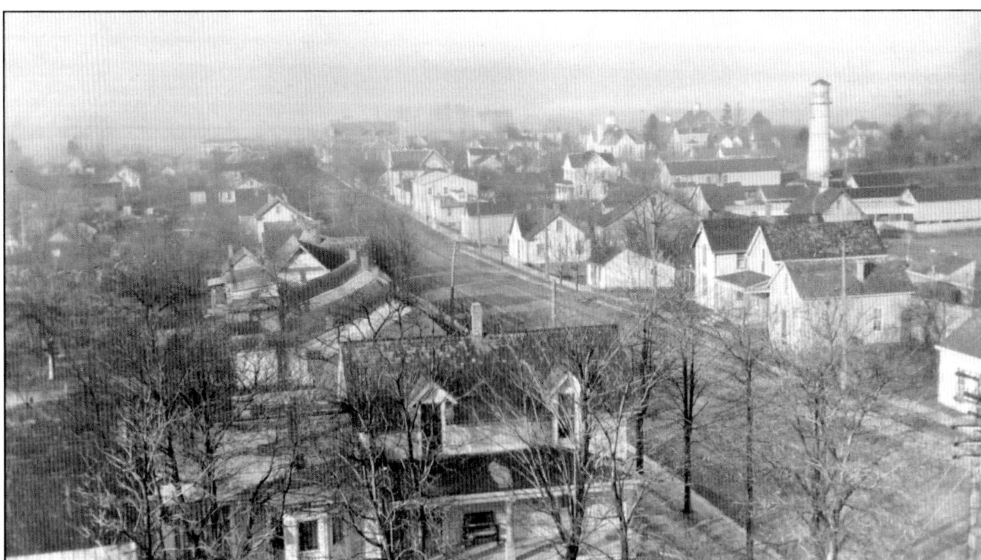

A bird's-eye view is offered up in a c. 1910 photograph postcard of the National Road in Lewisville. (Courtesy Rep. Tom Saunders.)

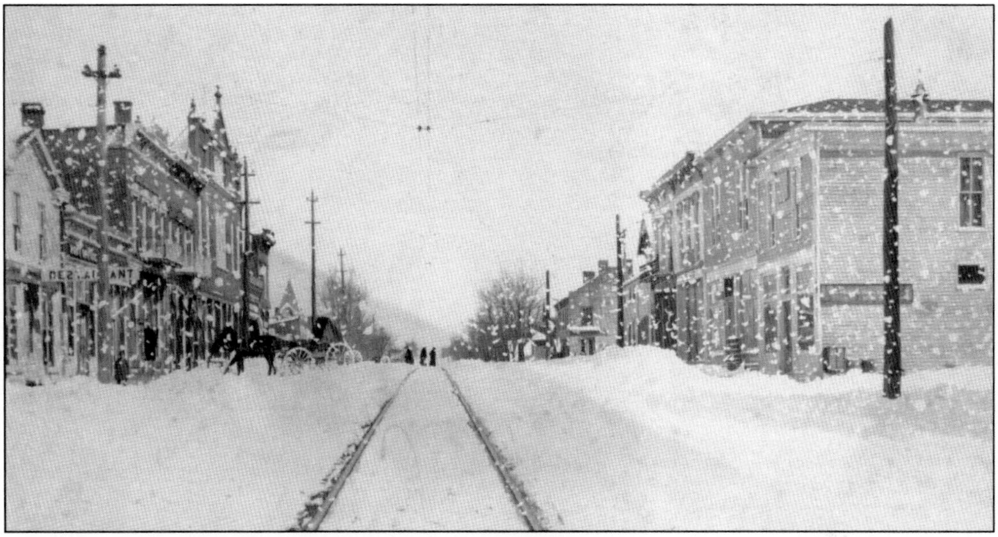

This is a c. 1915 wintertime view of the National Road in Lewisville. The interurban tracks are exposed, but the road itself is obscured by snow. Three women in Victorian dresses walk down the tracks in the center of the street, presumably because the sidewalks are impassable. (Courtesy Rep. Tom Saunders.)

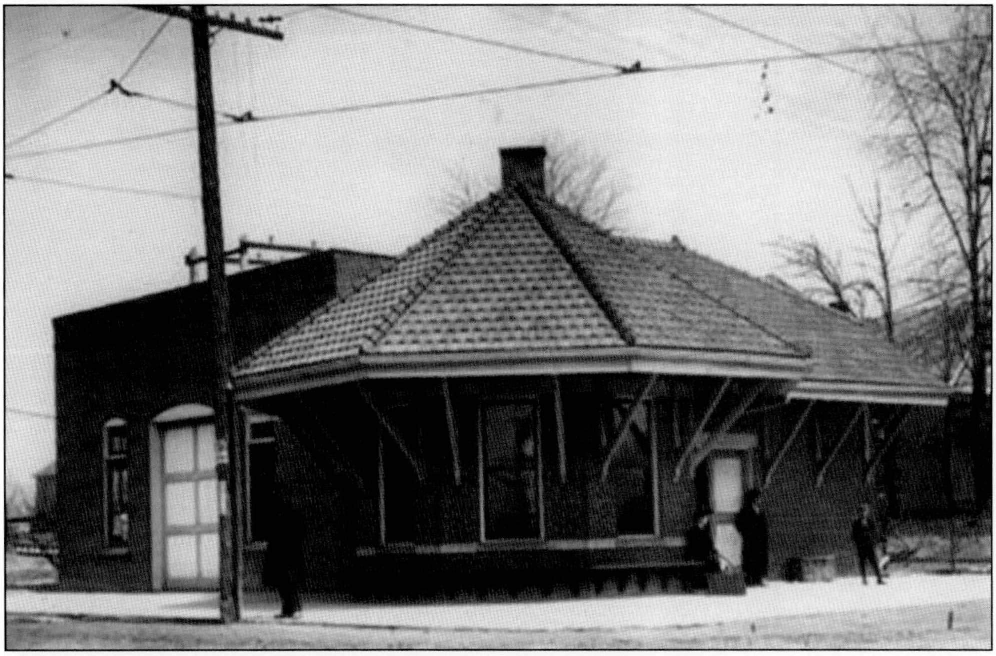

The Dunreith Rail Station on the Terre Haute–Indianapolis & Eastern interurban line is seen here in 1909. The station not only marked a waypoint on the east-west route that ran parallel to the National Road route, it was the right-of-way spur on the north-south Dunreith to Spiceland route in Henry County, paralleling the west side of the Old Spiceland Road. The Terre Haute, Indianapolis, and Eastern Traction Company was the second-largest interurban in the state at the height of the interurban era. This system included over 400 miles of track, with lines emanating from Indianapolis to the east, northwest, west, and southwest, as well as streetcar lines in several major cities. (Courtesy Kathy Miller.)

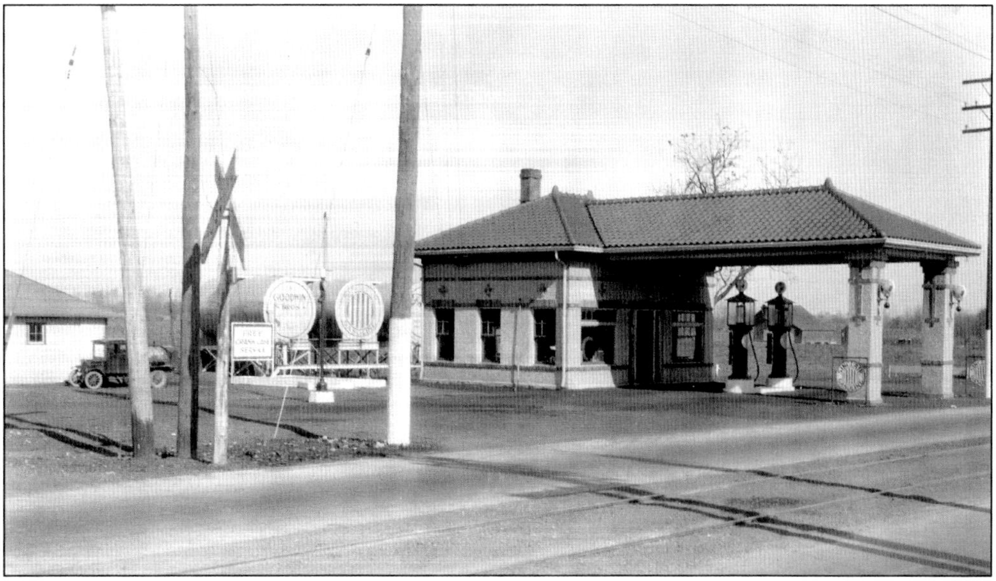

The Goodwin Brothers Sinclair Gas & Oil Service Station near Dunreith is pictured in the 1930s. The original glass gravity pumps and Sinclair glass globe toppers are intact. The interurban tracks can be seen in the foreground. (Courtesy Knightstown History Room.)

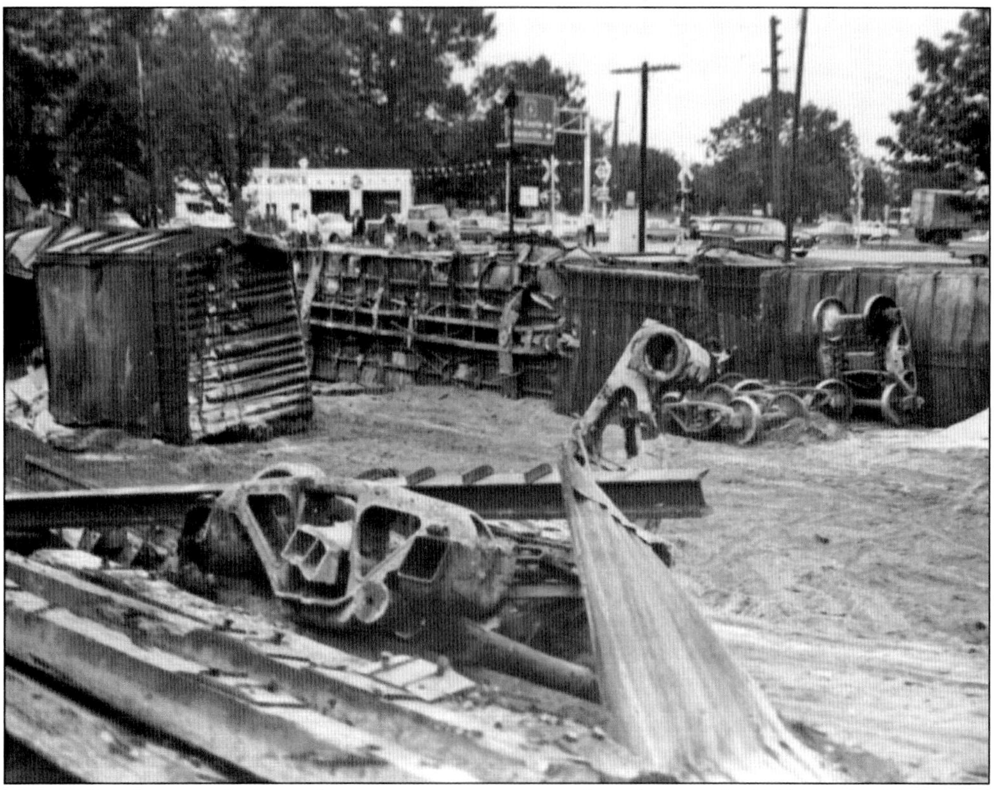

This 1960s photograph shows the remains of a train wreck in front of the D-X Gas & Oil Service Station at the intersection of the National Road and State Road 3 near Dunreith. (Courtesy Knightstown History Room.)

Three

HUDDLESTON FARMHOUSE

The 1840s was the peak of travel on the National Road in Indiana. For those who lived in-between pike towns, the road was an important commercial enterprise as well. Entrepreneurial men who wanted to take advantage of the commerce that it provided established inns such as the Huddleston Farmhouse. John Huddleston, a Quaker from North Carolina, moved first to Fountain City north of Richmond before relocating outside of Cambridge City and building his home and inn right along the road. Travelers would rent out rooms and purchase the goods they needed for their journey, and Huddleston became quite wealthy because of the National Road. He provided a place for oxen and horses to drink and rest, and in the barn on the grounds travelers could have their wagons repaired. Huddleston also made cheese and brooms and sold many goods from his small store on the first floor of his home.

The National Road connected Huddleston with Indianapolis, Richmond, and Dayton, Ohio. Also passing through Cambridge City near Huddleston Farmhouse was the Whitewater Canal, so Huddleston was also able to carry his goods to Cincinnati and the Ohio River. Because of this prime location, the Huddlestons enjoyed a higher standard of living than most of their contemporaries. This can be seen still today as one visits the site and walks through the home.

Today, Huddleston's property is owned by Indiana Landmarks and operated as a national interpretive center for the Historic National Road that also showcases a slice of life of a common family along this national corridor. It is one of the most preeminent sites across the byway, where one can visit an original traveler's inn along the Historic National Road. Indiana Landmarks received the property from Eli Lilly, who also helped establish a large endowment for the organization's preservation efforts. Indiana Landmarks is the nation's largest and most comprehensive statewide preservation not-for-profit organization. The services it provides makes Indiana a leader in preservation advocacy, and because of their support, the Historic National Road has the Indiana National Road Association and the National Road Heritage Site at Huddleston Farmhouse.

Huddleston Farmhouse is the office for Indiana Landmarks' eastern region, as well as the headquarters for the Indiana National Road Association and the National Road Alliance, which is the Six State National Road Organization. These organizations advocate for the preservation and promotion of the Historic National Road and landmarks across Indiana. Without them, recent strides, such as the removal of downtown Greenfield and the Richmond Depot from the 10 Most Endangered List compiled by Indiana Landmarks, would not have occurred. Instead, these landmarks are part of an overall economic redevelopment in their respective neighborhoods and an attraction for heritage tourism along the byway.

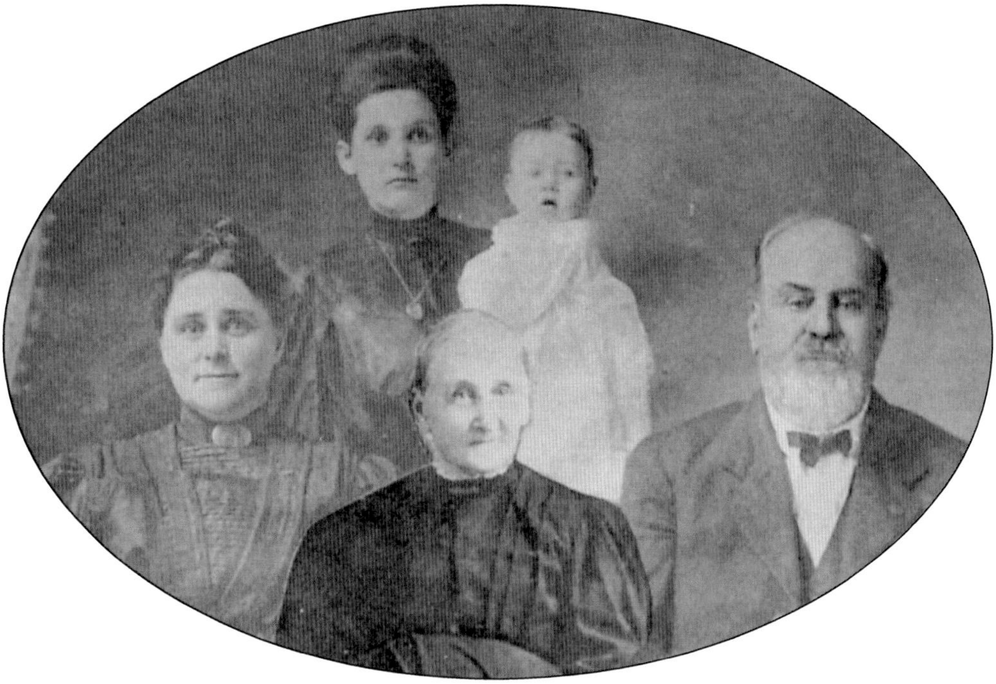

Susannah Huddleston (center) is part of a composite with family members, presumably her son Henry and his family. When Susannah's husband, John, died in 1877, the farm property was passed to Henry Huddleston. (Courtesy Indiana Landmarks.)

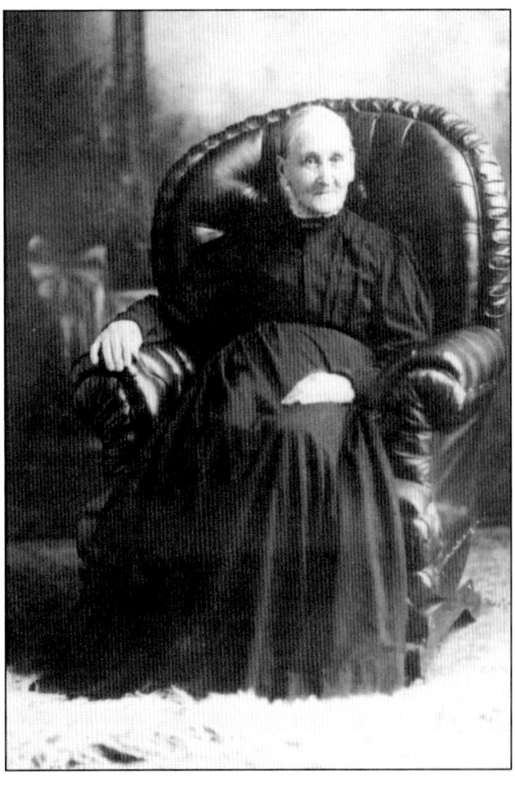

This photograph of Susannah Huddleston was taken sometime in the 1880s. Susannah Moyer (or Myer) was born in 1812. In 1830, she married John Huddleston and would proceed to have 12 children over the next 19 years (1832–1851). Her husband, John, died in 1877, and Susannah died in 1892. Both are buried in East Cemetery in Dublin, Indiana. (Courtesy Indiana Landmarks.)

The Huddleston Farmhouse Inn stands tall in the 1930s. John Huddleston began purchasing farmland in 1837 along the National Road in Cambridge City in Wayne County, Indiana. Upon this land, John and Susannah built a three-story, Federal-style home that they later turned into an inn for travelers on the National Road from 1850 to 1875. Weary travelers making the difficult trek westward on the National Road in the early 1800s stopped at the family inn for provisions, shelter, and to feed and rest their horses. (Courtesy Indiana Landmarks.)

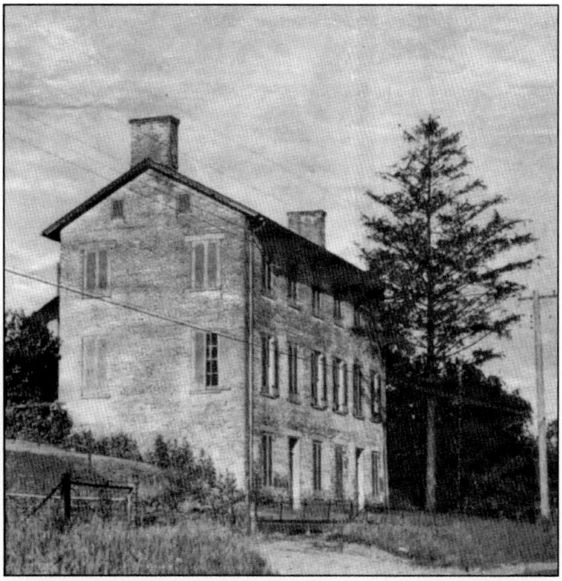

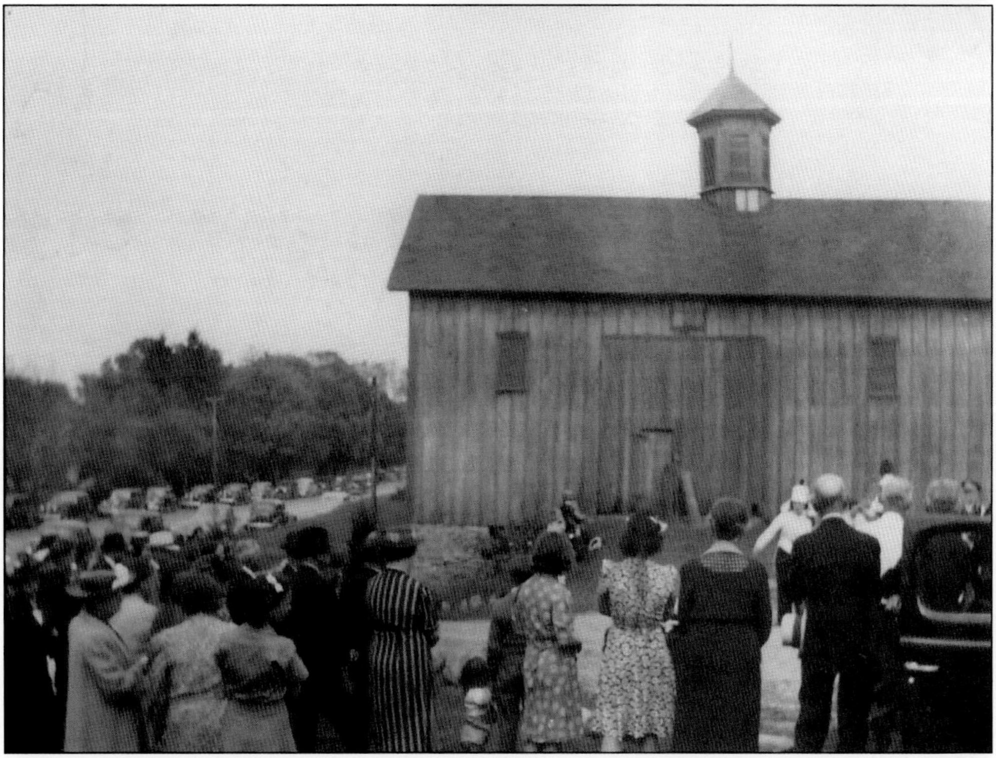

Here is a Daughters of the American Revolution scene outside of the barn during the dedication of the Huddleston Farmhouse in 1936. The image is part of a pamphlet, created in 1962 and printed and distributed at the house, that states, "The house was at one time a stage coach stop. In the carriage barn, the coaches were hoisted and the wheels greased. Part of the hoist still remains. The barns are very well constructed of mammoth beams, all hand hewn and pegged together." Several 1930s sedans can be seen lining the sides of the National Road on the left. (Courtesy Cambridge City Library-History Room.)

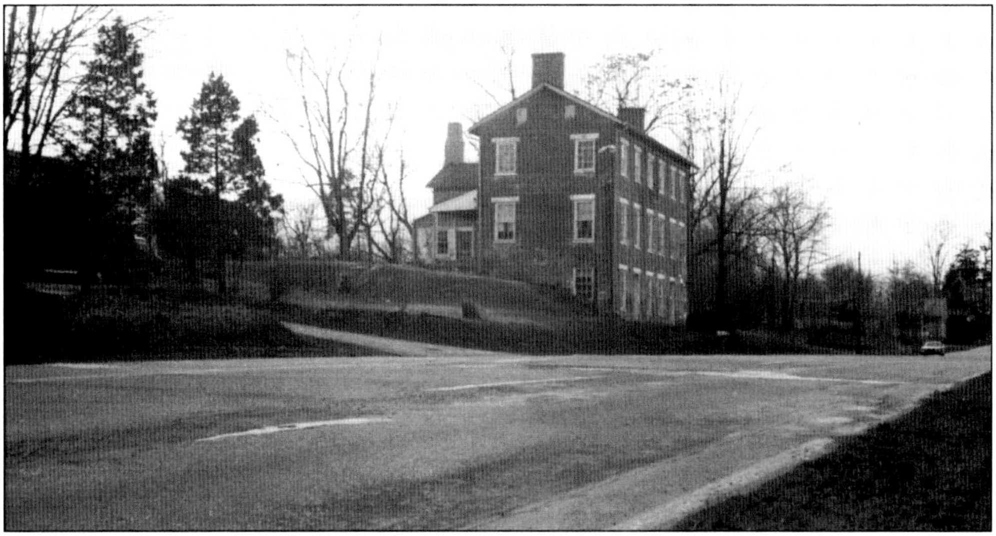

This 1975 Historic American Building Survey photograph is captioned, "Huddleston House (East & North Facade) Looking West from the National Road (US 40)." The walls of the house are 14 inches thick and contain many of the hand-blown, wavy glass windows. It is interesting to note how the road's edges meet the grass on both sides with no berm to separate the road from its surrounding landscape. At that time, the National Road would have conformed to the geography, making the journey more part of the natural environment. (Courtesy Indiana Landmarks.)

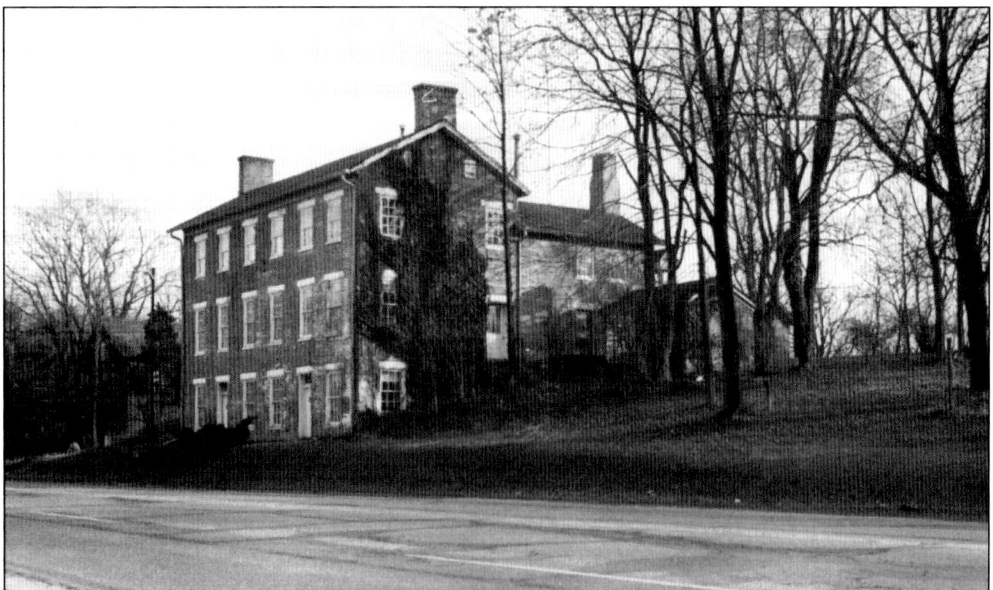

The Huddleston Farmhouse is captured in an April 4, 1975, *Richmond Palladium-Item* photograph. The 125,000 bricks used to build the house, as well as the Dublin United Brethren Church just up the National Road, were all made by hand on the property. The doors on the first floor lead into the traveler's kitchens that were rented by pioneers for a night in from the cold. The springhouse up the hill fed a trough that John Huddleston planted at the edge of the road to entice travelers to stop, water their oxen, and make purchases in the general store located between the two traveler's kitchens on the first floor. (Courtesy Indiana Landmarks.)

Pictured pre-restoration, a c. 1975 image is captioned "Huddleston Farmhouse Inn Museum Eastern Regional Office Historic Landmarks Office." The view is facing the east side of the building with the old signs in place. Owned and restored by Indiana Landmarks during the 1970s, the 1841 Huddleston Farmhouse Museum offers visitors a glimpse of the daily lives of John and Susannah Huddleston and their 12 children, as well as the travelers who crowded the porches and yard and rented the farmhouse's two travelers' kitchens for cooking and sleeping. (Courtesy Indiana Landmarks.)

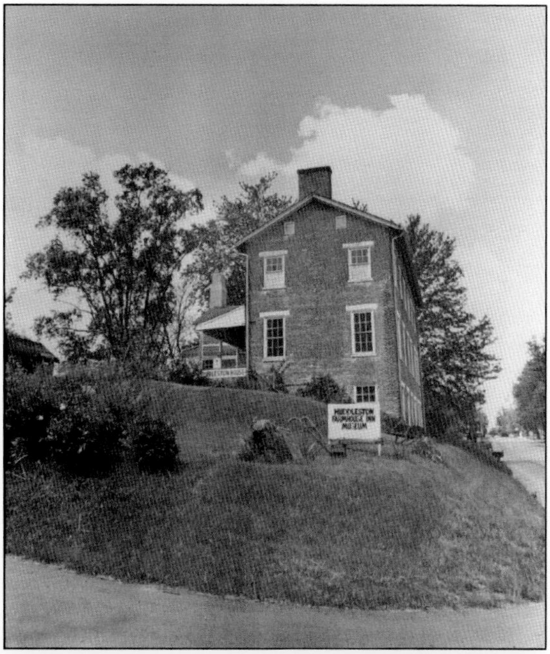

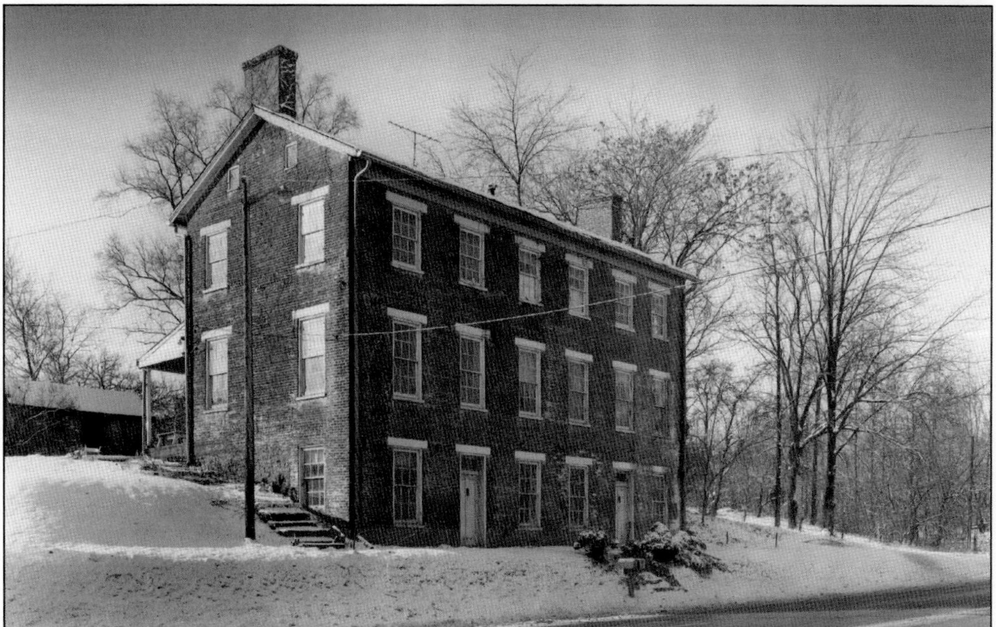

This January 1975 Architectural & Engineering Record photograph is captioned, "Huddleston Farmhouse Inn Museum Eastern Regional Office Historic Landmarks Office." The view faces the front of the building. Some of the original literature noted, "No form of liquor was ever tolerated in the house." Although the Huddleston family was made up of Quakers, travelers from all over the country who were on the heading west influenced them. Visitors from many cultures came to the inn, and evidence has been found that séances were performed on the premises. This illustrates how the National Road transported ideas and beliefs as well as people. (Courtesy Indiana Landmarks.)

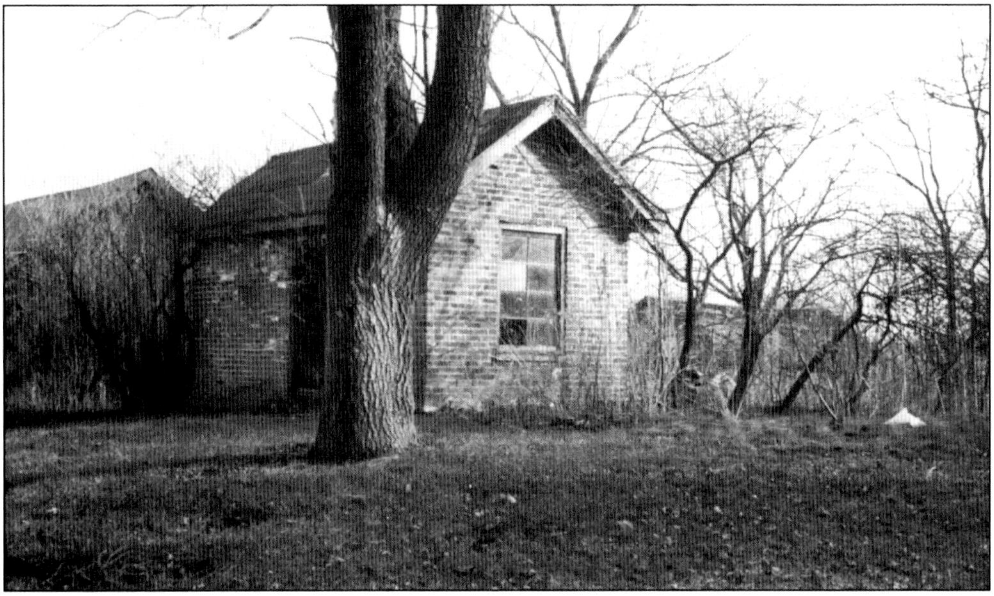

A 1975 Historic American Building Survey photograph caption reads, "Original Smokehouse in the foreground—Wagon shed at left—Hog barn in the background." According to the 1850 federal agricultural census, Huddleston had one of the most productive farms in the township, producing 20 tons of hay, 200 pounds of cheese, and 100 pounds of butter. Along with his farming and lodging business, Huddleston helped support his family by carting goods to and from Cincinnati and working on the National Road. Family histories state that Huddleston refused to carry tobacco or liquor on his trips to and from the city. (Courtesy Indiana Landmarks.)

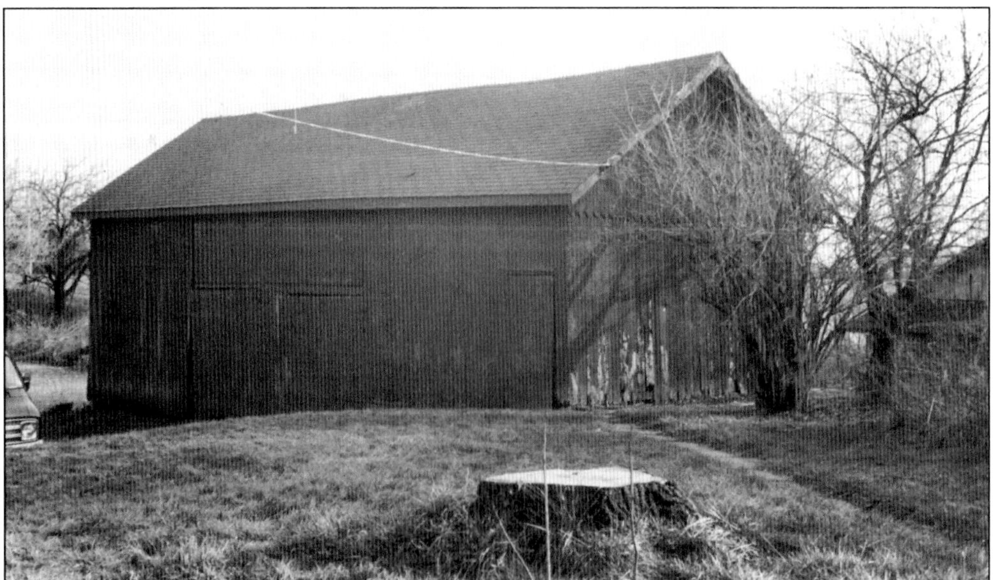

This 1975 Historic American Building Survey photograph has the caption, "Wagon Shed, Huddleston Farmhouse Hog barn in background." The farmhouse was once a carriage stop, and in this "carriage barn" the coaches were hoisted and the wheels greased. Evidence of the original hoist still remains visible on the massive hand-hewn rafters, held together by wooden pegs, that are in the barn. (Courtesy Indiana Landmarks.)

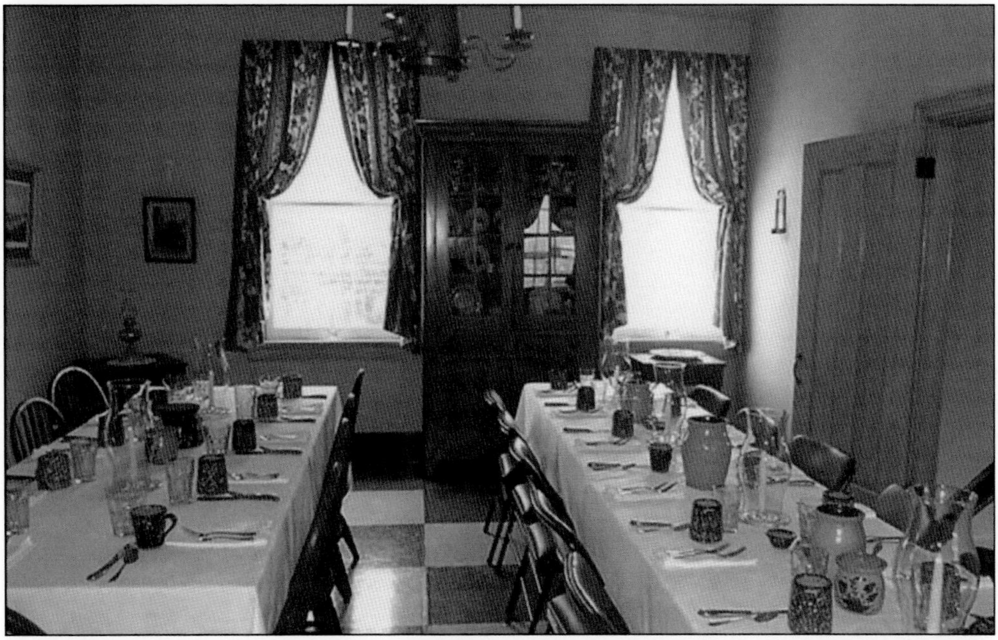

A typical table set-up for Huddleston Farmhouse dinners is seen here around 2000. Beginning around 1990 and continuing through 2008, the Huddleston Farmhouse Museum hosted popular Hearth Dinners. The dinners featured authentic menu items that would have been in use during the inn's heyday. Today many visitors to the museum remember these intimate gatherings fondly. The meals utilized the original fireplace for preparation and featured utensils and settings authentic to the period. (Courtesy Indiana Landmarks.)

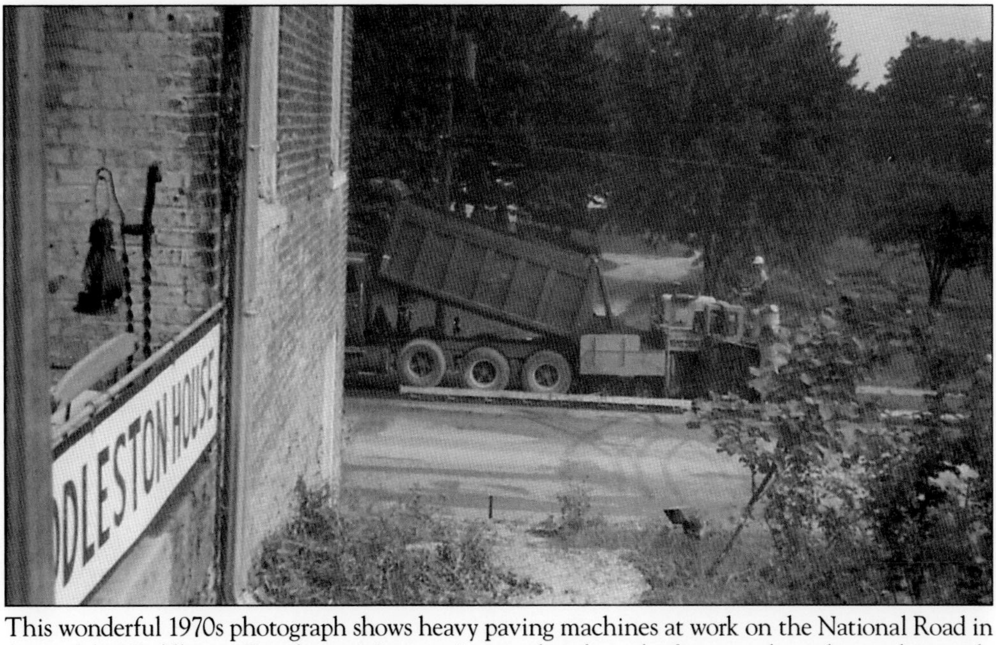

This wonderful 1970s photograph shows heavy paving machines at work on the National Road in front of the Huddleston Farmhouse Museum. It was taken from the front porch on the northeast side of the building. Construction on the road continues today, and sidewalks and curbs are now in front of the home and the road between Dublin and Cambridge City. (Courtesy Indiana Landmarks.)

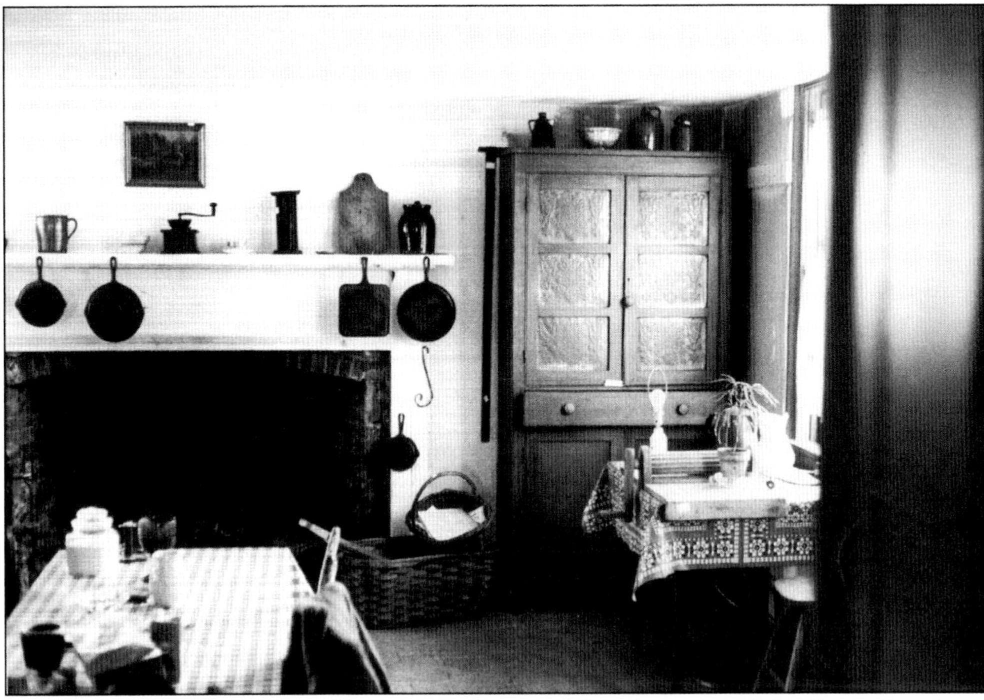

This 1975 Historic American Building Survey photograph has the caption, "Huddleston Farmhouse kitchen." An interesting story survives about Quaker Susannah Huddleston's kitchen. A group of immigrants that had stopped at the farmhouse the night before had departed at sunrise and left behind bread they had baked in the oven at the inn. "Hastily saddling a horse," according to Lee Burns in his history of the National Road in Indiana, "He [Huddleston] followed them with the bread, only to discover that their hurried departure had been caused by the fact that they had taken his best set of harnesses." (Courtesy Indiana Landmarks.)

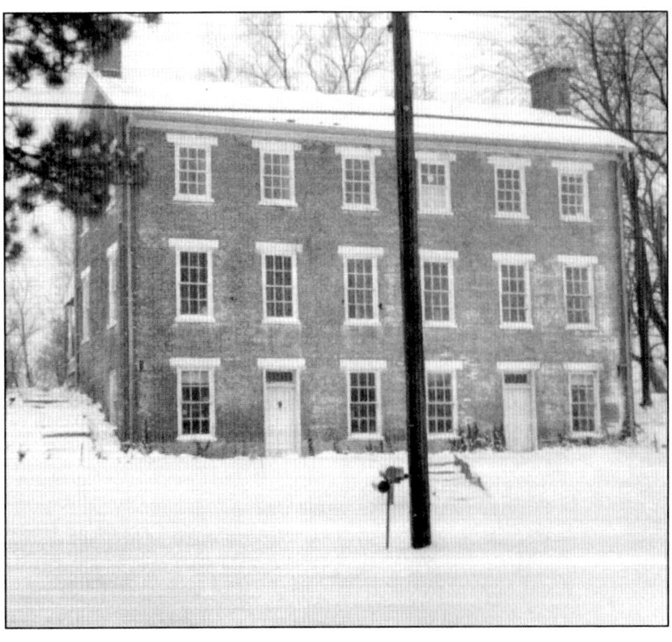

A c. 1975 wintertime photograph depicts the front of the Huddleston Farmhouse Museum. Although covered in snow in this view, the large stone slab stairs on each side of the house are the original massive fieldstones gathered in creeks and quarries of surrounding Wayne County. They show the wear made by thousands of steps over almost two centuries of guests, visitors, and family members. (Courtesy Indiana Landmarks.)

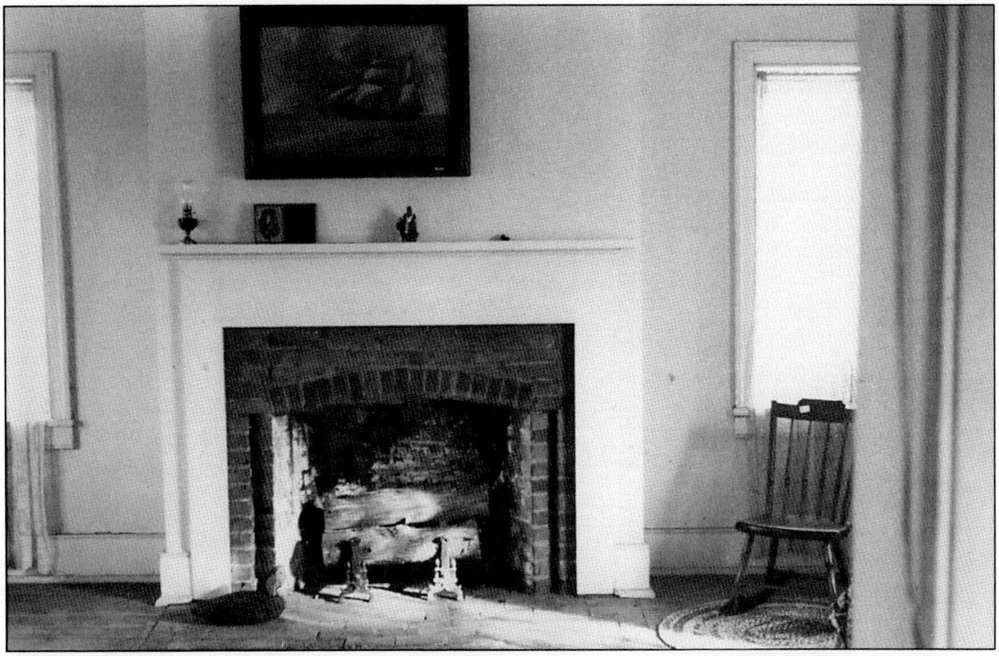

"East Room 3rd Floor" is the caption of this 1975 Historic American Building Survey photograph. The Huddleston Farmhouse has 14 rooms and seven fireplaces. This former bedroom is now the office of Indiana Landmarks eastern regional office. Today, the upstairs rooms are not restored to the period but now used as offices for preservation efforts in the region, for the interpretive center, and the Indiana National Road Association. (Courtesy Indiana Landmarks.)

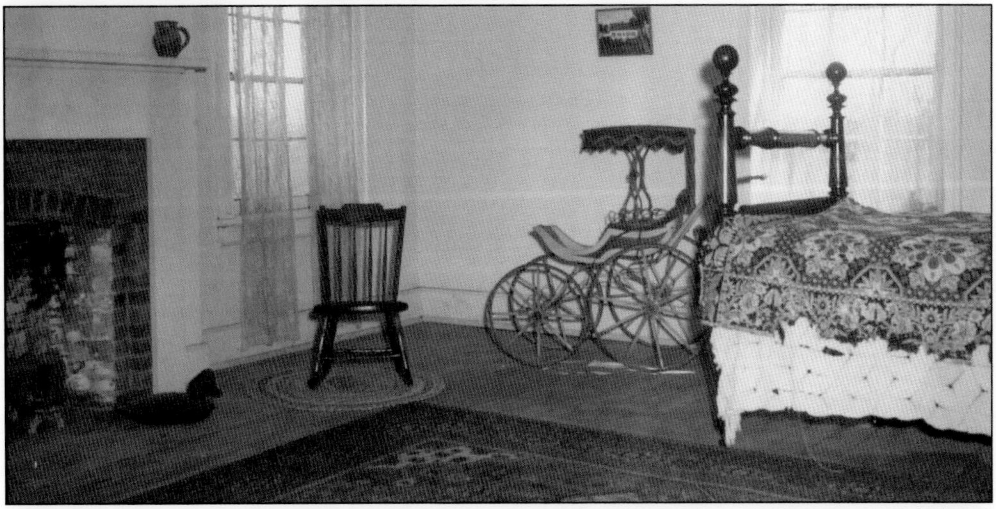

This 1975 Historic American Building Survey photograph is also captioned, "East Room 3rd Floor." There were 12 children in the Huddleston family, and each one found his or her space in this and a middle room on the third floor. The room on the west side of the house was John and Susannah's, which is where John died in 1877 after being kicked in the head by a mule. The last Huddleston descendent to live in the home was Charlie Huddleston, who also died in the home. The museum is furnished with objects authentic to the period, many on loan from the Indiana State Museum and historic in their own right. Only two pieces in the house are authentic to the Huddleston family: a cradle and Bible page listing the family tree. (Courtesy Indiana Landmarks.)

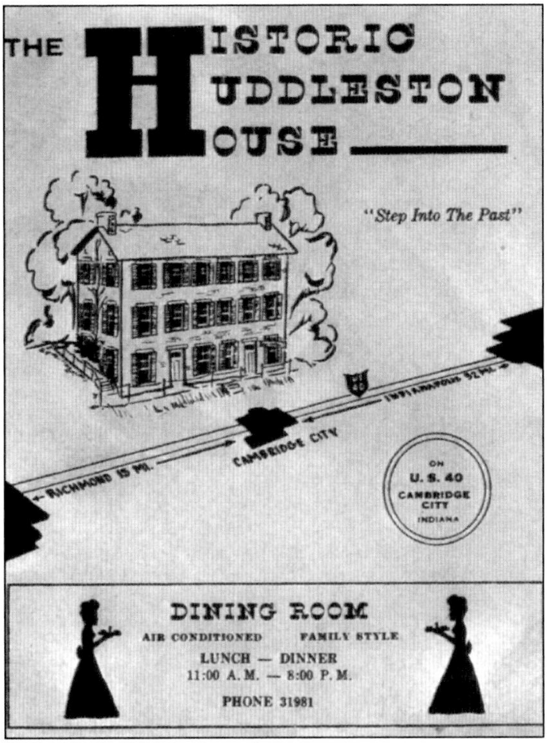

A 1962 Huddleston Farmhouse brochure claims that three presidents (Abraham Lincoln, Martin Van Buren, and James K. Polk) stayed in the inn and that inn owner John Huddleston pulled Van Buren's coach out of the mud after it became stuck outside. The flyer also noted the Huddleston family's role in the famed Underground Railroad and claimed that there was a tunnel used to hide escaped slaves under the house that ran a quarter-mile south behind the house to the railroad tracks still in place on the property today. Clearly history happened here, but there is no evidence that any of these events listed in the 1962 brochure actually happened on the property. (Courtesy Kathy Miller.)

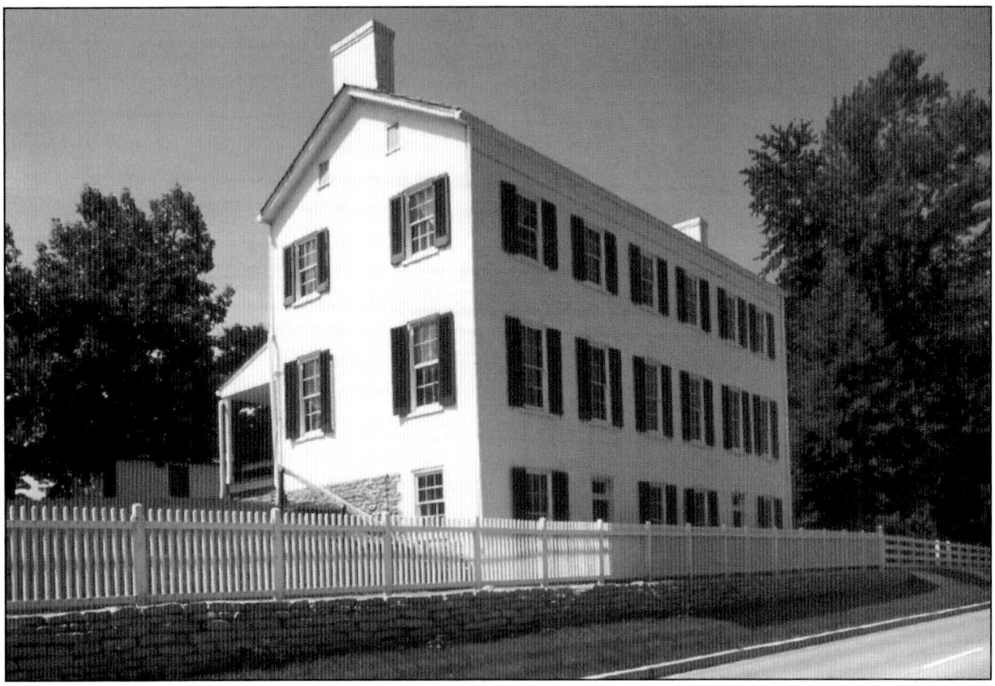

The Huddleston Farmhouse Museum looks southwest in this modern-day image. The site now serves as the National Road Heritage Site. Byway travelers today may now experience a slice of life along the road by seeing how the Huddlestons lived while also learning about the 900-mile, 200-year history of the National Road. (Courtesy Rhonda S. Hunter.)

Four

Knightstown to Greenfield

Named after Pennsylvanian Jonathan Knight, who surveyed the National Road in Indiana beginning in 1825, Knightstown is most identifiable by its square in the center of town. Bordered by historic structures from the 1800s on one side and a 1920s gas station on the corner of the other side, the town spans two important eras of the road. However, the most important landmark in town is the Knightstown Academy, one of the first preservation successes in the state, and the attached Hoosier Gym where the movie *Hoosiers* was filmed. The gym has a beautifully restored basketball court, with bleachers on either side, where one can still play a game of basketball. This is truly a piece of Hoosier heritage.

Once listed on the 10 Most Endangered List by Indiana Landmarks, downtown Greenfield has slowly worked and continues to work to preserve its unique downtown architecture. From a restored Carnegie Library, to an operating performance art center in the old Art Deco movie theater, to the monumental Masonic Lodge, Greenfield is a town local hero James Whitcomb Riley would be proud of. The famed poet was born in this town in 1849, and the community honors him with the large Riley Festival each year and a statue of him on the courthouse lawn. The Masonic Lodge's future, once in question, now serves as a home to many artisans, and its impressive upstairs lodge room with restored stained-glass windows is truly the best place for events in town.

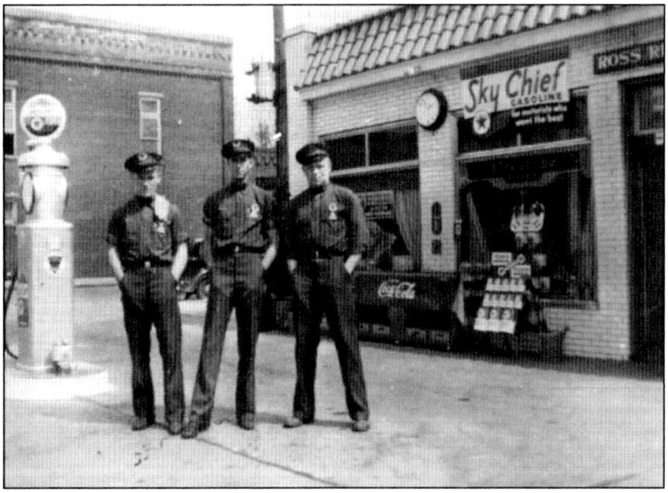

The Texaco Gas station at the southwest corner of Main and Jefferson Streets in Knightstown is pictured in 1939. From left to right are Phil Moore, Jim Maxwell, and Lyle Sheffield. Ross Reddick, whose name can be seen above the bay door of the garage, owned the station. Note the glass Sky Chief globes above the pump and the Coca-Cola ice chest dispenser. (Courtesy Knightstown History Museum.)

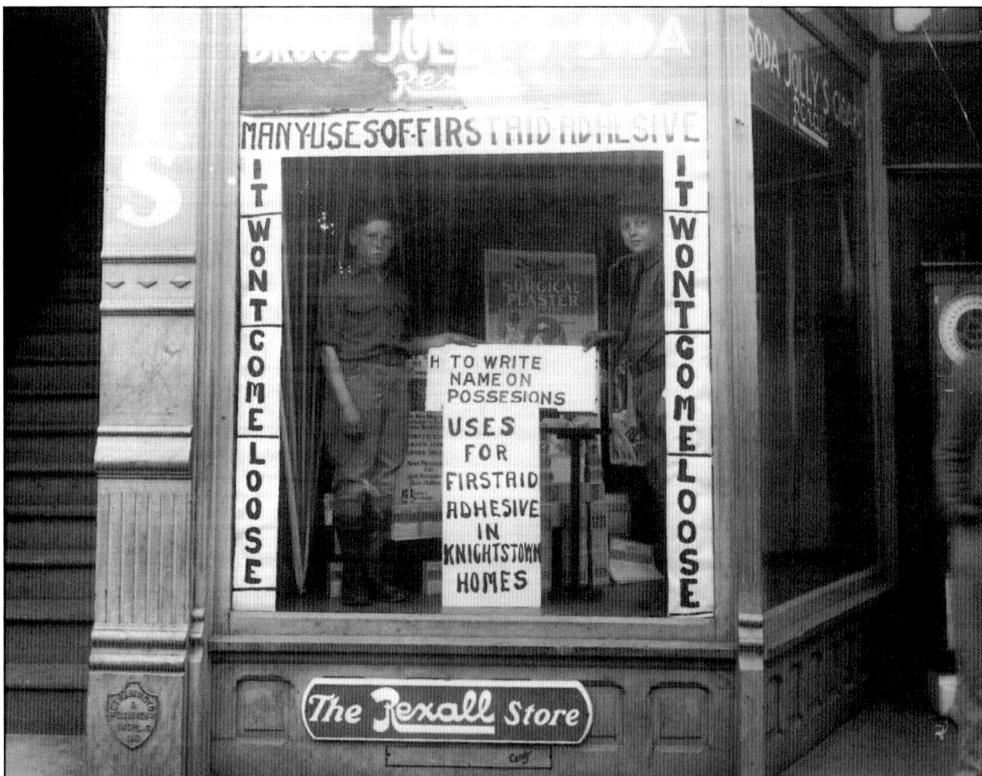

Two Boy Scouts pose in the front window of Jolly's Rexall Drug Store and soda fountain on Main Street in Knightstown around 1927. The window display was for Firstaid zinc oxide surgical plaster adhesive, and the two young men have handwritten signs for the product that read, "Many uses of first aid adhesive—It won't come loose." The signs would change as passersby walked in front of the window. The large space above Jolly's Drug Store, known as Bell's Hall, was used as the high school gym and for two years was home to the Knightstown basketball team until an independent gym was opened on December 1, 1922. The stairs that led to the upper-floor gymnasium can be seen on the left. (Courtesy Knightstown History Museum.)

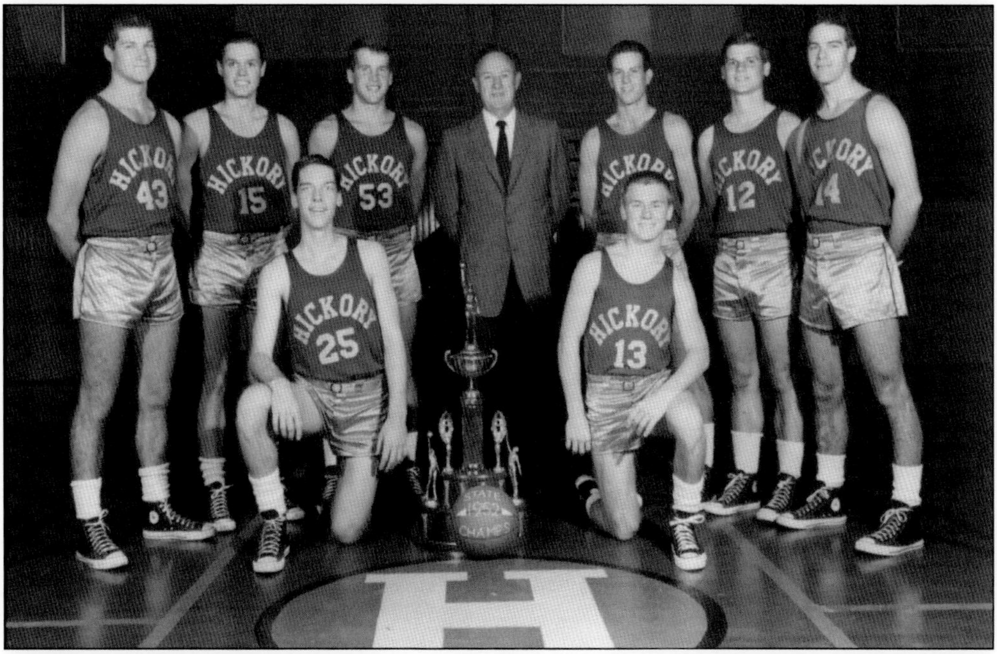

The Hickory High School basketball team from the 1986 movie *Hoosiers* poses in the old gym in Knightstown, Indiana. The fictional team was based in part on the 1954 state champion Milan High School team and filmed in the historic Knightstown Gym on the National Road. Considered by many the greatest basketball film ever made, the 1922 gym retains the look used in the film and is known today as the Hoosier Gym. (Courtesy Knightstown History Museum.)

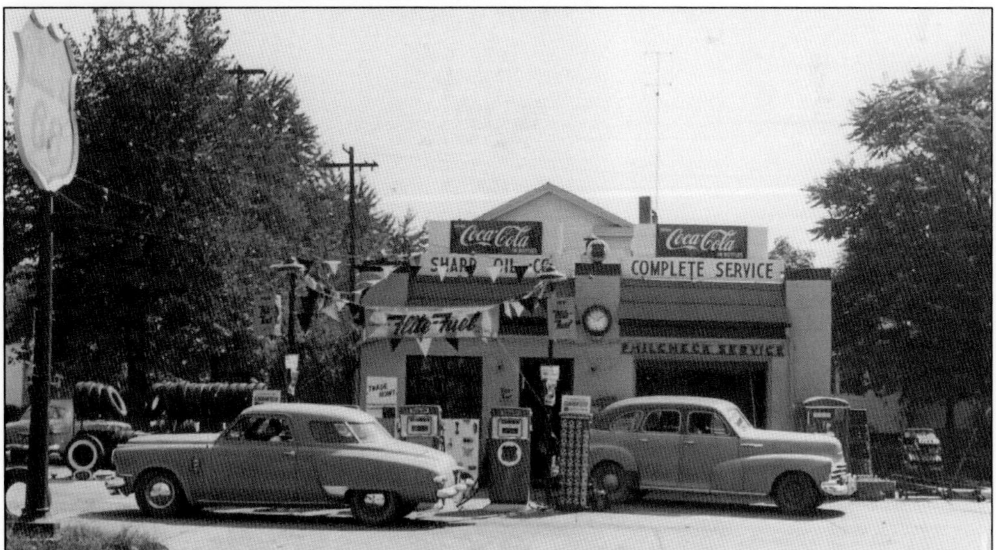

The Sharp Oil Company Phillips 66 gas station on the National Road west to Knightstown is pictured sometime around 1954. The banners advertise the new Phillips 66 Flite Fuel premium gasoline that was available between 1953 and 1959. Those were the days of high-compression engines, and the premium gasoline of the time was usually 100 octane or even a bit higher, the same as aviation fuel. Notice the large Coca-Cola signs attached to the roof of the single-bay service station. (Courtesy Knightstown History Museum.)

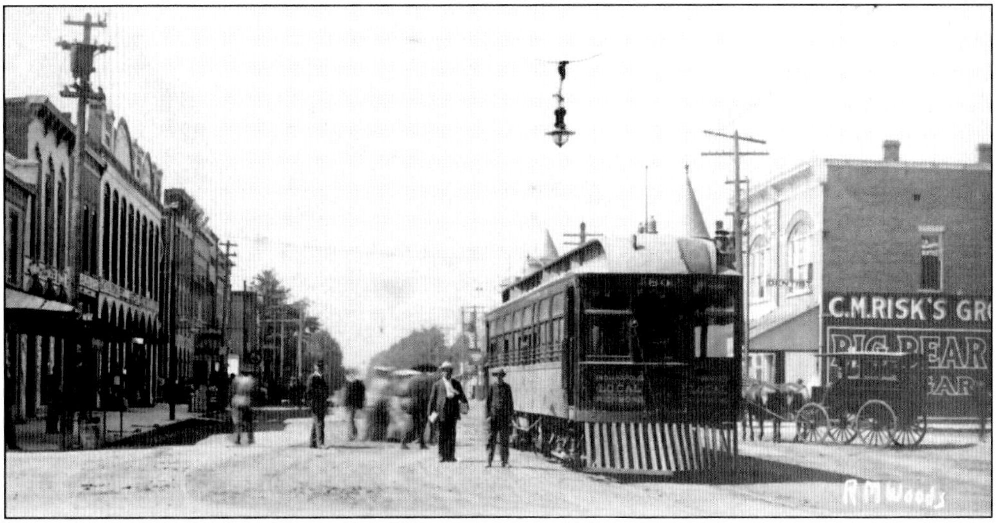

This view looks west on the National Road as the Knightstown interurban train arrives from Indianapolis in 1912. Car No. 80 features two signs above the cowcatcher on front that each read, "Indianapolis-Local-Richmond," and the uniformed driver is posing on the left as the passengers climb on and off the train. The C.M. Risk Grocery Store pictured on right features a huge sign for "Big Bear Cigars" on the side of the building. A hansom cab pulled by two horses waits patiently in front of the sign, and the early first-generation electric stoplight can be seen above the train car suspended by the same wires that supplied power for the interurban itself. (Courtesy Knightstown History Museum.)

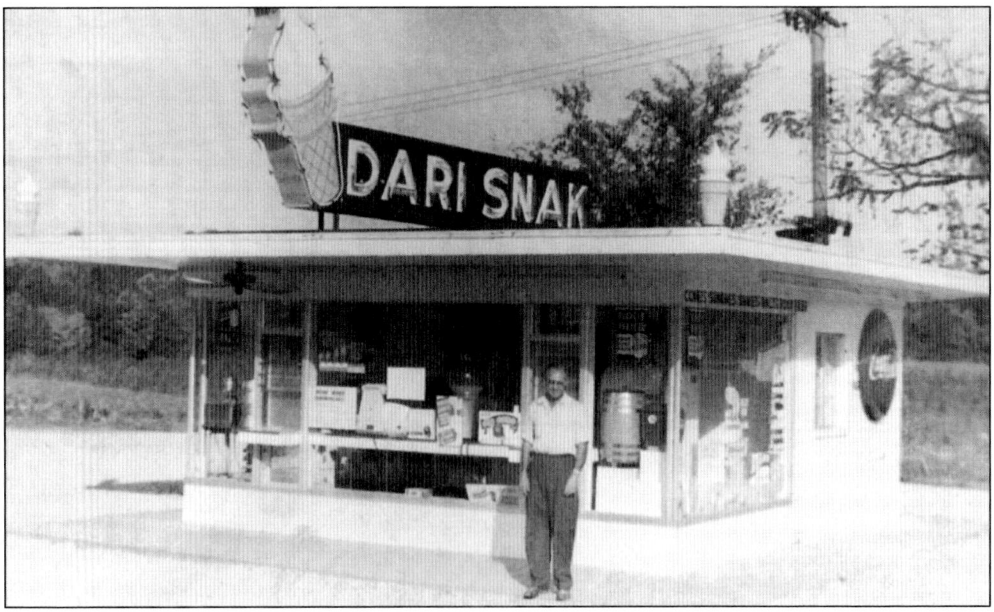

Raysville, platted in 1827 and named in honor of Indiana governor James B. Ray, is located one mile east of Knightstown and rests along the route of the old Historic National Road. This photograph of the Raysville Dari-Snak Drive-In was located at US 40 and Mill Road and was taken in 1954. Owner Roy C. Ramsey stands proudly outside one of its two walk-up windows. Notice the huge convex Coca-Cola sign on the side of the building, as well as the huge wooden root beer barrel inside the front window. (Courtesy Knightstown History Museum.)

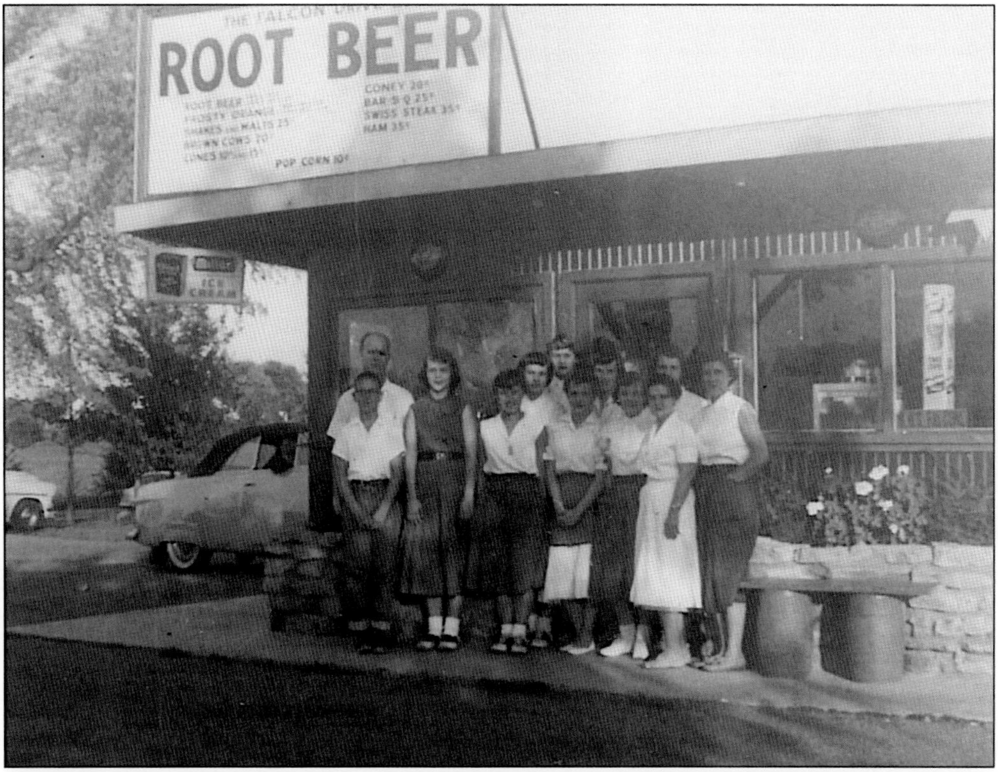

The Falcon Drive-In was located on the National Road at Mill Creek. Owner Joe Sullivan is in the second row on the far left. Notice the Miller Ice Cream sign hanging from the end of the building. The Miller Dairy was located east of Knightstown on the National Road in Cambridge City. Taken in the 1950s, the building featured many smaller-sized concave Coca-Cola signs under the eaves and offered Coney dogs for 20¢ and Swiss steak or ham for 35¢. (Courtesy Knightstown History Museum.)

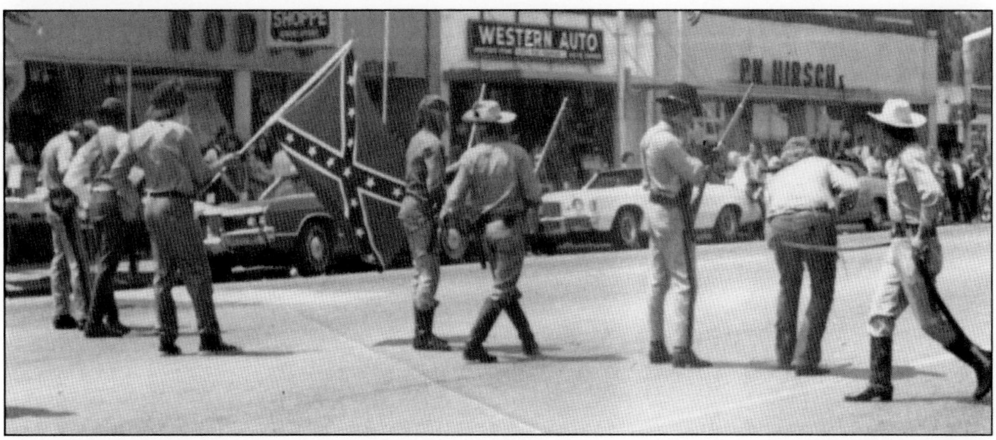

The 1972 Frontier Days street parade and celebration in Knightstown featured a Civil War reenactment that took place in the middle of the National Road. This was the highlight of the 150th-year celebration of the town. The Western Auto store and P.N. Hirsch store signs can be seen in the background. The Chuck Taylor All-Star high-top tennis shoes worn by the man holding the flag add to the authenticity of the era. (Courtesy Knightstown History Museum.)

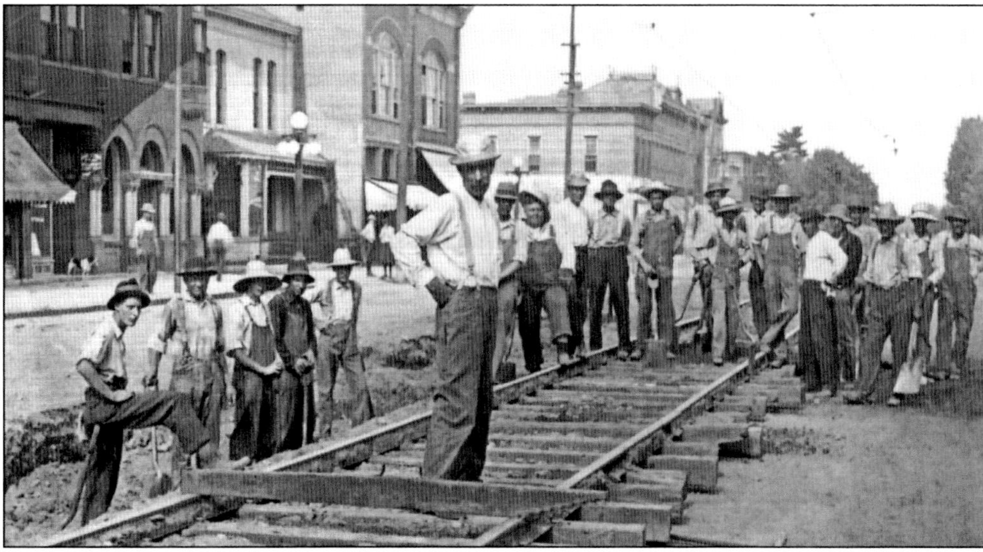

This fantastic image is of the interurban tracks being laid down the center of the National Road in Knightstown sometime in 1905. To minimize the cost of construction, interurban tracks typically ran along the route of a public highway in rural areas. Tracks could easily be added to existing roads by laying steel in the road without disrupting automobile and horse traffic. Often, when an interurban was first constructed, the adjacent National Road was unpaved and became bottomless mud during wet summer months or in winter. Horses would struggle to move people and wagons, and often the interurban might be the only reliable daily transportation both for moving people as well as farm–to town–to market products such as vegetables, fruit, meat, and fresh milk. (Courtesy Knightstown History Museum.)

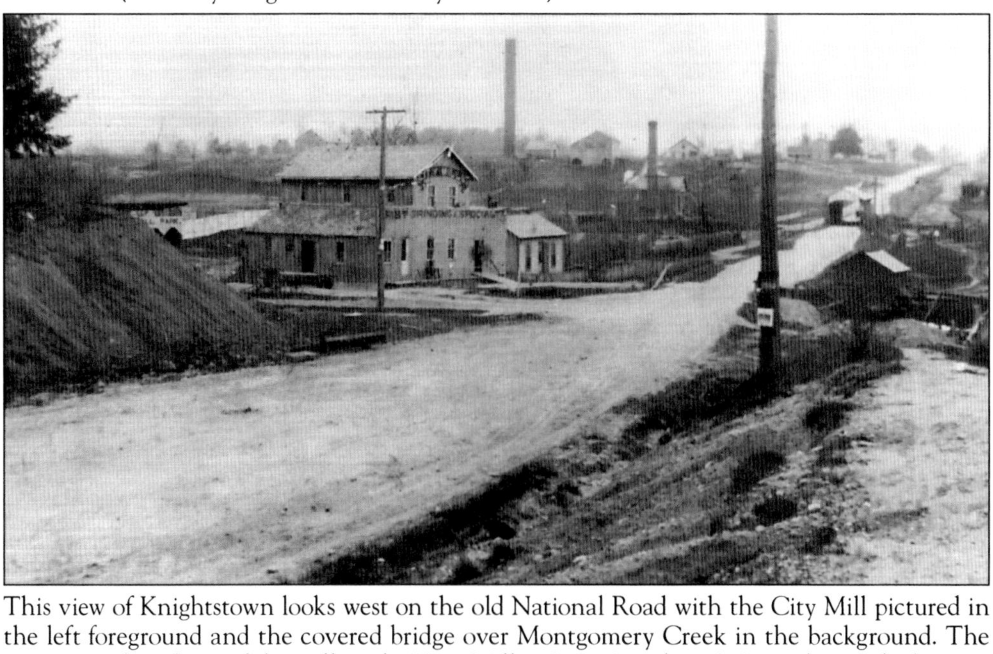

This view of Knightstown looks west on the old National Road with the City Mill pictured in the left foreground and the covered bridge over Montgomery Creek in the background. The sign painted on front of the mill reads, "City Mill—Grist Grinding A Specialty" with the City Mill Park visible behind the old mill. The Knightstown Power Station occupies the site today. (Courtesy Knightstown History Museum.)

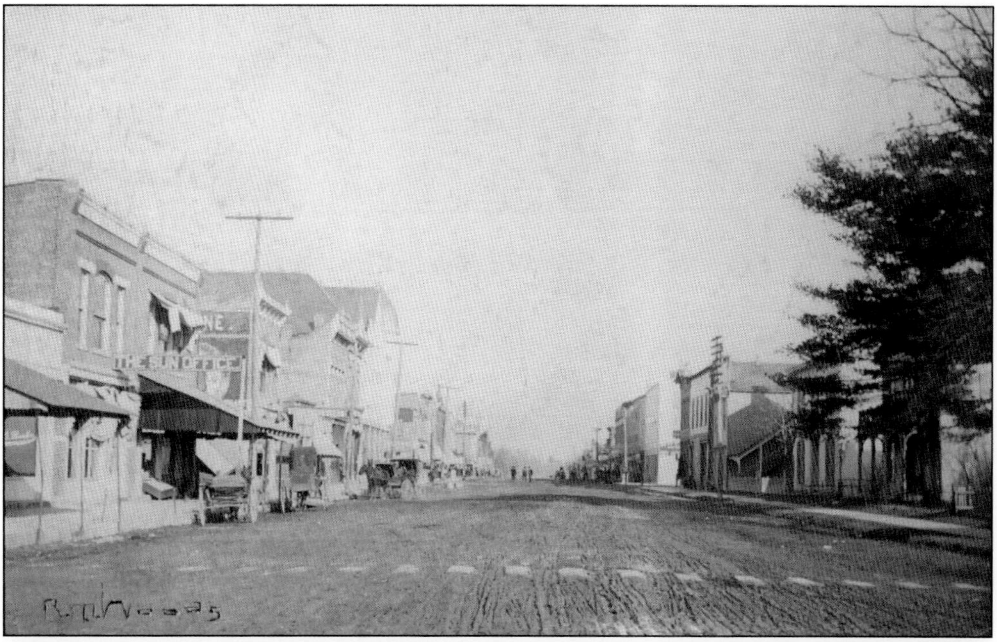

Main Street on the western edge of Knightstown is pictured around 1900. The offices of the *Sun* newspaper can be seen on the left. Visible in the foreground is the dirt street with no interurban tracks yet, but it does have a unique line of paving stones spaced a foot or so apart for pedestrians to keep their feet dry. The lower left has photographer R.M. Woods's signature. (Courtesy Knightstown History Museum.)

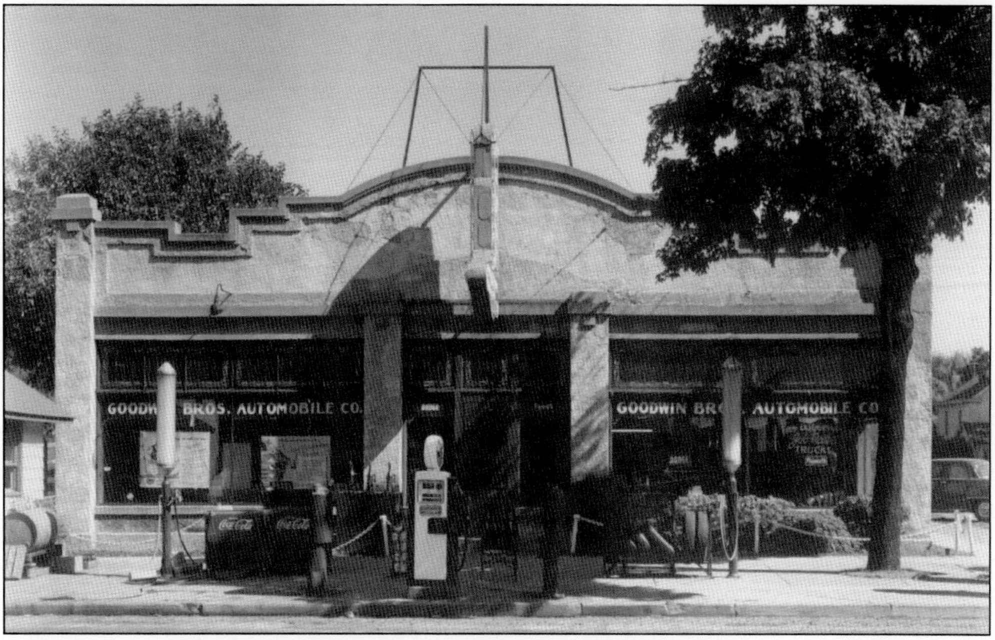

Pictured is Goodwin Brothers Automotive Service Station in Knightstown as it looked in the 1940s with a double Coca-Cola cooler out front. The old-fashioned gravity pumps are still intact with the new pump inset in the center. Goodwin Brothers was also a Dodge/Plymouth motorcar dealer; signs can be seen in the windows. (Courtesy Knightstown History Museum.)

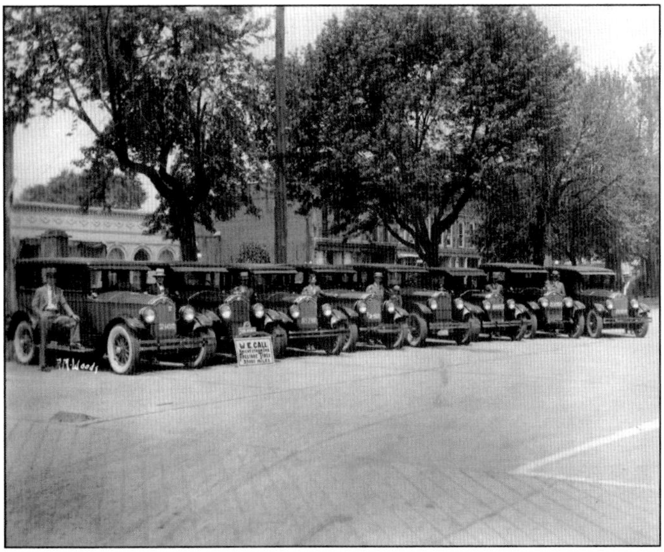

A 1926 photograph depicts a gathering of automobiles on the town square in Knightstown. A sign is propped up out front that reads, "W.E. Call Knightstown, Ind. Firestone Tires 29,000 Miles" with photographer R.M. Woods's name on the front. (Courtesy Knightstown History Museum.)

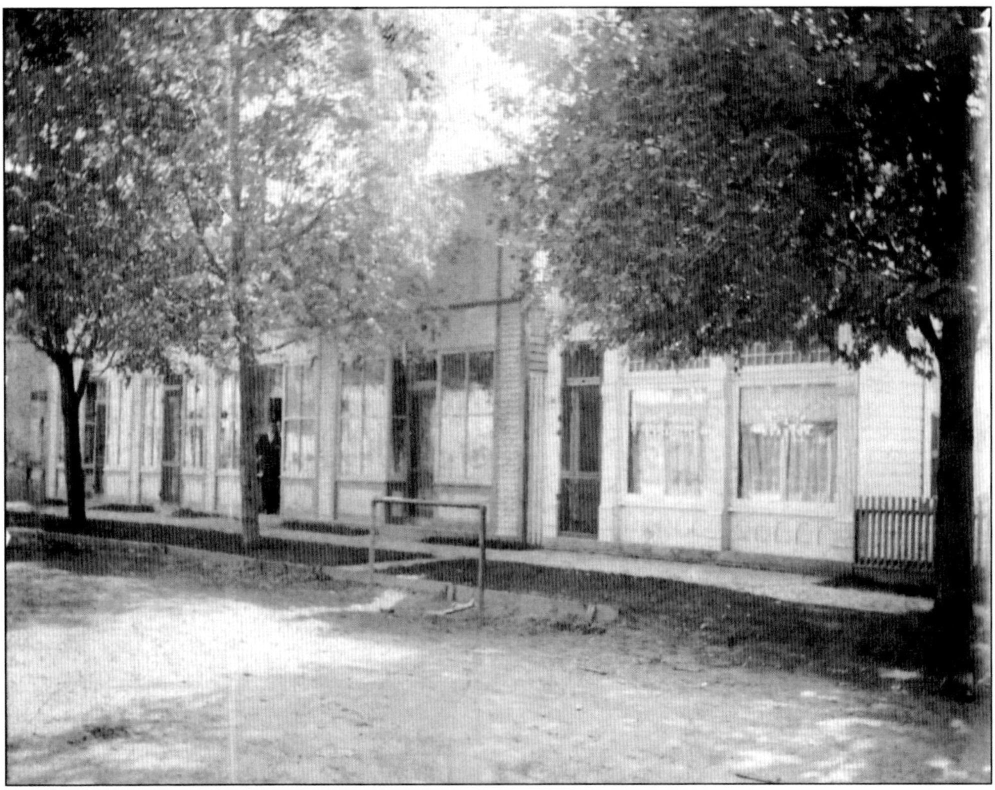

This rare 1915 cabinet photograph of a Knightstown street scene on the National Road includes a hitching post for horses on the street. The image, taken by the Fowinkle Studio in Knightstown, has been identified as "left, old building razed to make place for 'Opto' building. Right Dr. Barrett's Office. North Jeff St. West Side" on the front and captioned on the back, "The old building, left side, along the alley, was formerly on the site of the P. Office Main St. It was used in my boyhood days by my father to keep finished carriages and buggies in for sales room on main st. W.M. Edwards 12/12/1927." (Courtesy Knightstown History Museum.)

An unidentified woman stands beside a cigar-store wooden Indian on the National Road in Greenfield, Indiana. The back of the image states, "Mom on the old National Pike in Greenfield, Indiana on our way to the World's Fair in New York City July 12th, 1939." The ornate wooden Indian has a tomahawk in his buckskin belt and holds a rifle at the ready. A Coca-Cola sign is sandwiched between cigar signs in the front window, and the awning reads, "Fishing Tackle." (Alan E. Hunter collection.)

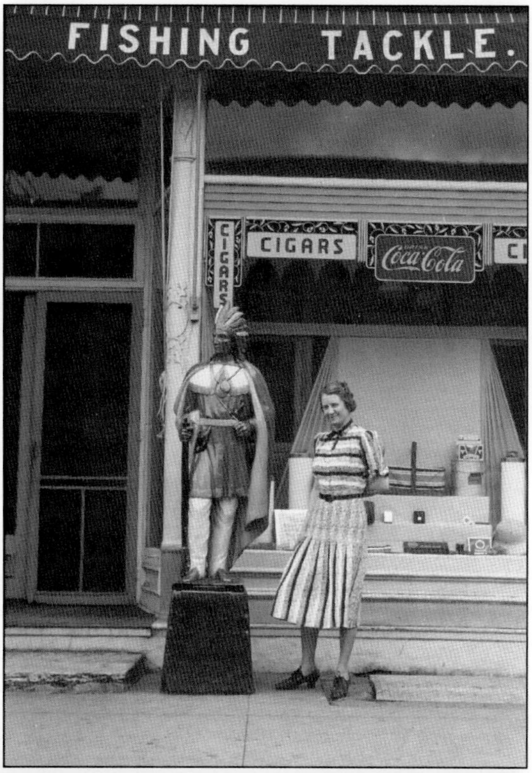

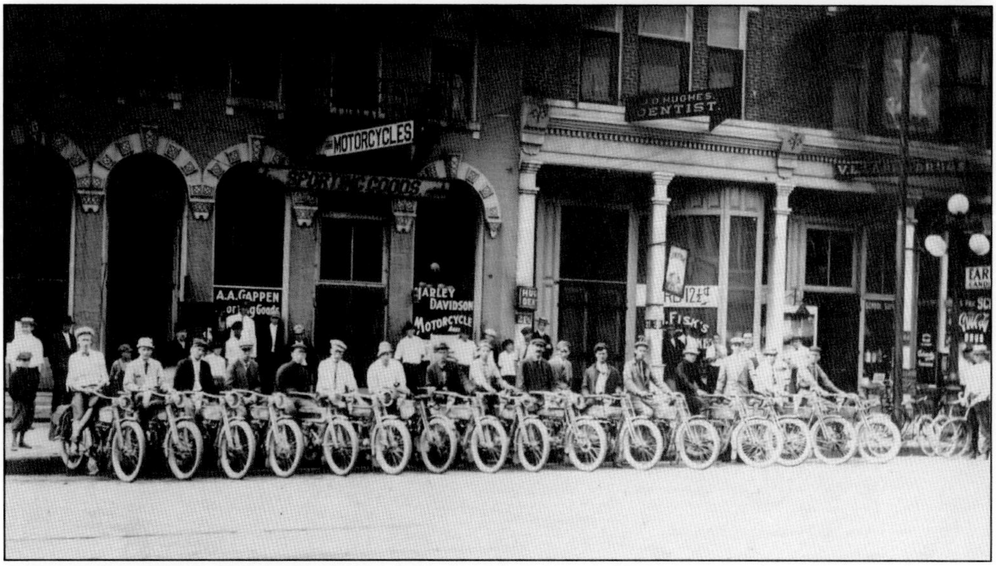

Sixteen 1914 Harley-Davidson motorcycles are lined up in front of the A.A. Gappen Sporting Goods Store located at 21 West Main Street on the south side of the National Road in Greenfield. The group, calling itself the Greenies, is posing at the starting point of a 40-mile road trip to the Decatur County Courthouse in Greensburg. The Gappen store window features a painted Harley-Davidson motorcycle sign as well as a porcelain sign hanging above the door. Dentist J.D. Hughes and Early's Drug Store are located just west of the store. A Coca-Cola sign can be seen in the front window of Early's on the right edge of the image. (Alan E. Hunter collection.)

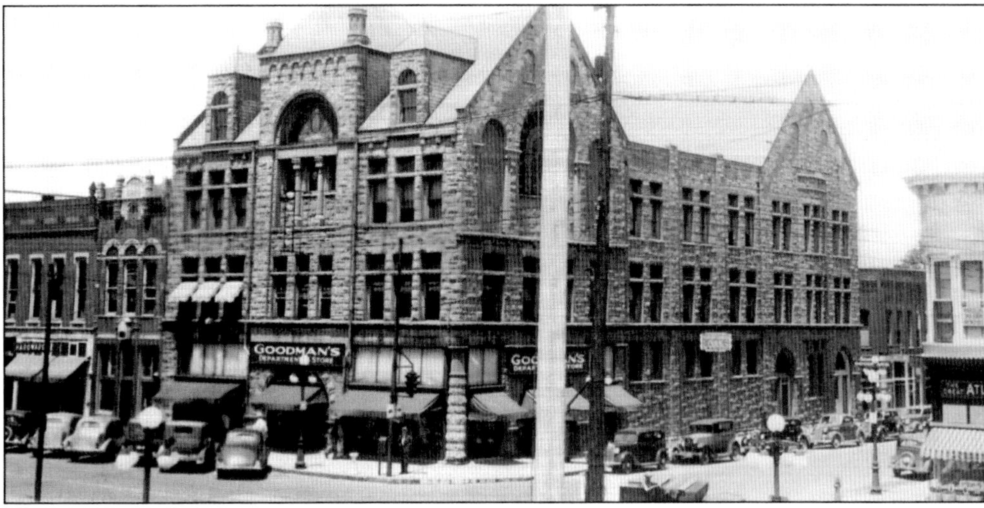

The Masonic temple in Greenfield was located at the corner of 2 West Main Street and the National Road. The temple was constructed in 1895 and designed by Indianapolis architect Louis H. Gibson in the Richardsonian Romanesque style. The main floor featured a series of department stores for over 75 years (pictured here as Goodman's), with professional offices on the second floor and the Masonic temple on the uppermost level. The building was recently refurbished but retains many of its original interior and exterior details. Newly reopened as the Creative Arts and Event Center, the main floor is home to an art gallery, the second floor features retail space and artist studios, and the top floor features a large, open space for banquets and weddings. (Courtesy Bob Hunt.)

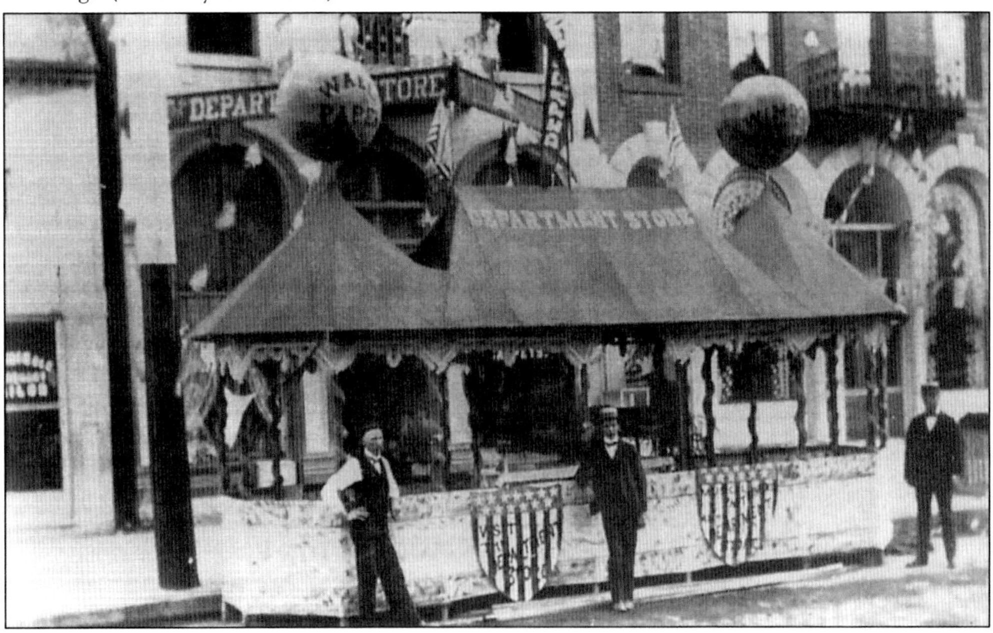

An 1899 photograph shows the ornate sidewalk display booth made for the Greenfield Street Fair by the department store located at 19 West Main Street on the south side of the National Road. The tailor on the far left was located on the ground level of Gooding's Tavern, one of Greenfield's most recognizable landmarks on the opposite corner from the Hancock County Courthouse. (Courtesy Joe Skvarenina.)

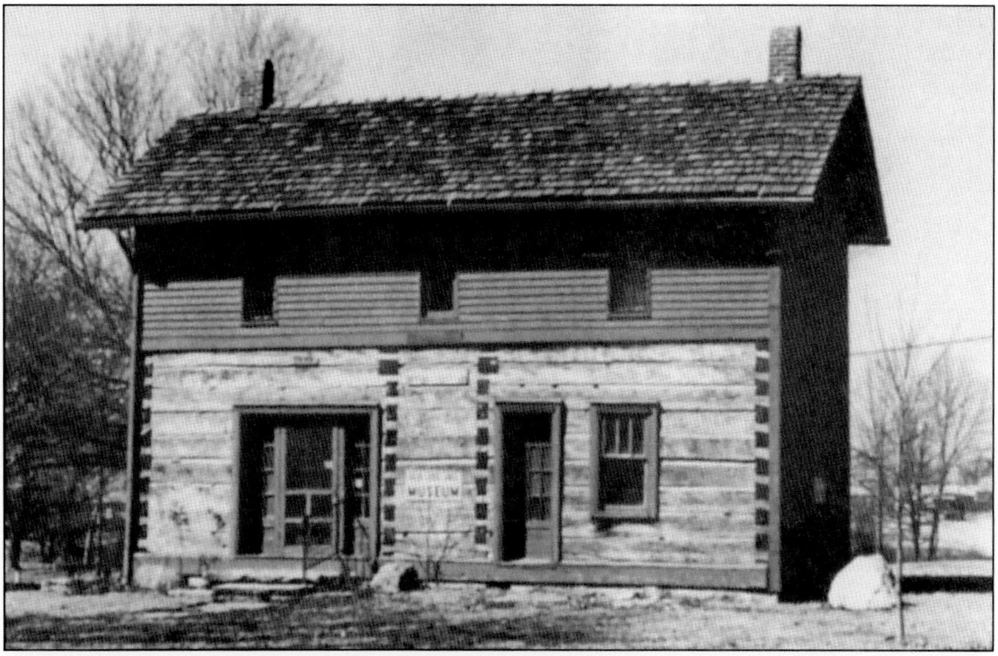

Built in 1853, the Old Log Jail served as the third county jail until 1874. The building was originally located on the south side of the public square downtown, south of where the present-day county courthouse lies. The jail was moved to its present location at the southeast corner of Riley Park near the intersection of US 40 and Apple Street. The building now serves as a museum and is maintained by the Hancock County Historical Society. The photograph was taken in 1967 just after the museum was opened and before the Chapel in the Park was moved directly behind it. (Courtesy Elayne Stewart.)

This c. 1870 photograph is of the old Greenfield Adelphian Band, which inspired the poem "The Old Band." Poet James Whitcomb Riley can be seen on the far right, holding the huge bass drum. The Adelphians not only played music but also staged plays. Young Riley starred in many of the plays and also painted most of the scenery and backdrops used in the productions at Greenfield's Old Masonic Hall on the National Road. (Courtesy Riley House Museum.)

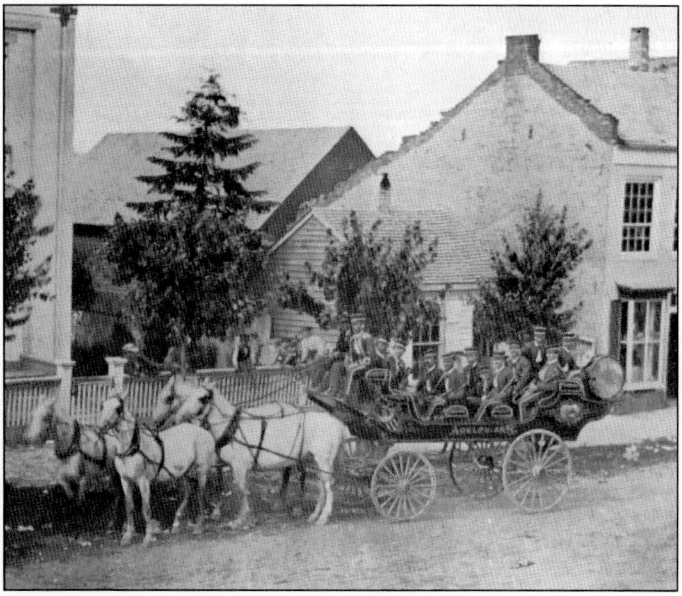

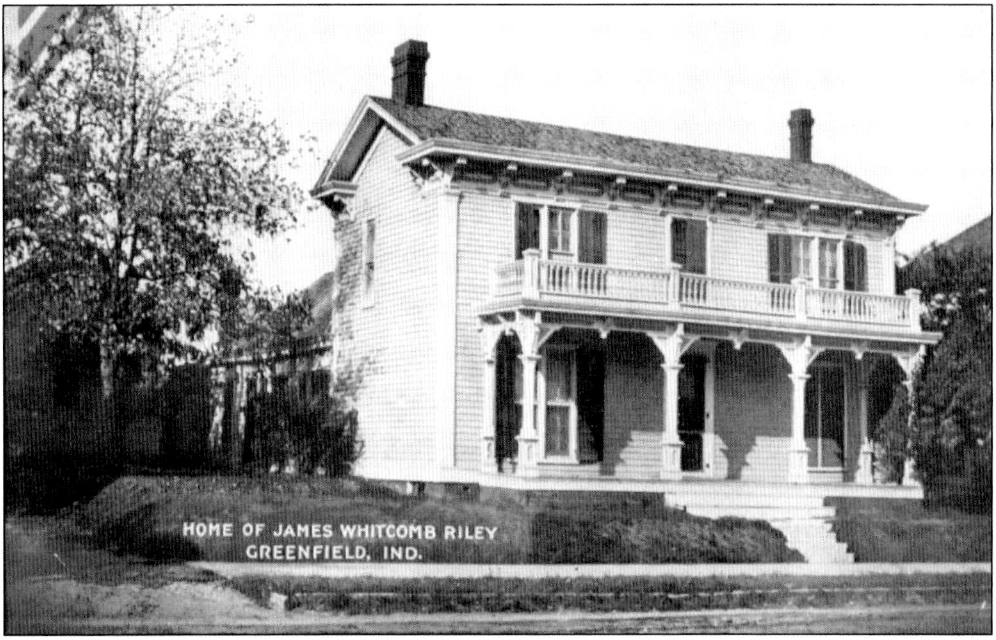

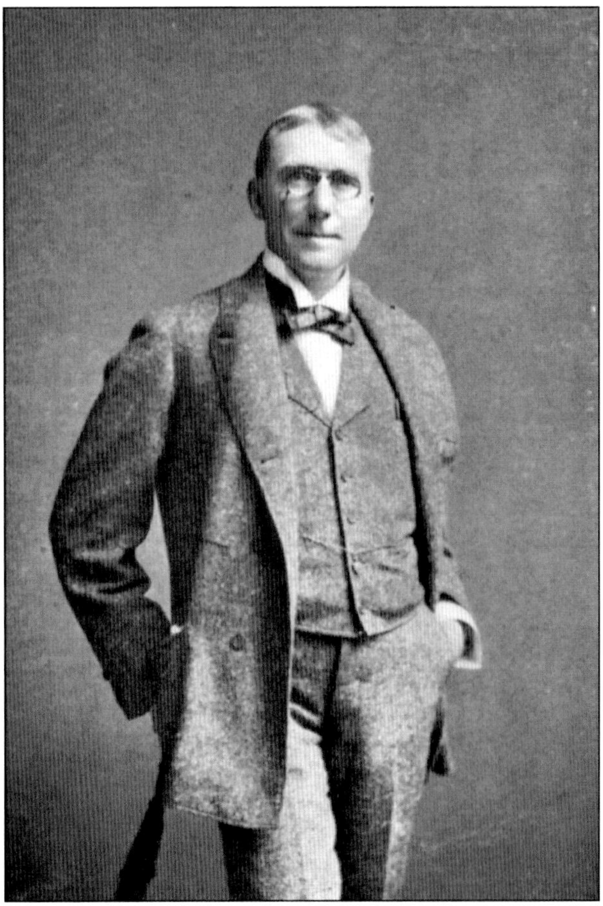

The Riley House is pictured around 1900. Poet James Whitcomb Riley was not actually born in the house but rather a cabin on the property on October 7, 1849. Although it was along the National Road, the residence was described as being "near lots of woodland animals, but very few people." The family sold the house in 1870, but James Whitcomb Riley bought the house back in 1893. Riley kept his residence in Indianapolis and never again lived in Greenfield house. (Courtesy Riley House Museum.)

Poet James Whitcomb Riley is pictured in 1889 at age 40. Before his death in 1916, Riley wrote over 1,000 poems, including "Little Orphant Annie," "When the Frost is on the Punkin," and the "The Bear Story." During his time, he was regarded as more important than Mark Twain. (Courtesy Riley House Museum.)

Five

Philadelphia to Cumberland

Philadelphia, the first town in Sugar Creek Township, was platted on April 11, 1838. During the 1870s and 1880s, a great deal of business transactions occurred in Philadelphia. It was an important little railroad town, with a sawmill, gristmill, a grain elevator, and a blacksmith shop. For a period of some 50 years, nothing much seemed to change in the little pike town, and the older citizens recalled in the 1930s, according to Indiana National Road Association literature, "It remains very much as it was from their earliest recollection." Today, Philadelphia is not known for who lives there, but rather for who is buried there. The inspiration for one of the most beloved characters in the history of American literature, Little Orphan Annie, was laid to rest in the town cemetery on the National Road.

Named after the starting point of the National Road in Maryland, Cumberland has emerged recently as an important town working to preserve its heritage. In the face of encroaching sprawl, the town has made it a priority to develop a unique streetscape, locally designate its historic core, and develop interpretation to promote its story to visitors who now may recognize a town that is separate from the onslaught of big-box stores and mass culture that lies just to the west of its borders. Cumberland marks the last pike town east of Indianapolis, and the experience of the road drastically changes from this point forward along the route, as travelers enter the big city and then head west toward Terre Haute, where the experience is more scenic and focused on the early-20th-century culture of the National Road.

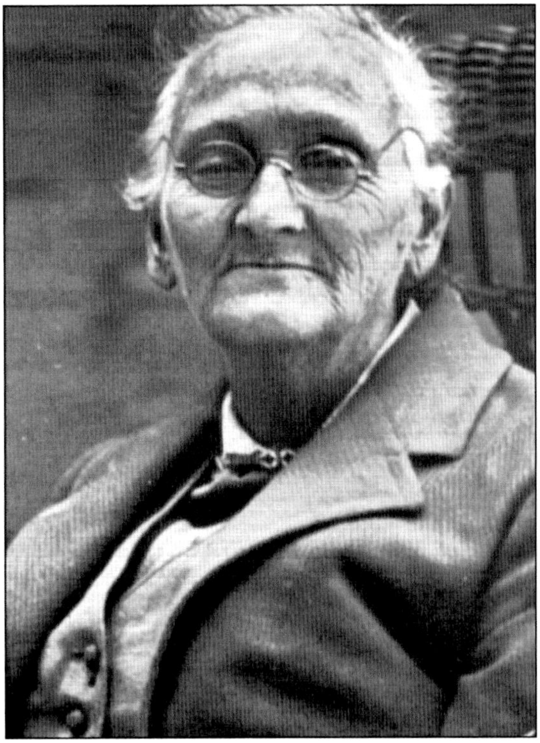

Pictured is Mary Alice Smith (Gray), the real-life inspiration for the James Whitcomb Riley poem "Little Orphant Annie." As a child of 10, she unwittingly provided the original character featured in poetry, stories, comics and comic strips, several plays, and even the Broadway play and movie *Annie*. Riley had a vivid recollection of her going up the stairs at night to her lonesome room in the attic, leaning down and patting each stair affectionately, and naming every one. Riley wrote another poem about her titled, "Where Is Mary Alice Smith?" He depicts the little orphan girl falling in love with a soldier boy who was killed and then herself dying of grief. In truth, Mary Alice went to work in a tavern on the National Road in the town of Philadelphia, where she met her husband, John Wesley Gray; their marriage produced seven children. (Allan E. Hunter collection.)

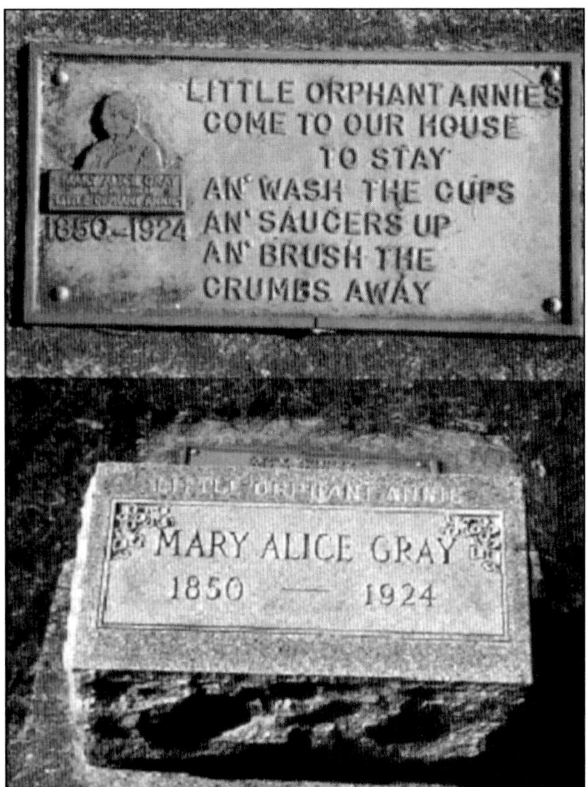

This is the grave of Mary Alice Smith, or Little Orphan Annie. She was born in Liberty in Union County, on September 25, 1850. She passed away quietly in her sleep on Friday, March 7, 1924. Her obituary began, "Little Orphan Annie has washed her last cup and saucer and brushed the last crumb away." Funeral services were held at 1 p.m. Sunday afternoon at the residence of her daughter, Mrs. L.D. Marsh, at 2225 Union Street, and her burial was in Spring Lake Cemetery in Philadelphia (about halfway between Cumberland and Greenfield). (Courtesy of Rhonda Hunter.)

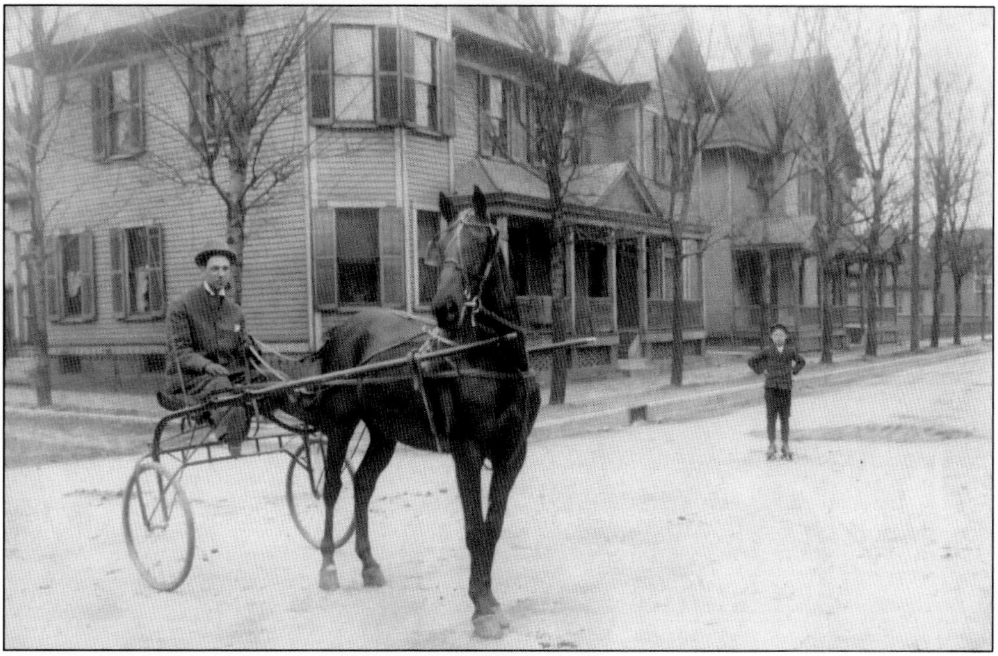

An unidentified man guides a racehorse from an attached sulky on the National Road in Philadelphia as his son looks on proudly a few feet away. The cabinet photograph is dated 1907 on the back. (Courtesy April and Mark Riggle.)

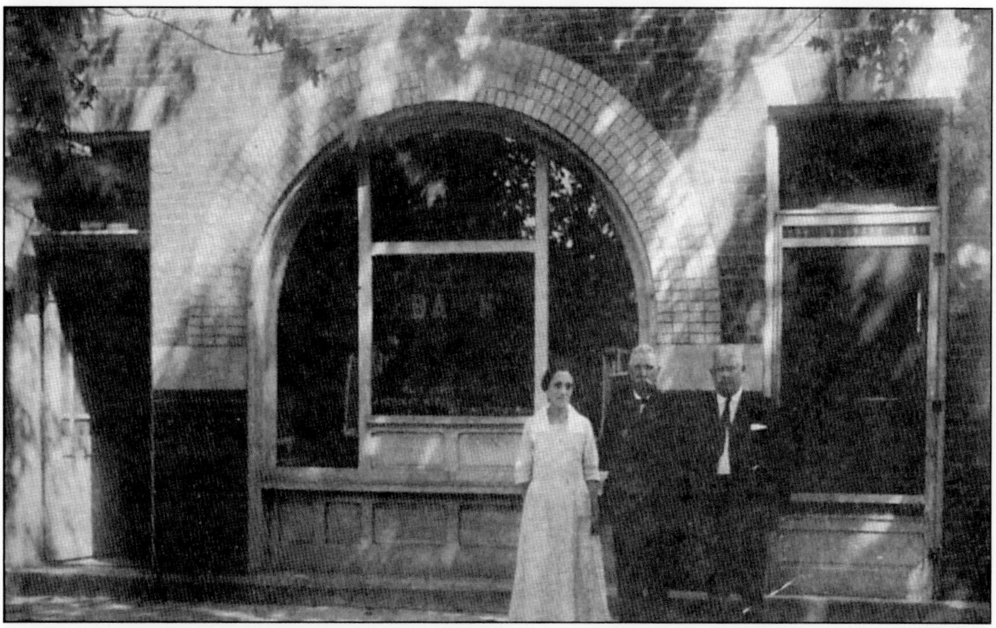

This is a c. 1900 view of the Cumberland Bank on the National Road. The most exciting thing to happen to Cumberland during the Great Depression was when three armed bandits robbed the bank in the summer of 1930. The bandits got away with $800 cash and waved to startled spectators as they drove slowly out of town with alarm bells ringing. The bank never really recovered and closed sometime in 1933. Cumberland did not get another bank until August 1963. (Courtesy Indianapolis Public Library-Warren Branch.)

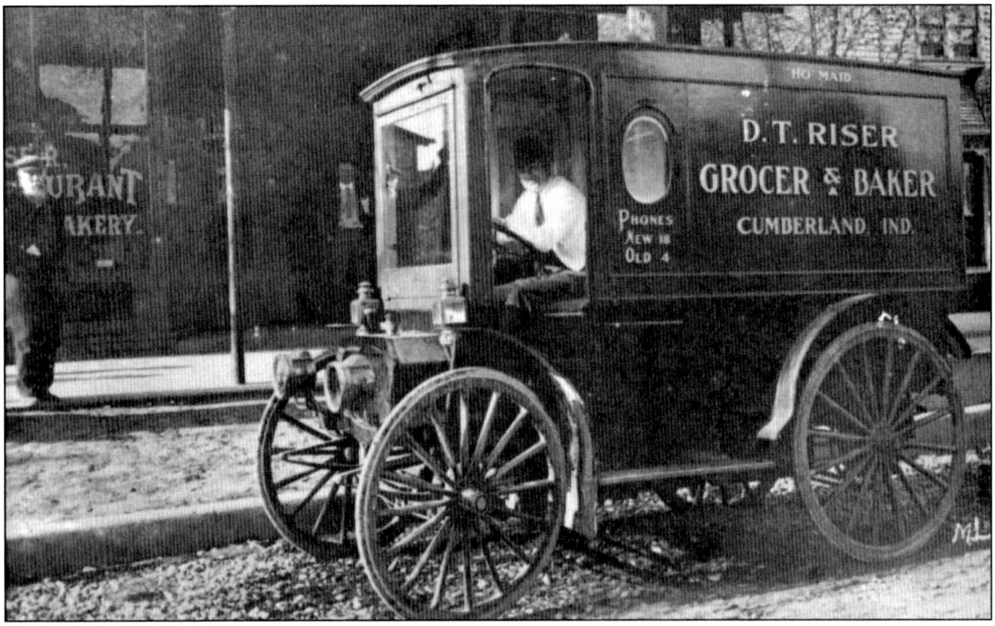

A c. 1910 image captures baker D.T. Riser, owner of D.T. Riser's Grocery & Bakery in Cumberland. Riser owned the first delivery truck in town and was known for delivering his fresh-baked bread all over the community. He was remembered for his friendliness and for his habit of passing town gossip to anyone who would listen. (Courtesy Indianapolis Public Library-Warren Branch.)

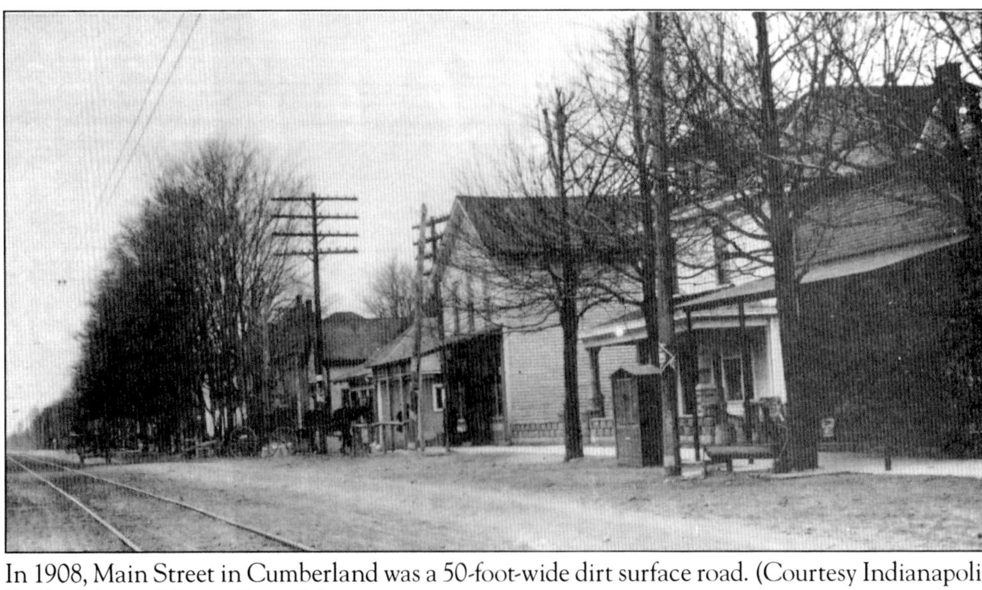

In 1908, Main Street in Cumberland was a 50-foot-wide dirt surface road. (Courtesy Indianapolis Public Library-Warren Branch.)

This is a 1900 view of a truck sinking a natural gas well in Cumberland. During the late 1880s, the discovery of natural gas in east central Indiana led to a gas boom in the area. The brief boom transformed much of east central Indiana from an agriculture-oriented economy to an economy that also included manufacturing. However, by 1905, the boom was mostly over, as much of the natural gas was wasted or mismanaged. (Courtesy Indianapolis Public Library-Warren Branch.)

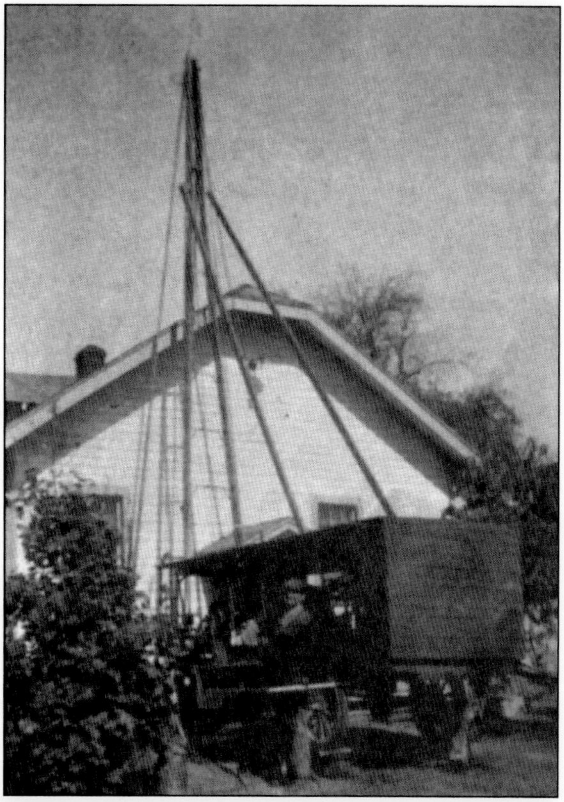

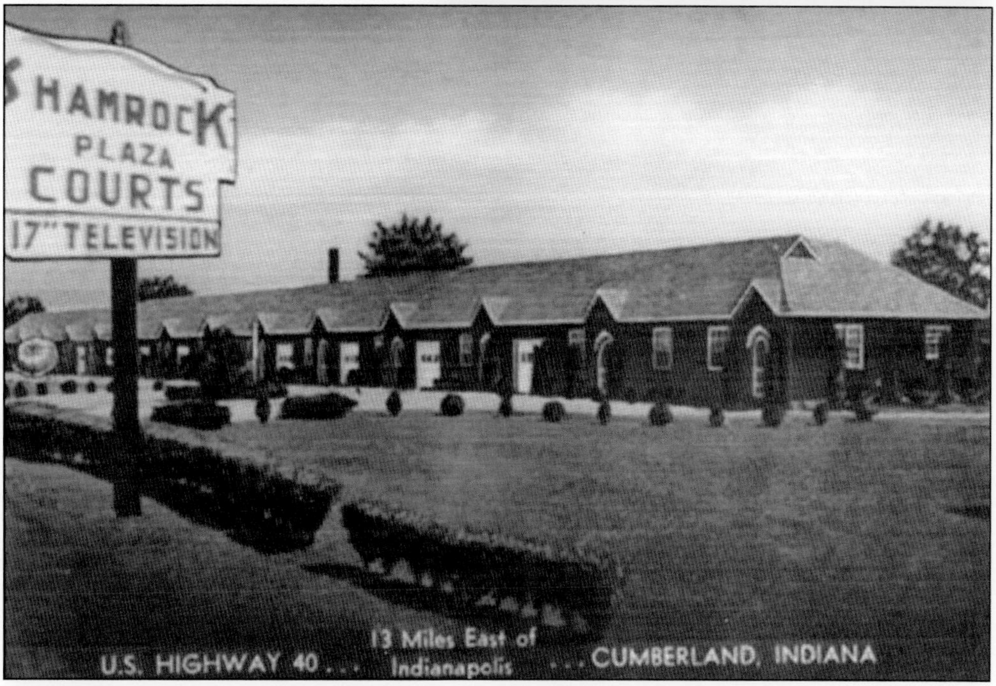

This 1950s color postcard shows the Shamrock Plaza Courts Motel in Cumberland. The motel's sign advertises that it has 17-inch televisions. (Alan E. Hunter collection.)

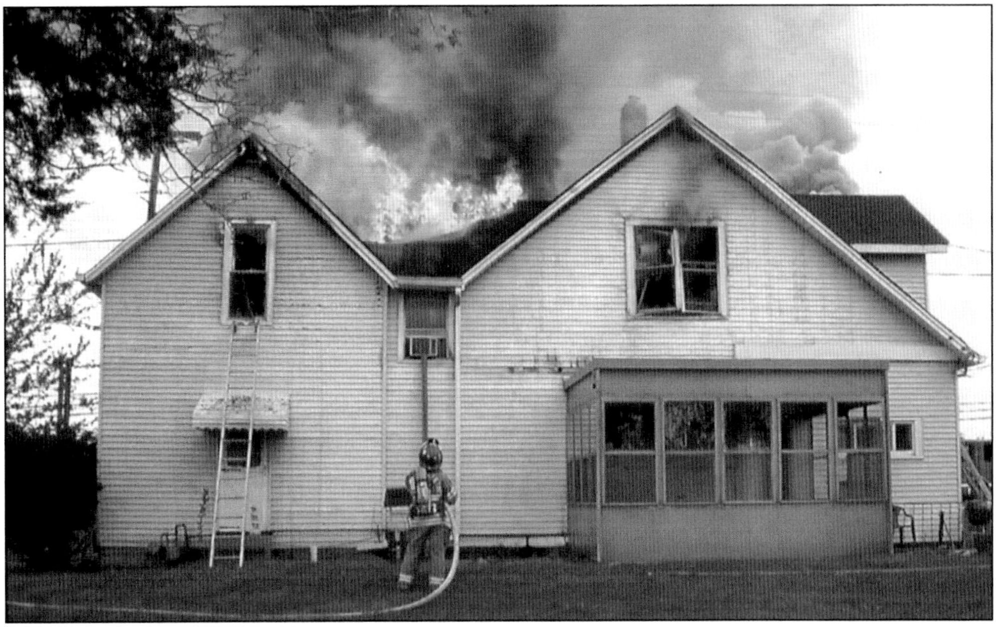

In 1989, Ron Sanders and his father, Alva Sanders, purchased a piece of land a half mile west of Cumberland, Indiana, on the south side of the National Road. Located at 7243 West US Highway 40, the property featured a family farmhouse as its most prominent landmark. On April 26, 2000, the farmhouse caught fire. (Courtesy Ron Sanders.)

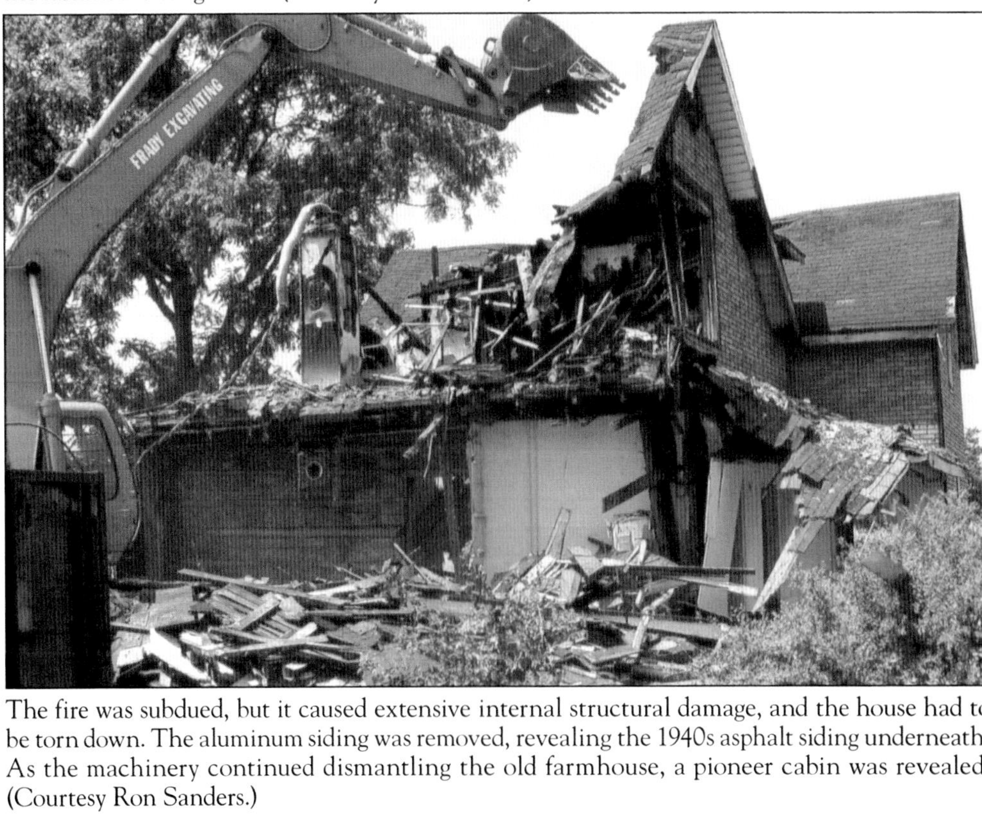

The fire was subdued, but it caused extensive internal structural damage, and the house had to be torn down. The aluminum siding was removed, revealing the 1940s asphalt siding underneath. As the machinery continued dismantling the old farmhouse, a pioneer cabin was revealed. (Courtesy Ron Sanders.)

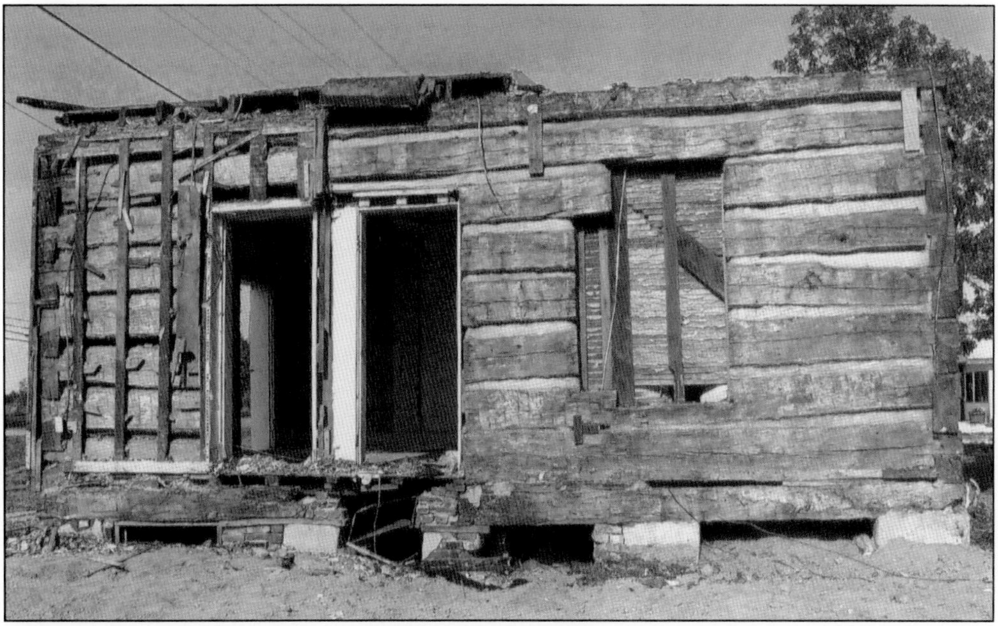

Heavy equipment continued to carefully deconstruct the area around the pioneer cabin. Soon the ancient shell of the original pioneer cabin was fully revealed. It is estimated that the cabin was built about 1820. Local legend claims that clergyman Henry Ward Beecher once stayed there during the time he was the pastor of the Second Presbyterian Church in Indianapolis (1839–1847). (Courtesy Ron Sanders.)

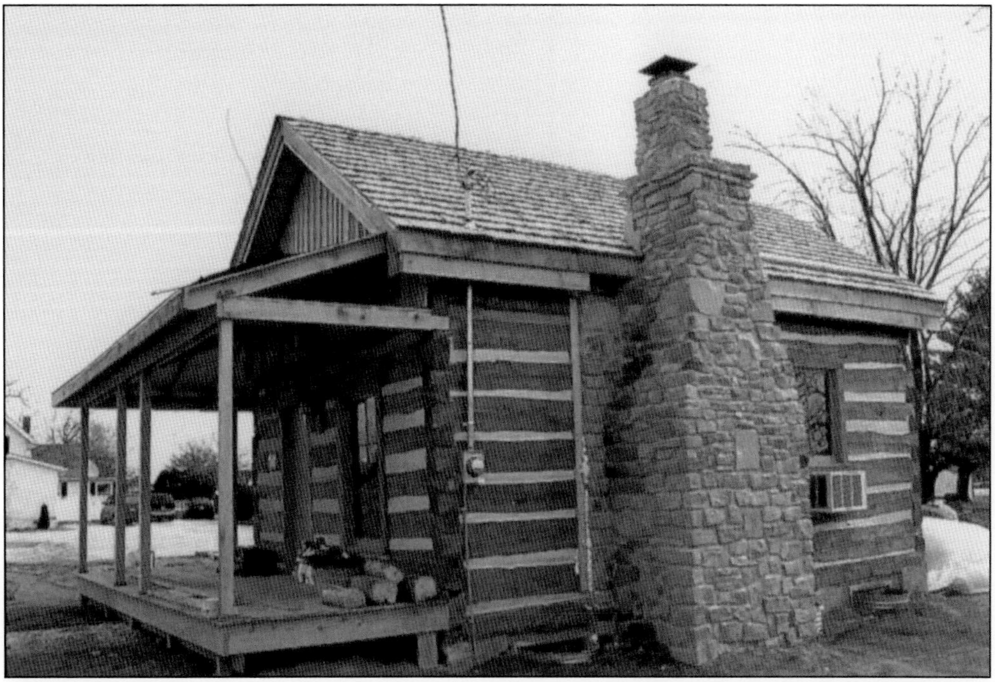

The pioneer cabin is fully restored with a new roof in place, and the reconstructed chimney made of Brown County stone stands proudly once again along the Historic National Road. (Courtesy Ron Sanders.)

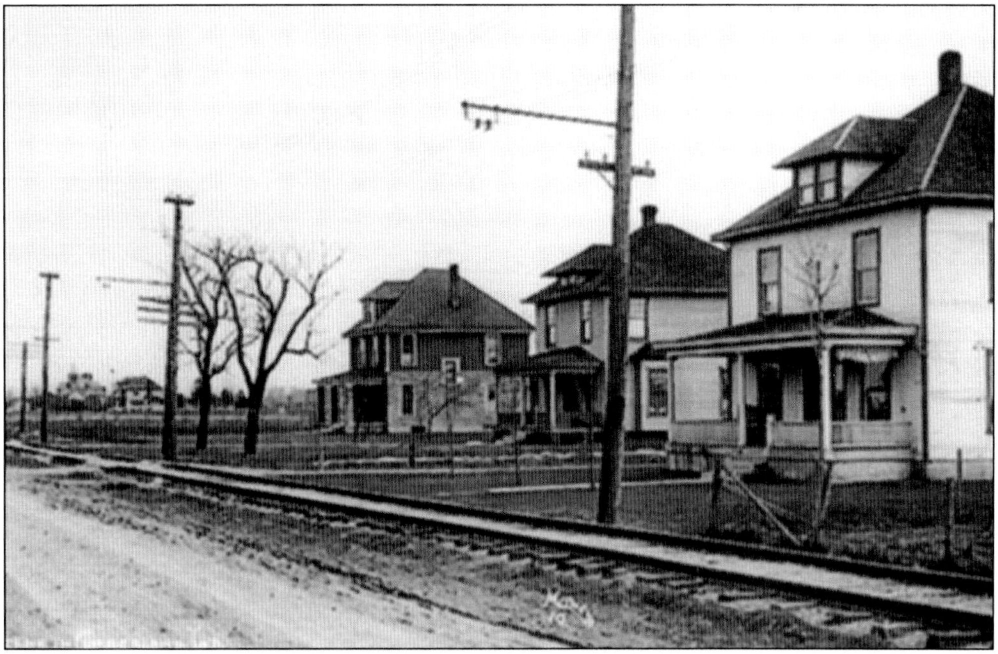

This is a c. 1910 real photo postcard of the National Road and the interurban tracks a quarter mile west of the iconic St. John United Church of Christ in Cumberland on the south side of the National Road. Located at 11000 East Washington Street, the property has long been Cumberland's most prominent landmark on the road. (Courtesy Indianapolis Public Library-Irvington Branch.)

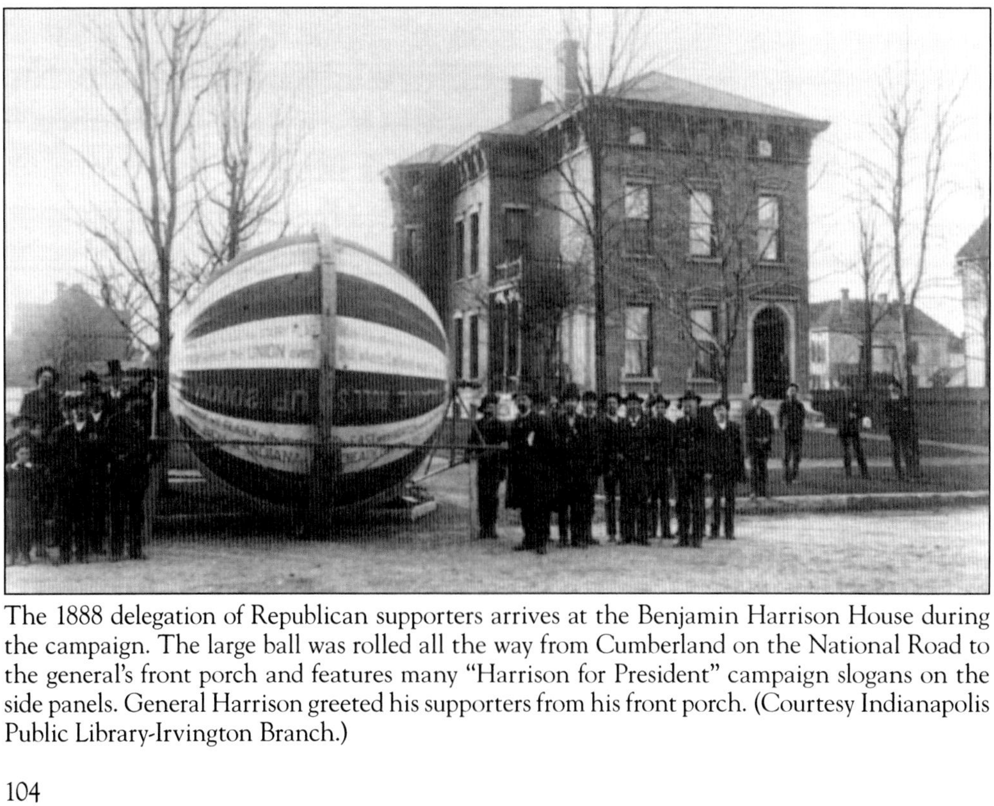

The 1888 delegation of Republican supporters arrives at the Benjamin Harrison House during the campaign. The large ball was rolled all the way from Cumberland on the National Road to the general's front porch and features many "Harrison for President" campaign slogans on the side panels. General Harrison greeted his supporters from his front porch. (Courtesy Indianapolis Public Library-Irvington Branch.)

Six

The Big City

Today, Indianapolis is the largest city in Indiana, though when the National Road was first constructed through town, it was smaller than Richmond and Terre Haute. Indianapolis became the state capital in 1820 after it was moved from Corydon, and it was not by chance that it was positioned next to the National Road. Founded in 1821, Indianapolis was designed by Alexander Ralston, an apprentice of Pierre L'Enfant. Nicknamed the "Circle City," Indianapolis is centered on historic Monument Circle. In the 1900s, as a part of the City Beautiful movement, noted landscape architect George Kessler created a plan for parklands and boulevards throughout the city, and the first Union Station was built in Indianapolis.

On the drive in from the east, travelers will pass through Irvington, another very unique neighborhood along the National Road. Irvington, founded in 1870, was once the location of Butler University. It is a planned neighborhood with winding streets that reflects the Romantic landscape-design era. Although the university left in 1928, the neighborhood expanded and incorporated some of its remains, including the Bona Thompson Library, now a center for art and culture.

Downtown, the Historic National Road is called Washington Street, and old and new mix here quite well. Original historic building facades are reused and incorporated into a successful downtown mall that is connected to the famous glass dome for the ArtsGarden that hovers above the Historic National Road. Other historic buildings are being rehabilitated, and this helps retain much of the original streetscape that one would have seen during the turn of the century.

Pres. Abraham Lincoln lectured in downtown during his trip to Washington, DC, to take over the presidency; candidate Robert F. Kennedy was campaigning there when Martin Luther King Jr. was assassinated; and Elvis Presley performed his last concert in Indianapolis. The National Road has been the site of many large-scale parades through downtown, and important neighborhoods such as Irvington are well preserved throughout the city.

While much of the Historic National Road's identity has been sacrificed on the edges of Indianapolis, Cumberland on the east and Plainfield on the west side continue efforts to protect their heritage by developing streetscapes and locally protecting their town. Both communities embarked on streetscape improvement projects, and Cumberland took it another step further by locally designating its downtown so that it may retain some identity in the face of urban development pressures.

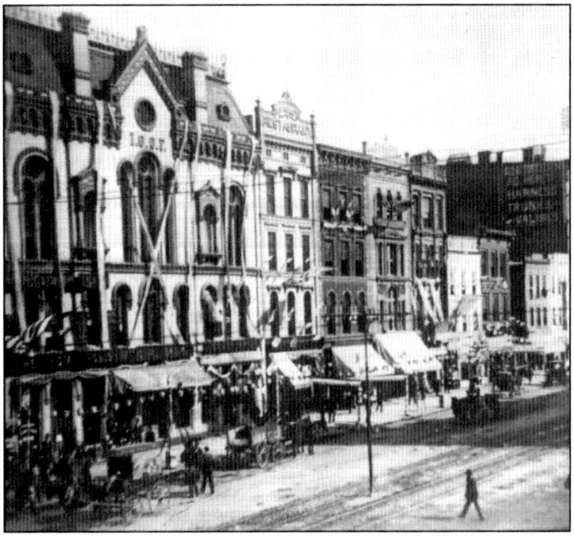

The north side of Washington Street looks east from Pennsylvania Street around 1890. On the left side of the photograph is the ornate Odd Fellows Building, which is draped in bunting, perhaps for a Flag Day parade. The Indiana National Bank occupies the ground floor of the building. The IOOF tore this structure down and replaced it with towering a 13-story headquarters, which still stands today. In 1908 and 1909, it was the tallest building in the city and was the first high-rise in Indianapolis to rise above 200 feet or 15 floors. The top floor contained a large auditorium. (Courtesy Indianapolis Public Library-Warren branch.)

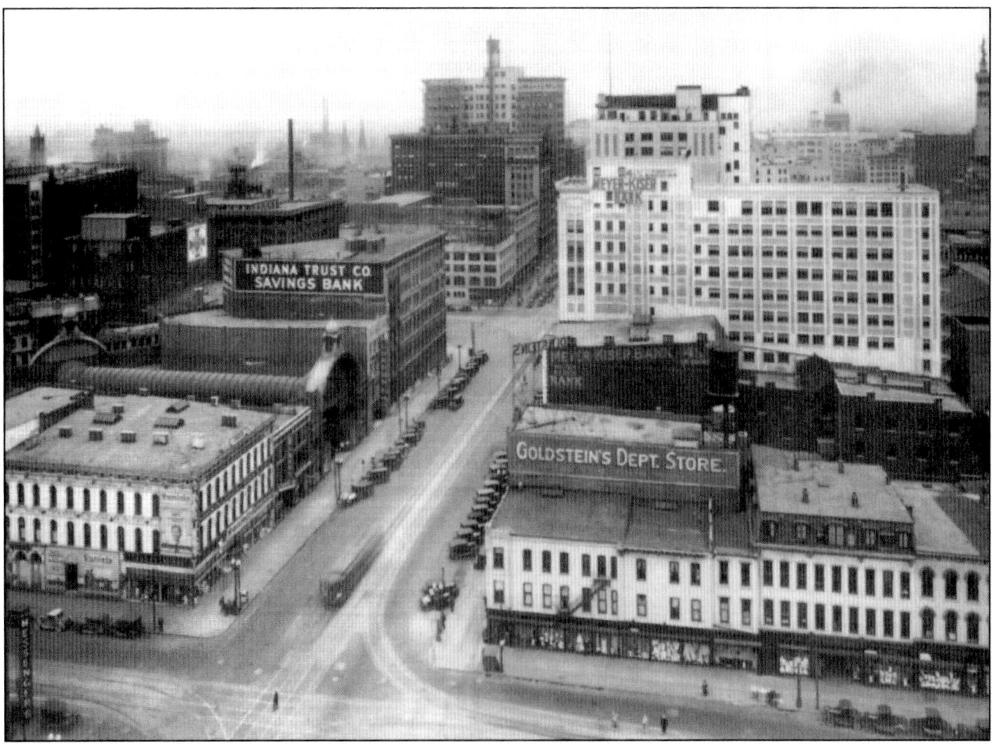

This aerial view of Washington Street looking west was taken sometime in the 1920s. Monument Circle and the Indiana State House can be seen in the upper right corner. The building with the arched roof is the Pembroke Arcade. Located at 133–137 East Washington Street, the Pembroke Building was designed by the renowned architecture firm of Vonnegut and Bohn. Inspired by architecture of the 1893 Chicago World's Fair, the Pembroke was a forerunner of the modern shopping mall and contained small retail shops. It featured heavy gold-leaf trim, pressed steel radiators, and a Louis Millet–designed glass-and-iron vaulted roof. It opened in the 1890s and was torn down in 1943. (Courtesy Indianapolis Public Library-Warren branch.)

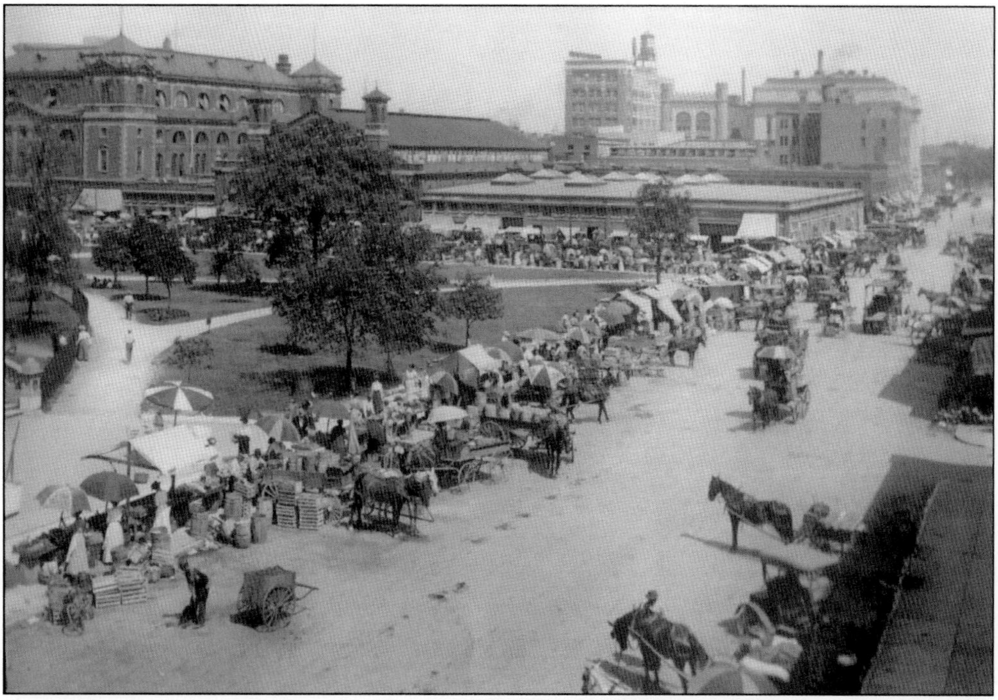

An overhead view of vendor stalls at the outdoor farmer's market at Alabama and Market Streets is captured here in 1912. The city market is partially obscured by trees in the background next to old Tomlinson Hall. The manure cart is visible in the lower left corner, and its owner can be seen scooping up horse droppings with a large scoop shovel. (Courtesy Indianapolis Public Library-Warren branch.)

This is a 1922 overhead view of vendor stalls at the outdoor farmer's market on Market Street looking east. The Gordon Sign Company and the Taggert Bread factory can be seen in the background. The bread factory had its own water tower that can also be seen in the upper center of the photograph. (Allan E. Hunter collection.)

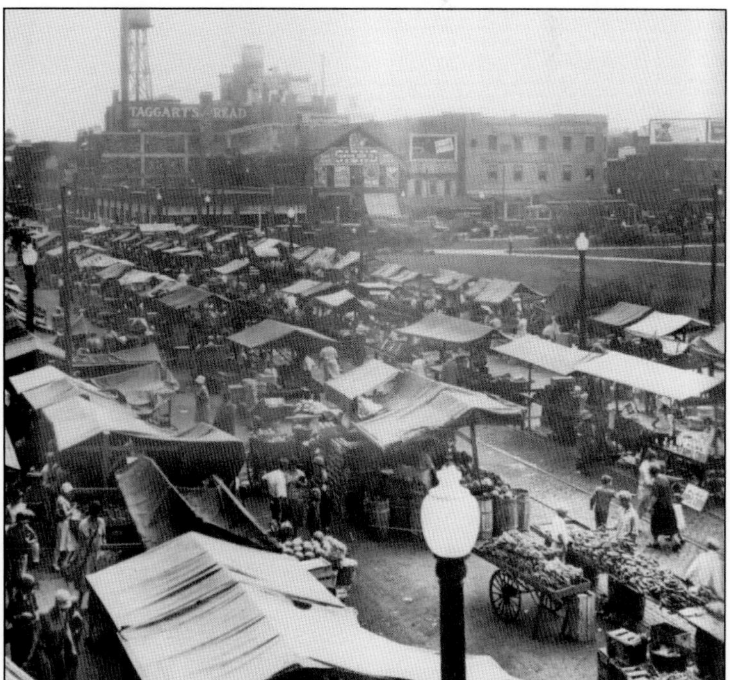

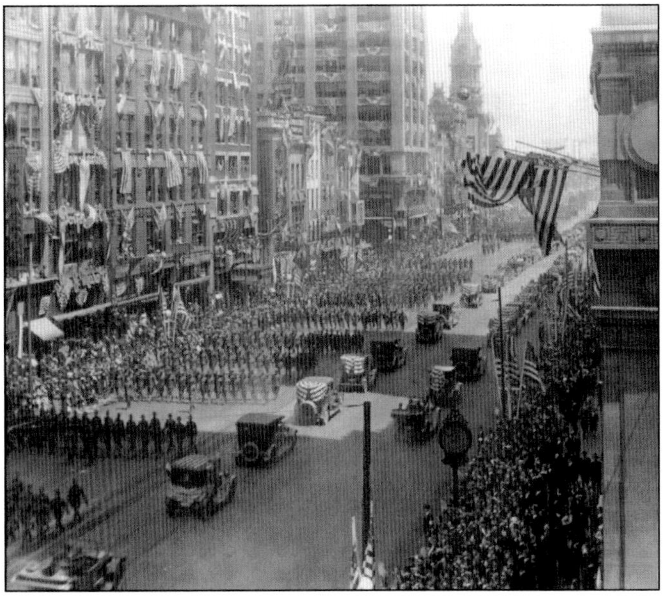

World War I veterans march east along Washington Street during the homecoming parade on May 7, 1919. The photograph's caption claims that the automobiles headed up the opposite side of the street are carrying wounded soldiers. Some of the businesses on the left side of the street include Howards Carpets, J. Marrot shoe store, and Vonnegut Hardware. The ornate building with the 80-foot-tall tower seen just to the right of center is the Vance Block. (Courtesy Indianapolis Public Library-Warren branch.)

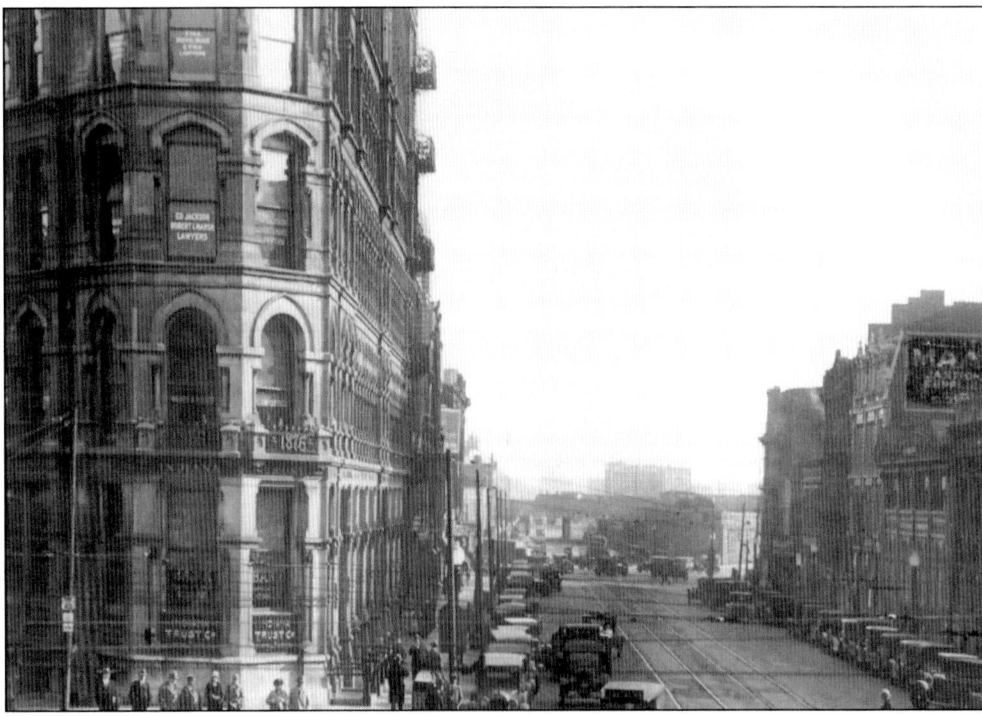

This 1920s view of the intersection of Virginia Avenue and Washington Street looks southeast from Washington Street. The ornate flatiron building on the left is the Indiana Trust Building, located at 117 East Washington Street, that was more commonly known as the Vance Block. The 1877 city directory carried an ad stating, "VANCE BLOCK, Corner Virginia Ave and Washington, containing 100 ELEGANT OFFICE AND STORE ROOMS Heated by Steam, Water Supply in Every Room. For Offices Apply at Room 42, 3rd Floor." The third-floor office window on the left lists the name of Ed Jackson, the disgraced Indiana governor with KKK ties, whose office was located here until 1937. (Courtesy Indianapolis Public Library-Warren branch.)

The tower of the Marion County Courthouse soars above East Washington Street in 1936. Dedicated on July 5, 1876, the elaborate Second Empire–style building was a city landmark until it was razed in the early 1960s. It cost almost $1.5 million to build, nearly twice the original estimate. Designed by architect Isaac M. Hodgson, the massive building fronted Washington Street and covered the block between Alabama and Delaware Streets. It featured five three-story bays, a central clock tower, and red granite pillars with an exterior of Indiana limestone. Marion County residents were never completely comfortable with the ostentatious buildings and their "bewildering profusion of colors, frescoes, and gingerbread trim." Notice the Coca-Cola sign in the lower center of the photo. (Courtesy Indianapolis Public Library-Warren branch.)

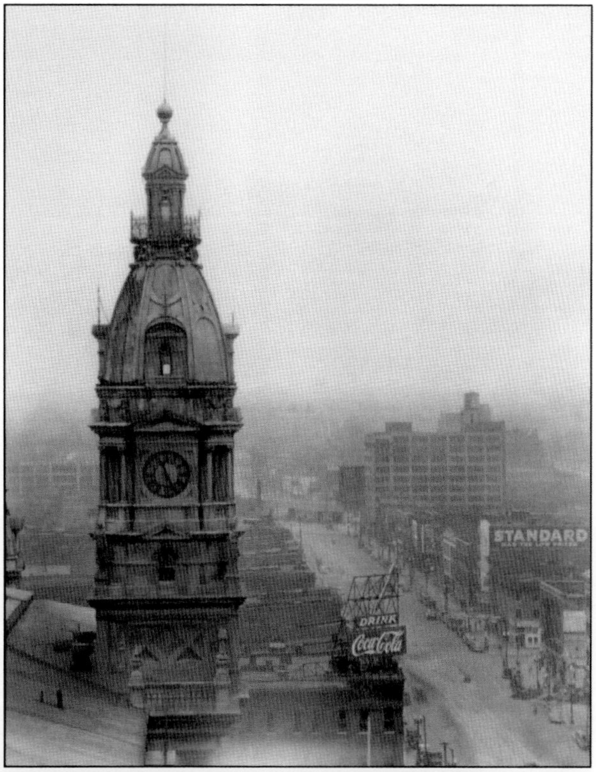

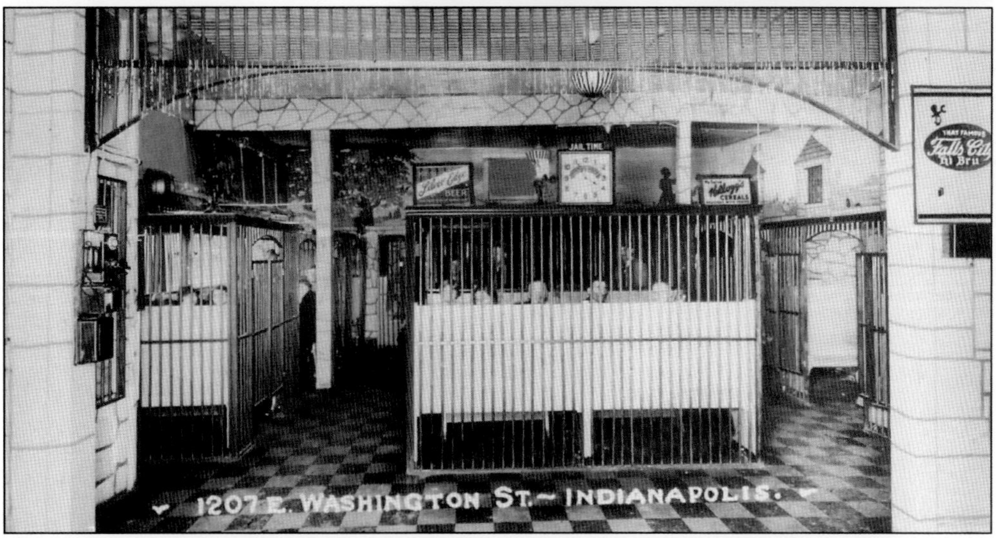

This 1934 real-photo postcard is of Fox's Jail House restaurant at 1207 East Washington Street in Indianapolis. Customers dine in booths that are constructed as jail cells with bars on the sides. The back reads, "Spend your time in Jail—eat—drink—music in a cell. Never a cover charge." Ads for Silver Edge beer, Falls City beer, and Kellogg's cereals adorn the wall. The square clock over the center booth displays "Jail Time." Note the wooden wall telephone on the left. These jail-themed restaurants were very popular in the Hoosier state, as gangsters like Bonnie and Clyde, Pretty Boy Floyd, Baby Face Nelson, and Hoosier John Dillinger roamed the Midwest as misconceived modern-day Robin Hoods. (Courtesy Bill Raney.)

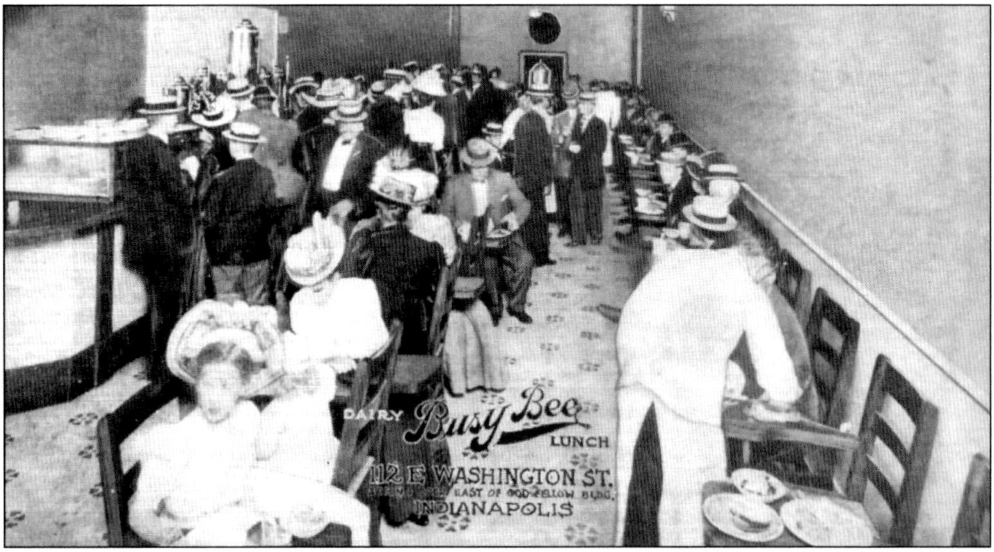

A postcard, postmarked 1934, shows the "Busy Bee Dairy-Lunch 112 E. Washington St. Indianapolis Second Door East of Odd Fellow Bldg." The unique design of the restaurant featured a cafeteria-style counter on the left where patrons walked the line, picking out their food. The right wall has a long line of old-fashioned wooden school desks, where patrons ate their plates of food. The left row of school desks is staggered (every other one) in front-to-back fashion. (Courtesy Bill Raney.)

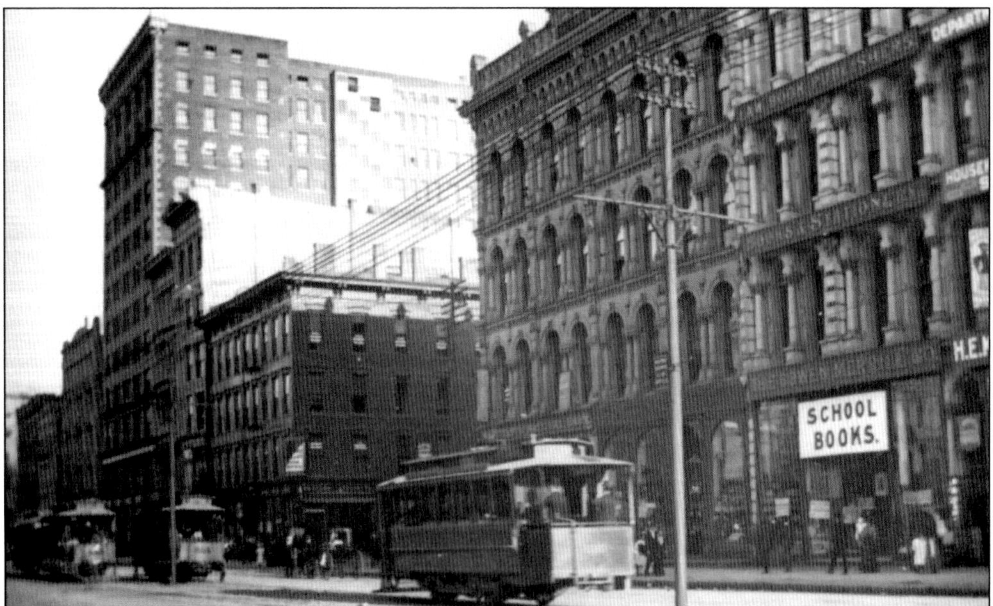

Streetcars pass by the five-story Bowen-Merrill Company, located at 9 and 11 West Washington Street. Bowen-Merrill was a publishing company that grew out of an Indianapolis bookstore, owned by Samuel Merrill, whose specialty had been in publishing law books. In 1883, it began publishing popular books by Indiana authors such as James Whitcomb Riley, George Ade, and Meredith Nicholson. Other authors in the Bowen-Merrill stable included Benjamin Harrison and L. Frank Baum of *The Wizard of Oz* fame. In 1903, the company was renamed Bobbs-Merrill under the leadership of William C. Bobbs. (Courtesy Indianapolis Public Library-Warren branch.)

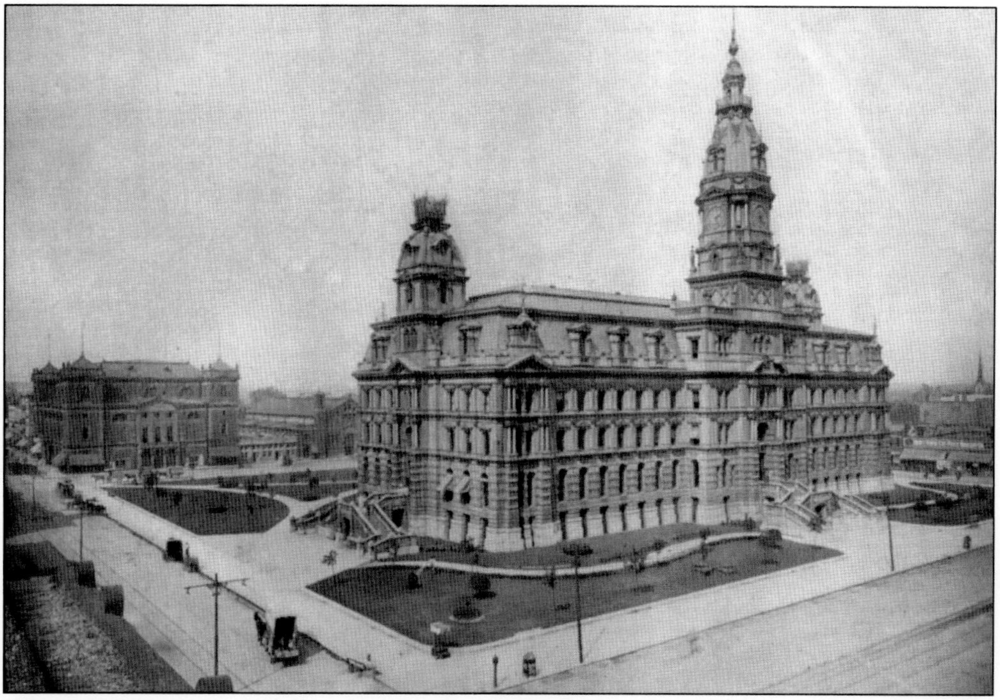

This is the Marion County Courthouse on East Washington Street in Indianapolis around 1900. The Second Empire—designed building featured a 97-foot-tall clock tower. It cost $1.4 million when it was built in 1876. The building was torn down in the early 1960s. Today, the 28-story Indianapolis City-County Building occupies the space. Tomlinson Hall and City Market can be seen in the background. (Courtesy Indianapolis Public Library-Irvington Branch.)

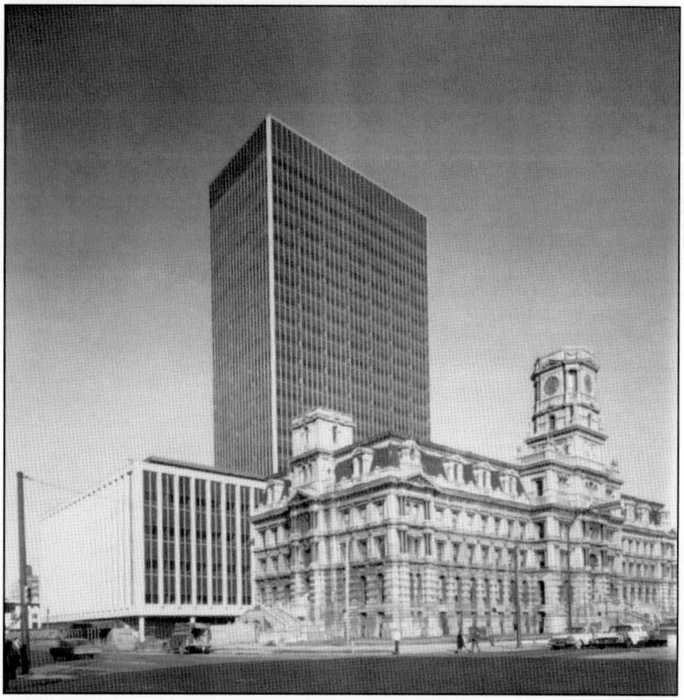

A 1962 photograph shows the old Marion County Courthouse at 200 East Washington Street with the new Indianapolis City-County Building that would replace it towering ominously behind. The two buildings stood side by side for several days before the grand old courthouse was demolished. (Allan E. Hunter collection.)

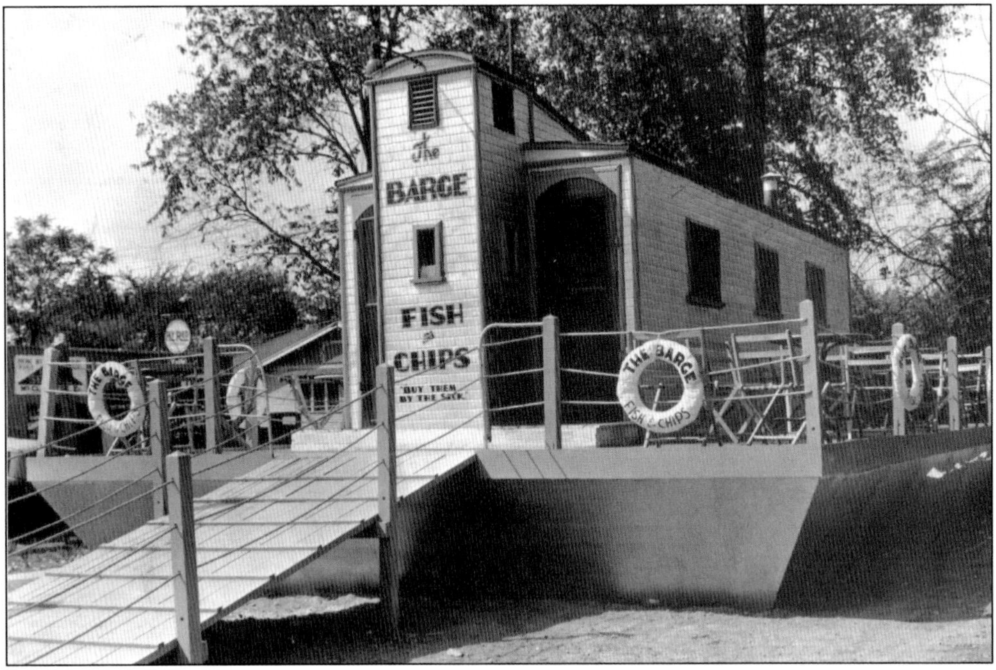

This 1935 image shows the Barge restaurant, which was located on the corner of Denny and East Washington Streets in Indianapolis. The restaurant was made from an old Indianapolis Railways trolley car designed to resemble a fishing boat in every detail, right down to the gangplank and life preservers on the roped railing. The sign reads, "The Barge Fish and Chips Buy Them by the Sack" on the front. A gas station can be seen behind the building featuring a "Hy-Red" gasoline sign. This is a wonderful example of lost roadside Americana on the National Road. (Allan E. Hunter collection.)

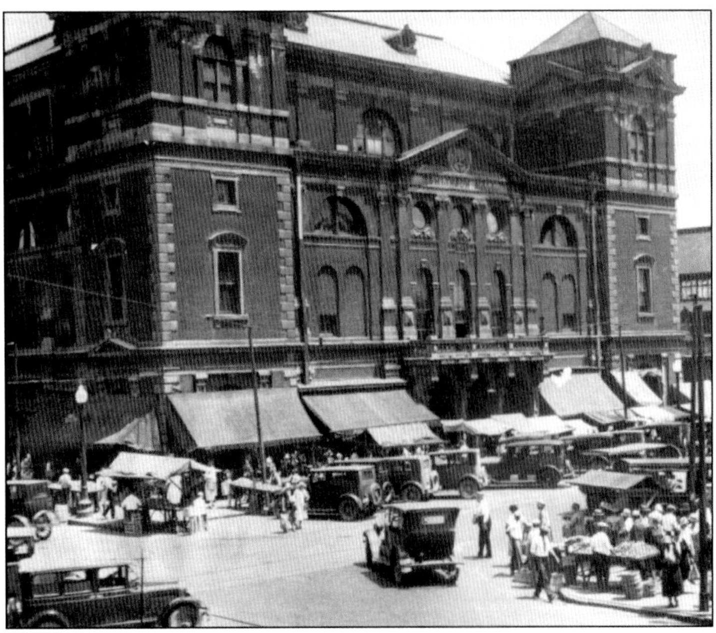

Tomlinson Hall is pictured in the depths of the Great Depression. In 1932 and 1933, the massive building served as a homeless shelter for unfortunate Hoosiers. An arch from the front of the building stands outside of the Indianapolis City Market and is the only visible sign of the grand old hall today. (Allan E. Hunter collection.)

This is a view of the Indianapolis Commercial Club at Washington and Meridian Streets in 1914. Several prominent Indianapolis businessmen created the club, and Eli Lilly was its first president. In 1914, the commercial club had an estimated 1,100 members. The building was constructed in 1891, and the Commercial club occupied the sixth, seventh, and eighth floors. (Allan E. Hunter collection.)

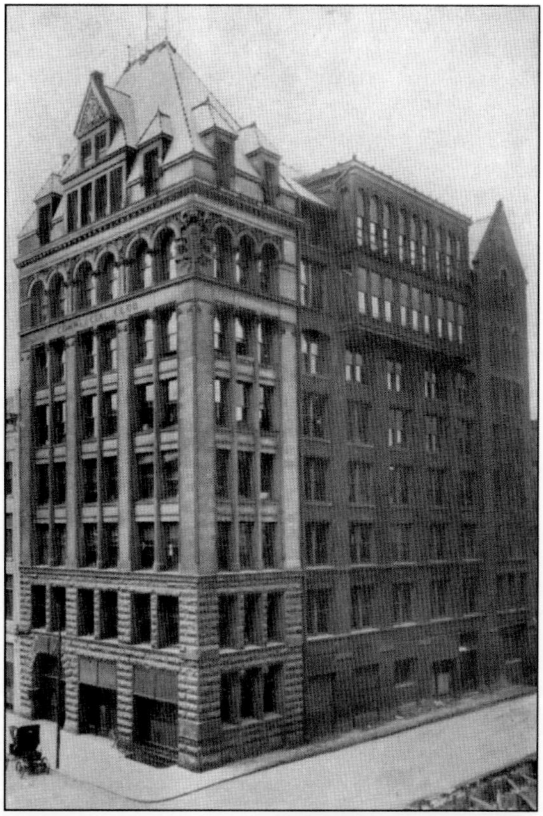

A 1904 photograph shows Washington Street from Meridian Street looking east. The interurban glides past a horse and buggy in the center of the street. The W.H. Block department building is on the left. (Allan E. Hunter collection.)

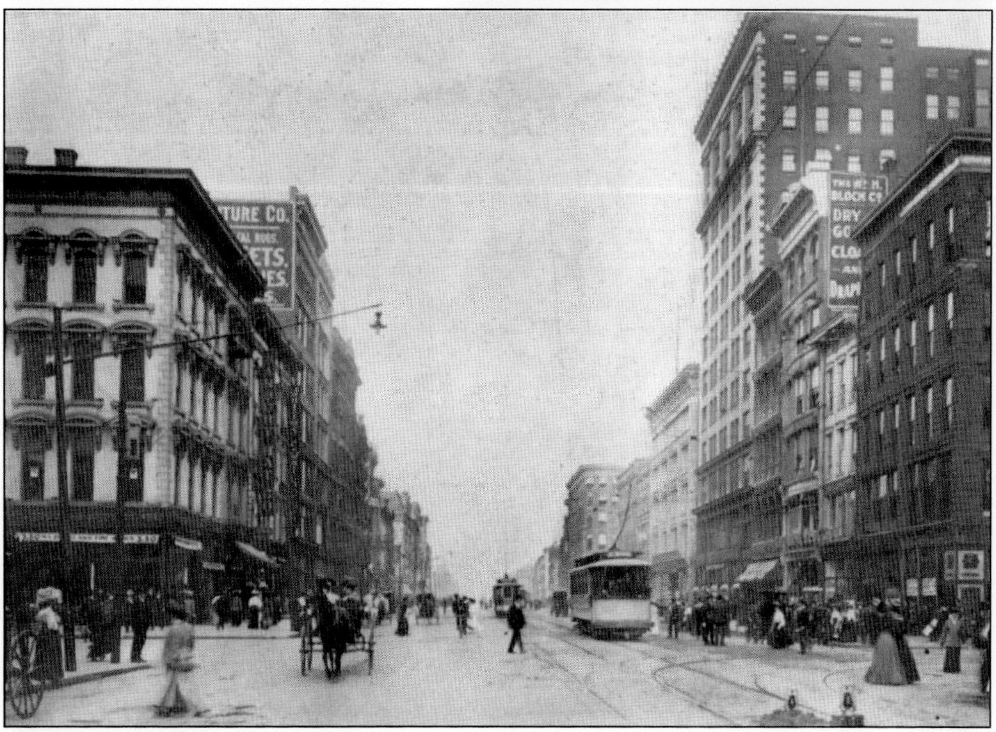

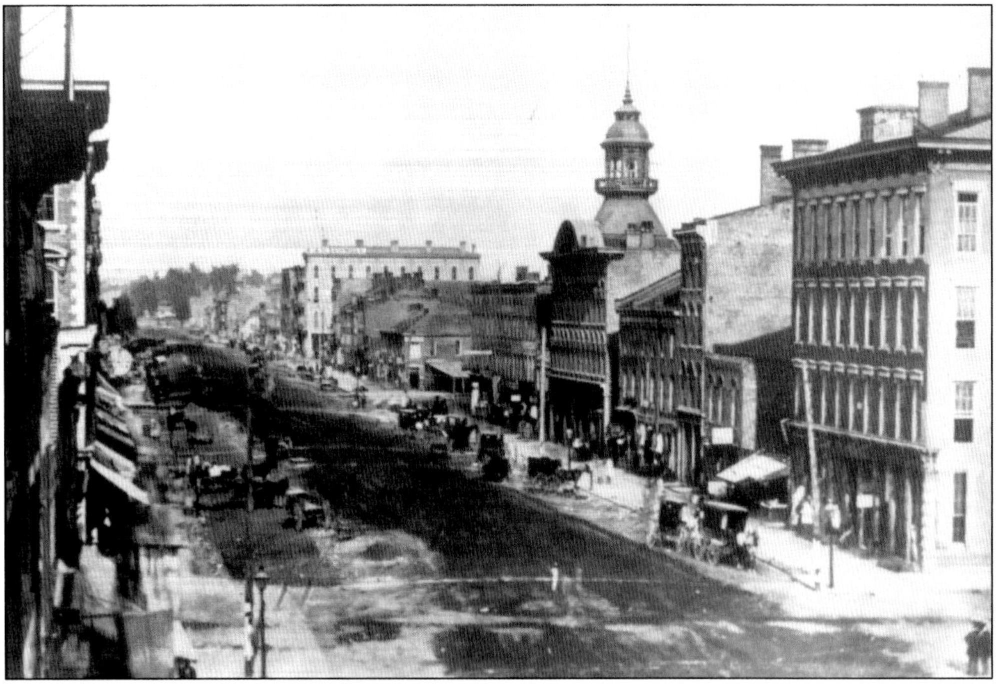

This rare 1862 glass-plate negative photograph of Washington Street looking east was taken during the Civil War. (Allan E. Hunter collection.)

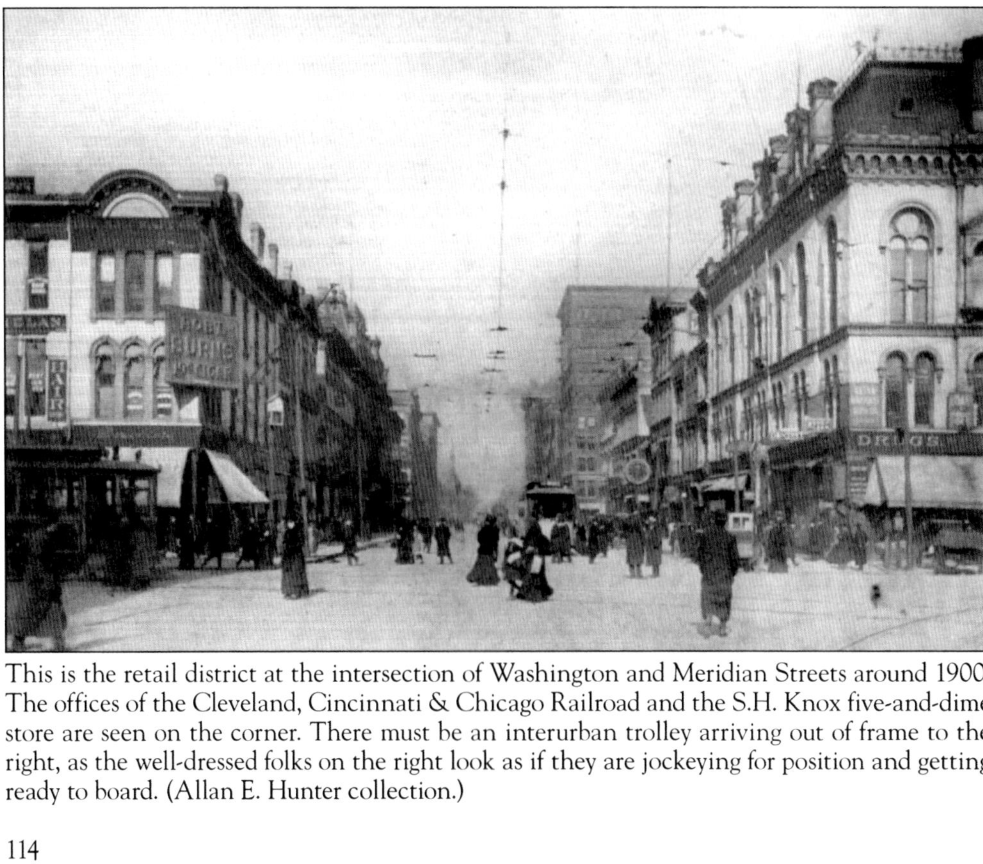

This is the retail district at the intersection of Washington and Meridian Streets around 1900. The offices of the Cleveland, Cincinnati & Chicago Railroad and the S.H. Knox five-and-dime store are seen on the corner. There must be an interurban trolley arriving out of frame to the right, as the well-dressed folks on the right look as if they are jockeying for position and getting ready to board. (Allan E. Hunter collection.)

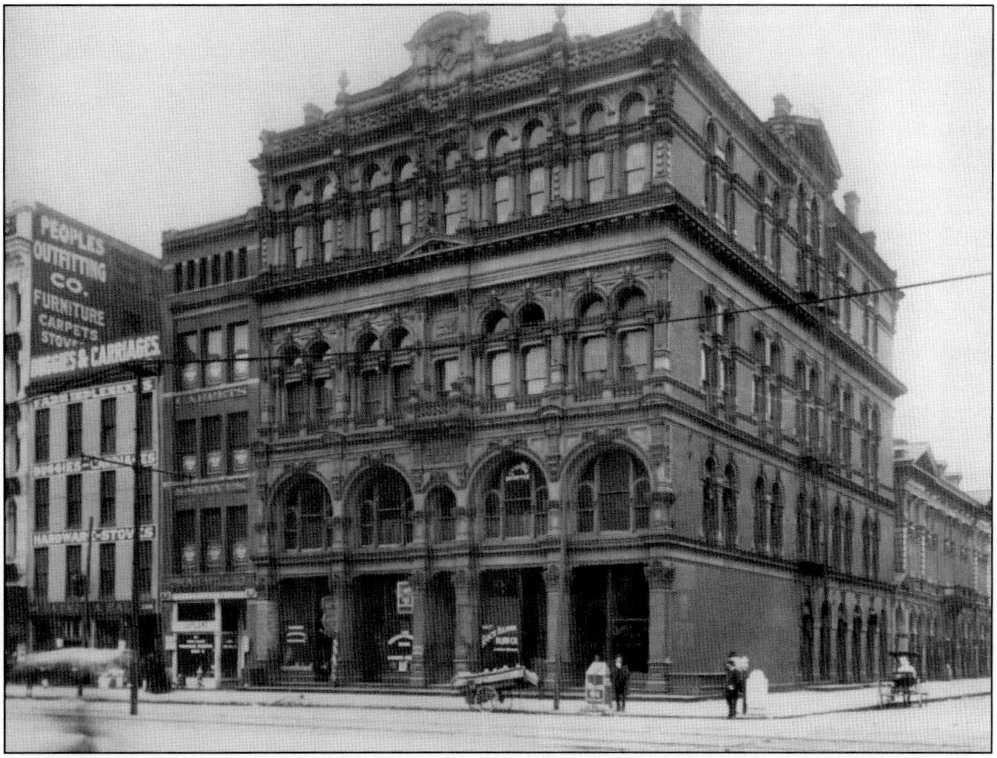

The Masonic temple, located at the intersection of Washington Street and Capitol Avenue, is pictured around 1910. A street vendor's cart can be seen in front of the building with its owner leaning against a mailbox as the uniformed policeman, on the corner just a few paces away, keeps a close eye on him. (Courtesy Indianapolis Public Library-Warren branch.)

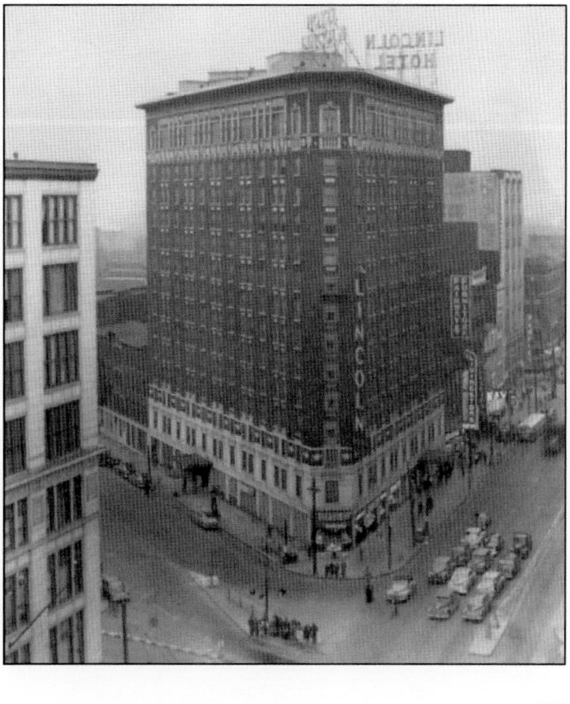

The Lincoln Hotel is pictured in the early 1950s. Indianapolis's premier architectural firm, Rubush and Hunter, designed the 14-story flatiron building located at the corner of Washington Street, Illinois Street, and Kentucky Avenue. Rubush and Hunter is widely acknowledged for changing the Indianapolis streetscape in the early 20th century. The building was razed in 1973, and the site is now home to Merchants Plaza and the Hyatt Regency Hotel. The entire intersection is now gone. (Courtesy Indianapolis Public Library-Warren branch.)

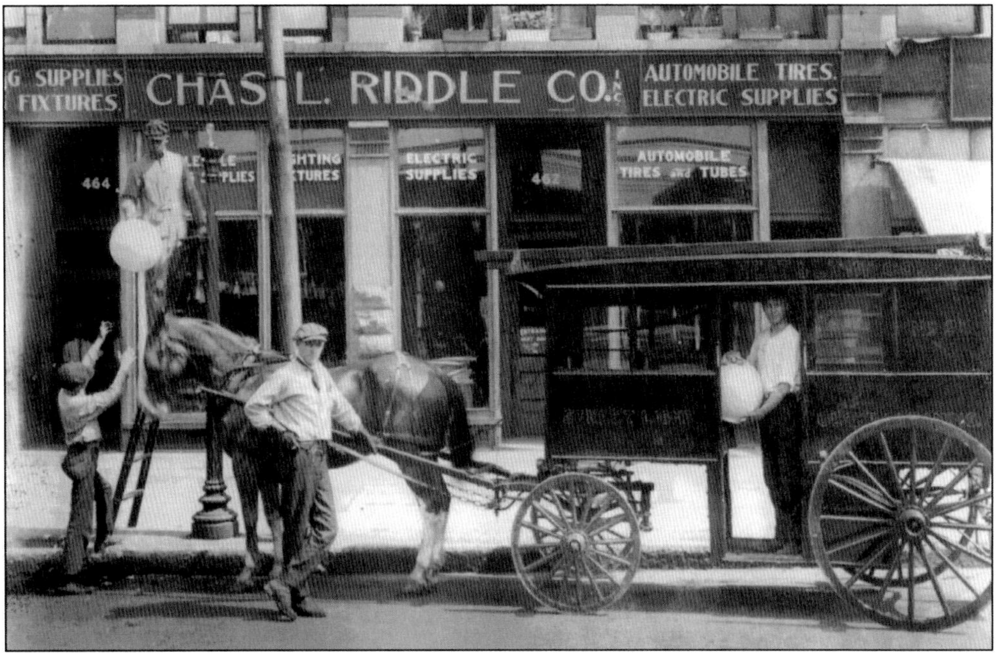

Workers in horse-drawn wagon No. 25 from the Merchants Heat & Light Co. Street Globe Cleaners are pictured cleaning streetlights in front of Charles L. Riddle Company at 462 West Washington Street in 1919. The Charles Riddle store sold automobile tires, tubes, and electrical supplies. Obviously posing for the camera, one man tends the horses, while another man atop a ladder hands down the large milk-glass lamp globe to a coworker on the ground as the last man waits with a clean globe inside the wagon. The photograph's original handwritten caption reads, "This simple job needed three men a boy a horse and a wagon." (Courtesy Indianapolis Public Library-Warren branch.)

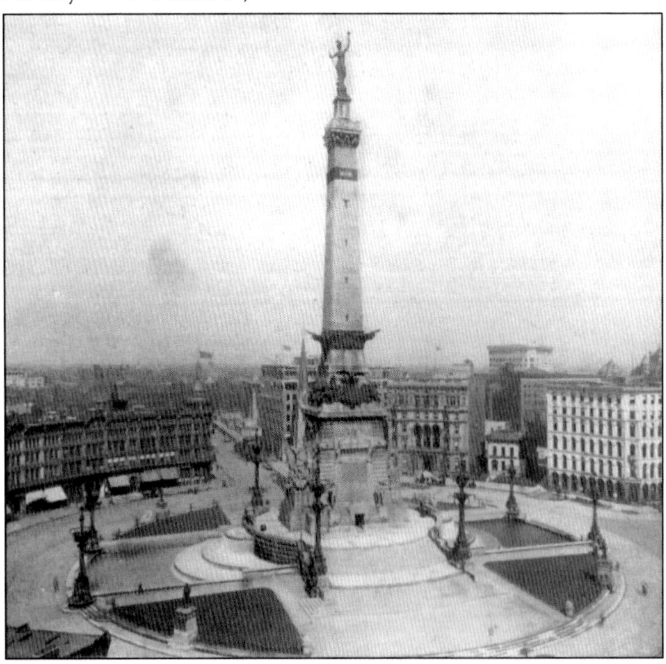

Located in the center of the city's original one-square-mile plat and considered to be the signature structure in Indianapolis, the Soldiers and Sailors Monument was dedicated on May 15, 1902. The poem "America, Messiah of Nations," written by James Whitcomb Riley for the dedication of the monument, was transformed into a march by John Philip Sousa. Both Riley and Sousa performed the poem and march at the dedication ceremonies. Gen. Lew Wallace was master of ceremonies for the event. The circle is shown here as it looked in 1914. (Alan E. Hunter collection.)

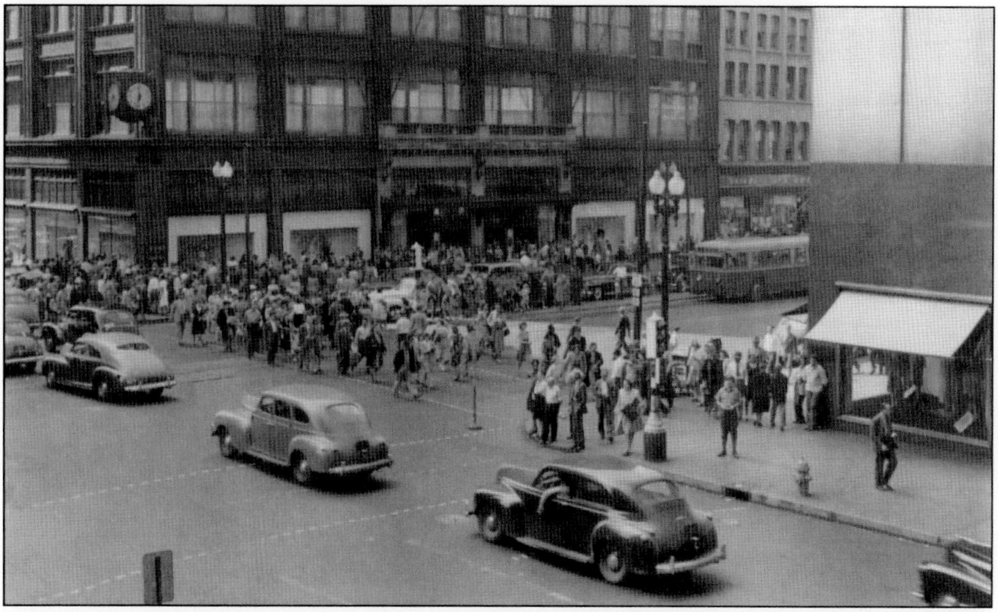

The intersection of Washington and Illinois Streets is pictured in the 1950s. This intersection was touted as being the "Crossroads of America" and is historically the most photographed intersection in the city. The H.P. Wasson and Company store can be seen on the right, and the L.S. Ayres and Company department store is the large building on the left. The city's most prominent department stores during the last century, Wasson's lasted at this location from 1883 until 1979, and Ayres was here from 1905 to 1992. Parisian department store now operates on the site, which is part of Circle Center Mall. Notice the clock on the corner of the building to the left. Each year during the Christmas season since the close of World War II, a cherub statue appears on the clock to greet pedestrians on the corner below. (Courtesy Indianapolis Public Library-Warren branch.)

Pictured is the Roosevelt Building as it looked in 1938. The architectural firm of Vonnegut, Bohn, and Mueller designed the distinctive narrow skyscraper (it was only 30 feet wide). Opened in 1923, it stood on the northeast corner of Washington and Illinois Streets. The building was imploded by the city on August 12,1990, to make way for a Saks Fifth Avenue store in Circle Center Mall, but Saks pulled out, and the lot remained vacant for years. The luxurious Conrad Hotel was built on the spot in the spring of 2006. To this day, it is the largest building in Indianapolis to be demolished not due to fire or structural problems. (Courtesy Indianapolis Public Library-Warren branch.)

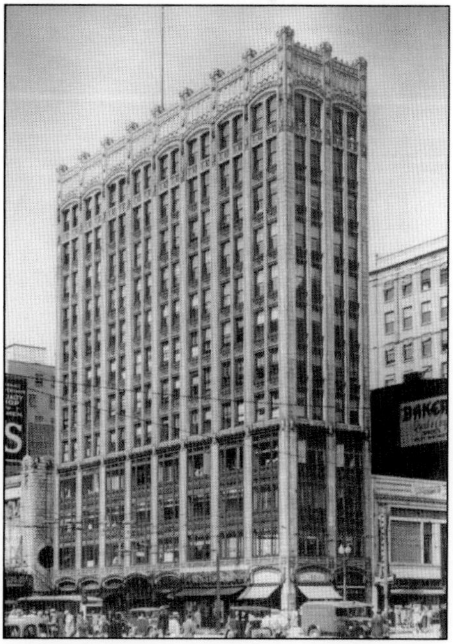

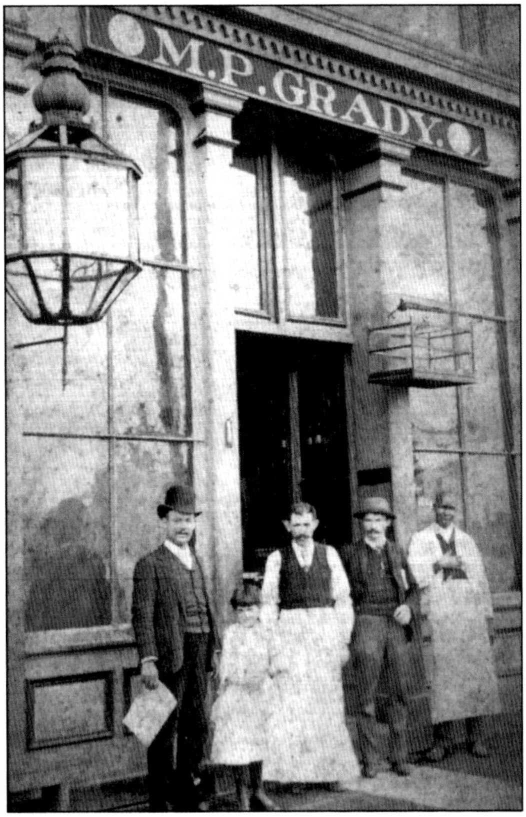

Shown is M.P. Grady's saloon on West Washington Street as it appeared in the early 1890s. The 1899 Indianapolis City Directory identifies the tavern's owner, Martin P. Grady, as a member of the Elks and an employee of the US Bureau of Animal Industry. (Courtesy Indianapolis Public Library-Warren branch.)

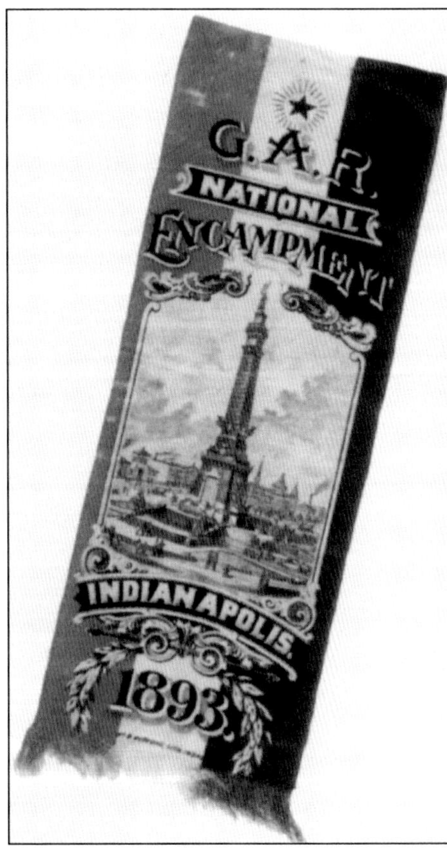

This is an 1893 GAR National Encampment ribbon worn by Civil War veterans while visiting Indianapolis. (Alan E. Hunter collection.)

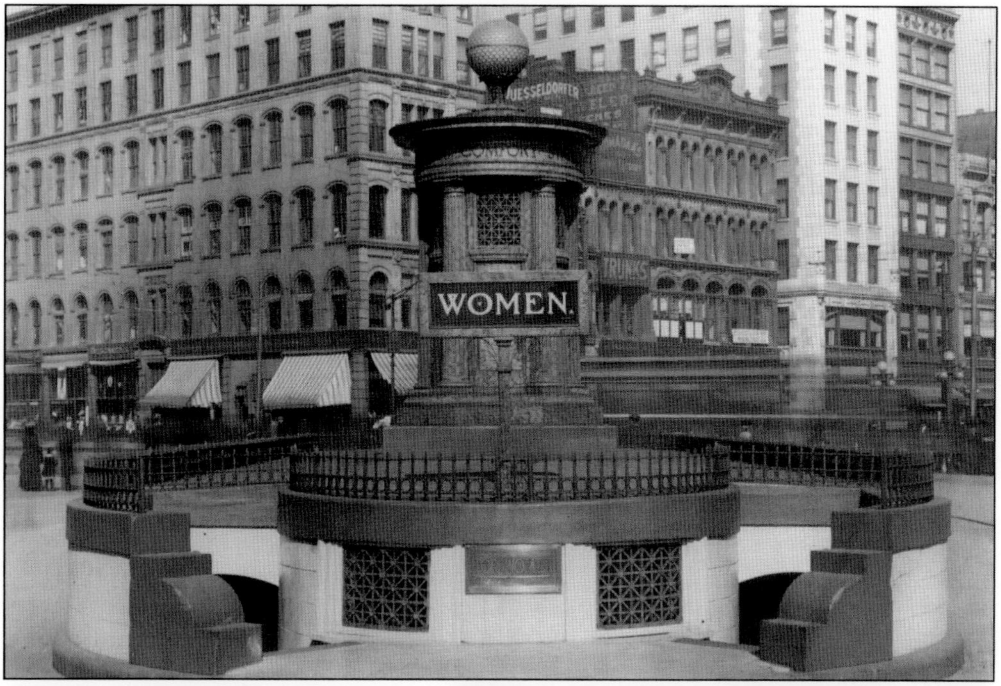

This 1911 photograph shows the women's comfort station, formerly located on the corner of Kentucky Avenue and West Washington Street in Indianapolis, with the men's station located just a few yards away. Second- and third-shift workers, whose hours prohibited them from using the facilities inside stores and office buildings, principally used these underground restrooms. Within months of their opening in 1910, women began to complain about their filth and terrible smell, and city council feared that they would become a haven for loafing; however, they lasted over 50 years before finally closing in 1963. Today, the site is home to the ArtsGarden outside Circle Center Mall. (Allan E. Hunter collection.)

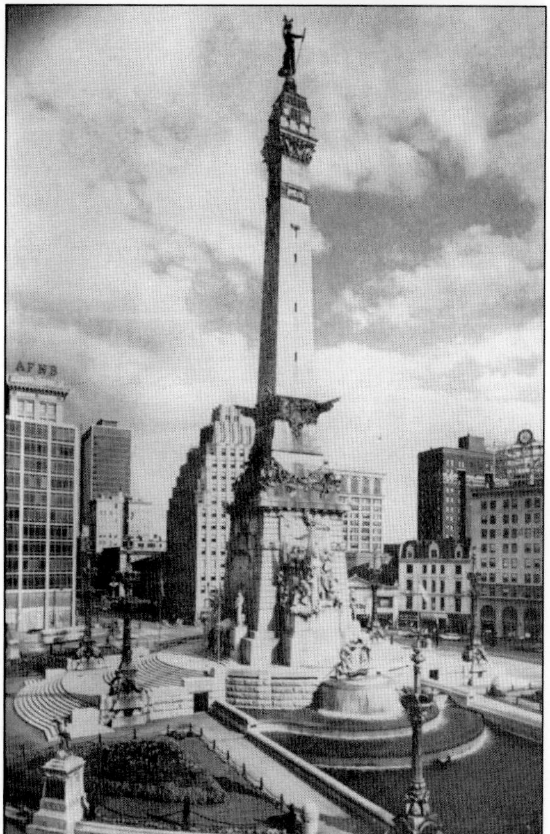

Monument Circle is pictured in 1964. The 28-story Indianapolis City/County Building, constructed just two years before, and the Indianapolis Power & Light Company and American Fletcher National Bank Buildings can be seen in the background. (Courtesy Indianapolis Public Library-Irvington Branch.)

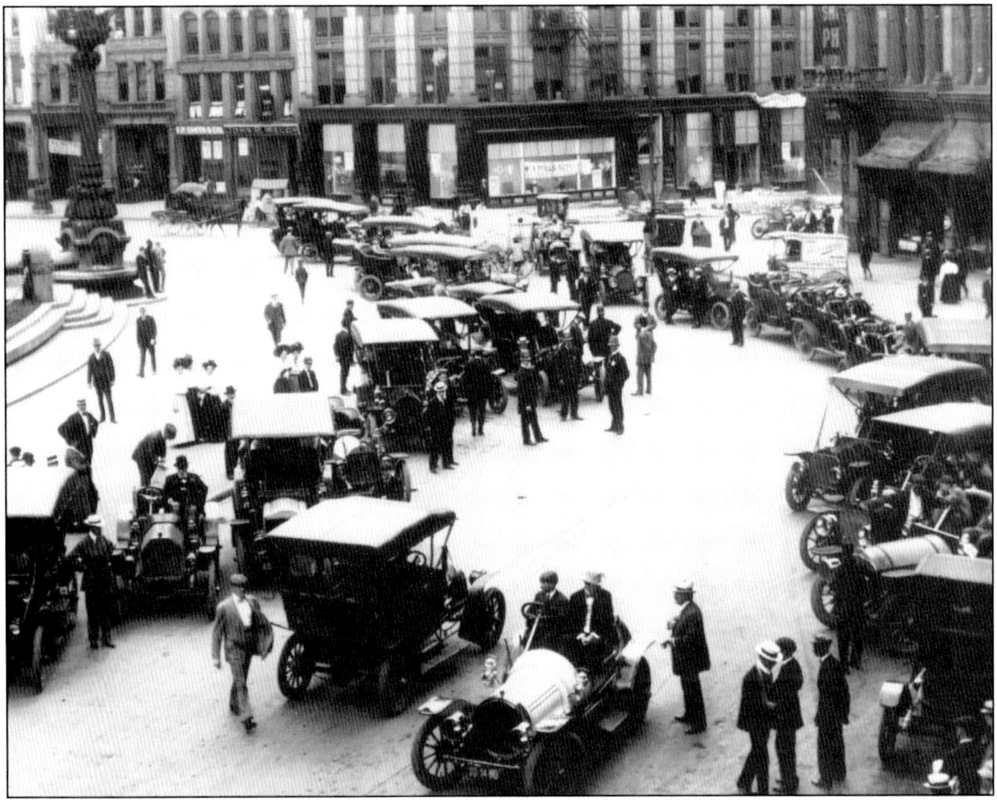

The Hoosier motor club had an automobile show on Monument Circle in June 1908. Four Indianapolis policemen in their English bobby-style hats can be seen in the center. A few horse-drawn buggies can also be seen wandering into the photograph behind the new automobiles. (Alan E. Hunter collection.)

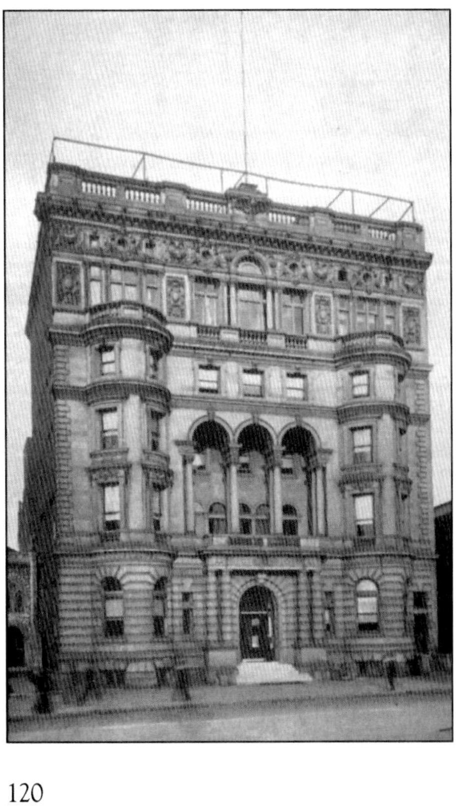

The Columbia Club on Monument Circle is pictured around 1914. The building was dedicated in 1900 and has functioned as a gathering place for Republican politicians for over a century in Indianapolis. (Alan E. Hunter collection.)

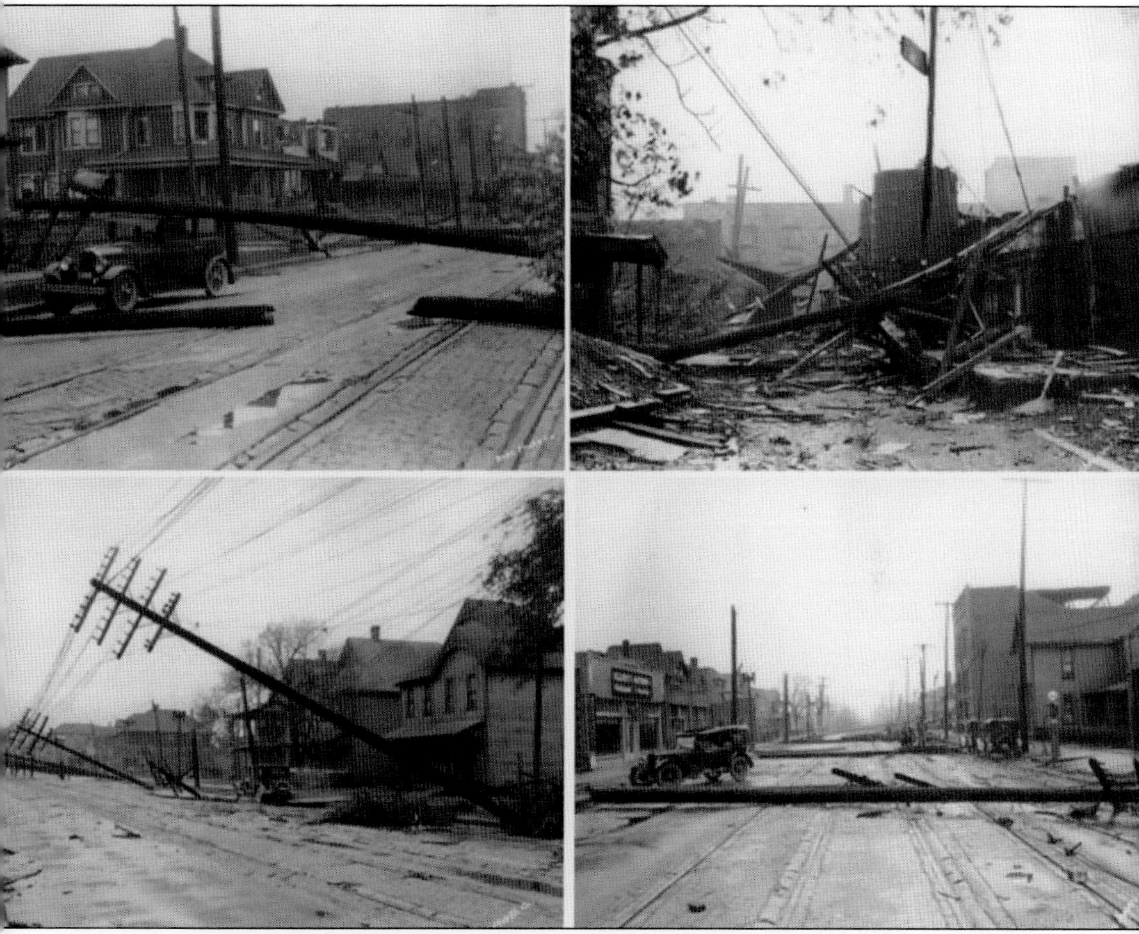

It is a common urban legend that tornadoes do not strike downtown areas of major metropolitan areas; this is definitely false. On May 18, 1927, a tornado damaged 200 East Washington Street and Hendricks Place. Note the interurban tracks running through the brick-lined street. The F-3 tornado moved through the heart of Indianapolis roughly traveling the route of the National Road, killing two young boys and injuring up to 200 people. One scene shows tornado damage in an alley at Pine and Washington Streets. Note the urban grain silos in the background. The worst destruction occurred on the city's east side, where 16 solid blocks were destroyed. Although devastating, the news was quickly pushed off of the front pages three days later by Charles Lindbergh's New York to Paris transatlantic flight on May 21–22, 1927. The lower right image shows the tornado damage at Washington and Rural Streets; note the toppled power line right next to the untouched gas pump with its glass globe top. (Courtesy Indianapolis Public Library-Irvington Branch.)

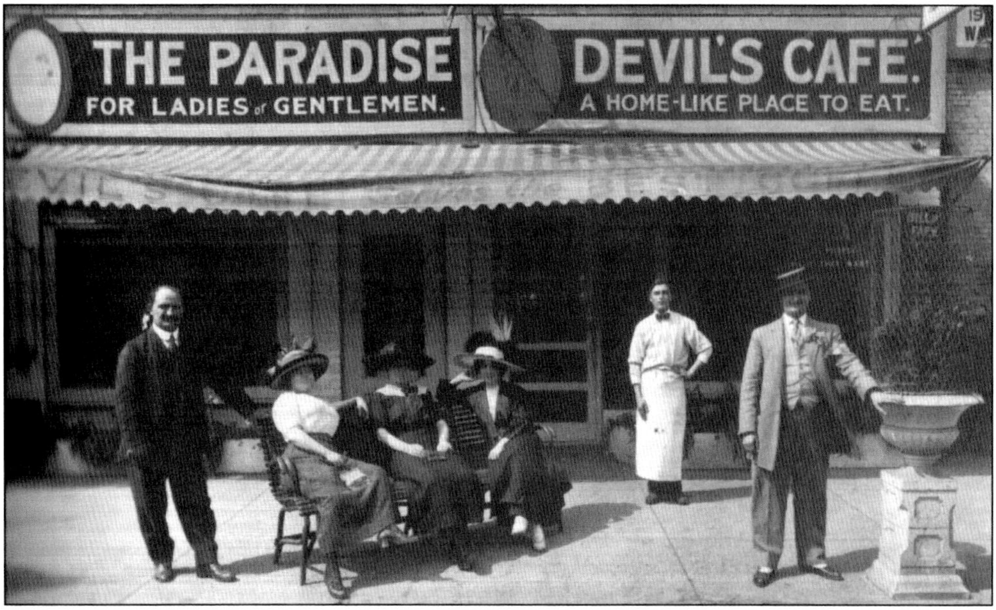

Here is a 1910 image of the Devil's Café at 108 West Maryland Street. Owner Pantelis Cafouros is pictured (far left) with his restaurant staff. Cafouros's wife (seated third from left), who did not speak English, believed "devil" corresponded to the French "de ville," meaning "in the city." When she found out its true meaning, she objected. (Allan E. Hunter collection.)

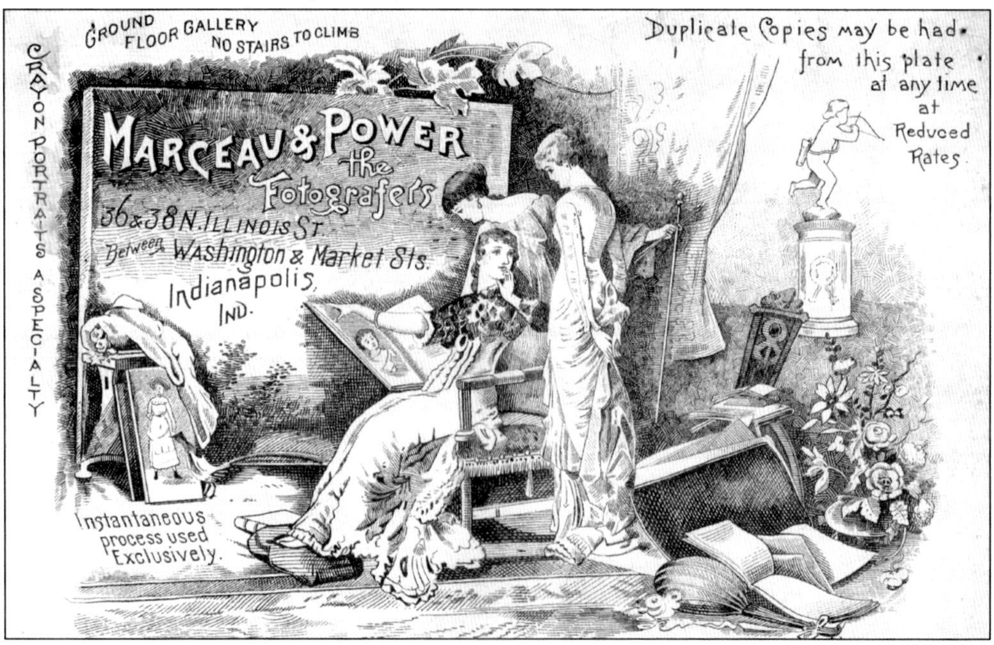

This is an ornate 1880s Victorian advertisement found on the back of a cabinet card from Marceau & Power the Fotografers photography studio located at 36 and 38 North Illinois Street between Washington and Market Streets in Indianapolis. During the golden age of studio photography (from the Antebellum Era into the Industrial Revolution), Washington Street in Indianapolis was the desired address for photographers and their studios, boasting no less then two dozen professional studios at any given time. (Alan E. Hunter collection.)

Burger Chef was a fast-food restaurant chain founded in 1954 in Indianapolis with several locations along the National Road and throughout the state. Its first hamburgers sold for 15¢. In the late 1950s, the chain created the first value combo with a hamburger, fries, and soft drink for the price of 45¢ (50¢ with a milk shake). The summer of 1965 issue of *Burger Chef News*, a corporate publication, announced the plan for the first "walk-in cafeteria style" Burger Chef restaurant to open in Indianapolis in September 1965. The newsletter featured an artist's rendering of the new-style building on the cover. It was more than twice the size of any other Burger Chef restaurant and featured a moving trail rail designed to help customers move along. (Alan E. Hunter collection.)

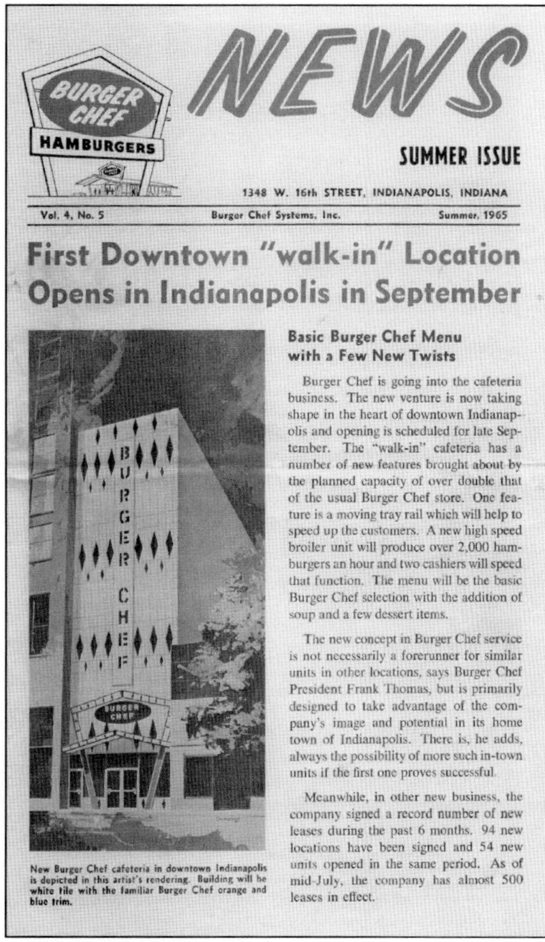

BURGER CHEF HAMBURGERS

NEWS

SUMMER ISSUE

1348 W. 16th STREET, INDIANAPOLIS, INDIANA

Vol. 4, No. 5 — Burger Chef Systems, Inc. — Summer, 1965

First Downtown "walk-in" Location Opens in Indianapolis in September

New Burger Chef cafeteria in downtown Indianapolis is depicted in this artist's rendering. Building will be white tile with the familiar Burger Chef orange and blue trim.

Basic Burger Chef Menu with a Few New Twists

Burger Chef is going into the cafeteria business. The new venture is now taking shape in the heart of downtown Indianapolis and opening is scheduled for late September. The "walk-in" cafeteria has a number of new features brought about by the planned capacity of over double that of the usual Burger Chef store. One feature is a moving tray rail which will help to speed up the customers. A new high speed broiler unit will produce over 2,000 hamburgers an hour and two cashiers will speed that function. The menu will be the basic Burger Chef selection with the addition of soup and a few dessert items.

The new concept in Burger Chef service is not necessarily a forerunner for similar units in other locations, says Burger Chef President Frank Thomas, but is primarily designed to take advantage of the company's image and potential in its home town of Indianapolis. There is, he adds, always the possibility of more such in-town units if the first one proves successful.

Meanwhile, in other new business, the company signed a record number of new leases during the past 6 months. 94 new locations have been signed and 54 new units opened in the same period. As of mid-July, the company has almost 500 leases in effect.

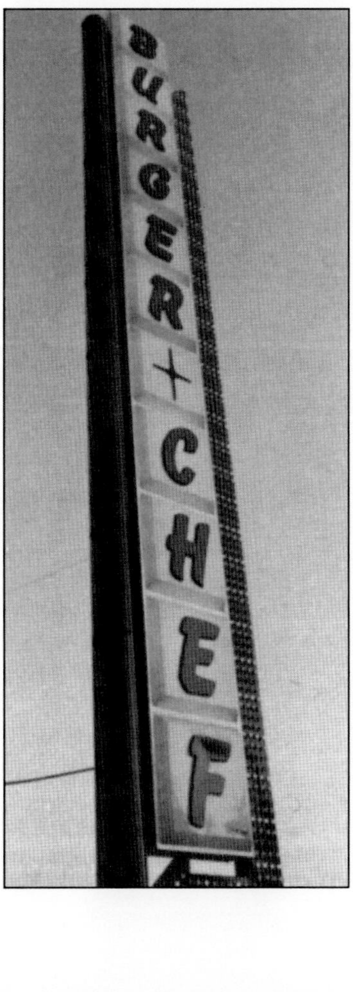

Burger Chef called this sign the "Downtowner." It was specifically designed for the downtown Indianapolis location and was one of the few signs Burger Chef used that did not feature a logo. The sign was described in company literature, "This lengthy giant is typical of signs used in downtown cafeterias and unique locations in existing buildings." Burger Chef was enormously popular and spread across both the West Coast and the East Coast, eventually becoming second only to McDonald's in terms of number of locations. (Alan E. Hunter collection.)

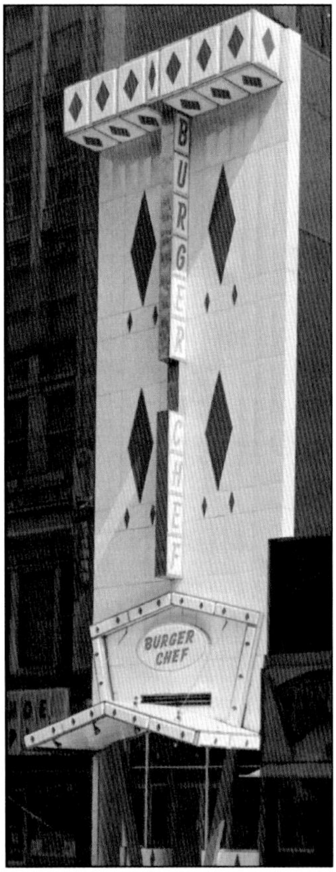

The Indianapolis downtown Burger Chef cafeteria-style restaurant was located at 6 East Washington Street. The building featured a white tile front with the familiar Burger Chef orange and blue trim. The front of the building featured no less than 40 neon backlit signs and spotlights, which gave it a glowing effect at night. (Alan E. Hunter collection.)

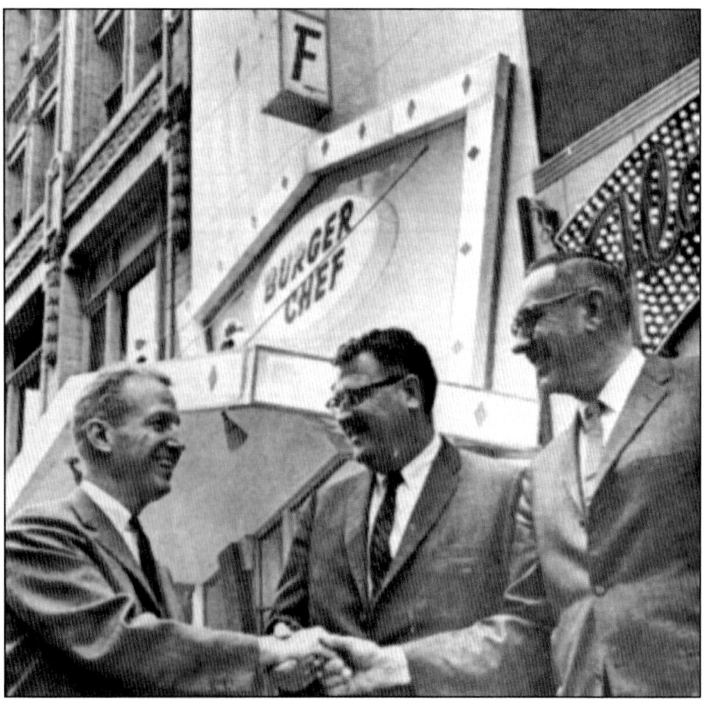

Indianapolis mayor John J. Barton (left) hands the keys of the new Burger Chef "Downtowner" Restaurant at 6 West Washington Street to company president Frank Thomas (center) and vice president Walter Lough in the spring of 1966. (Alan E. Hunter collection.)

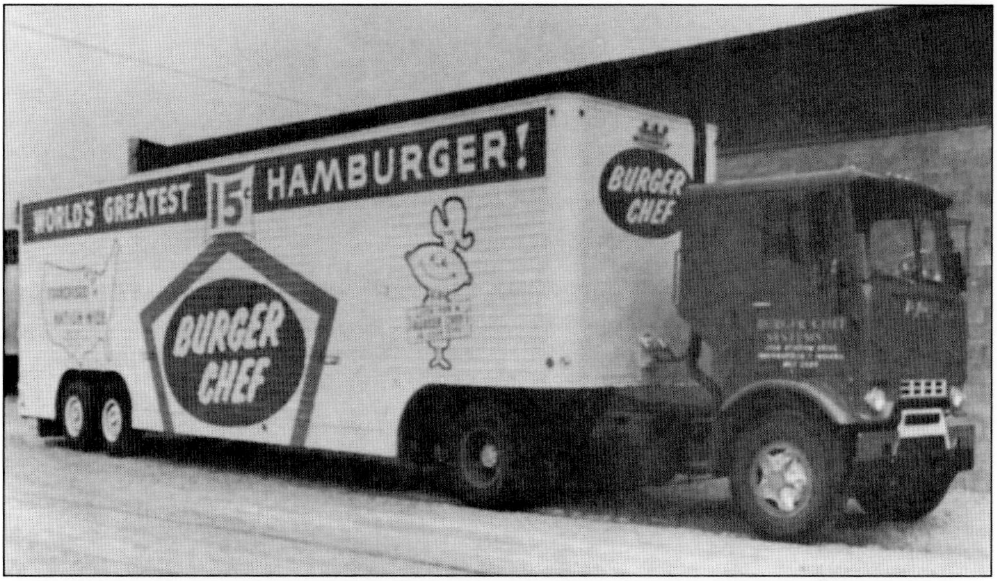

This is a Burger Chef truck and trailer from the early 1960s. Headquartered in Indianapolis with locations all along the National Road from Richmond to Terre Haute, these trucks were a familiar sight. (Alan E. Hunter collection.)

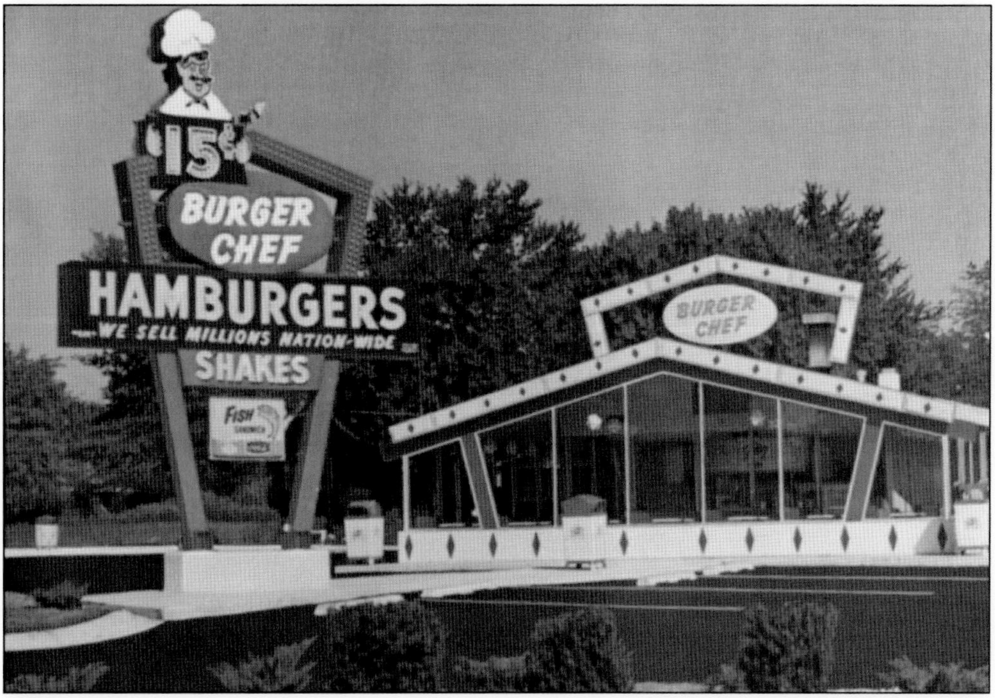

A Burger Chef restaurant from around 1960 is pictured. The company offered a signature double-burger called the Big Shef, and later a quarter-pound hamburger called the Super Shef. Later on, it pioneered the Works Bar, where customers could dress their hamburgers with condiments and vegetables exactly as they wanted. The bar required that customers order their hamburgers "with" or "without"; "with" hamburgers were dressed by the kitchen staff and "without" by the customer. (Alan E. Hunter collection.)

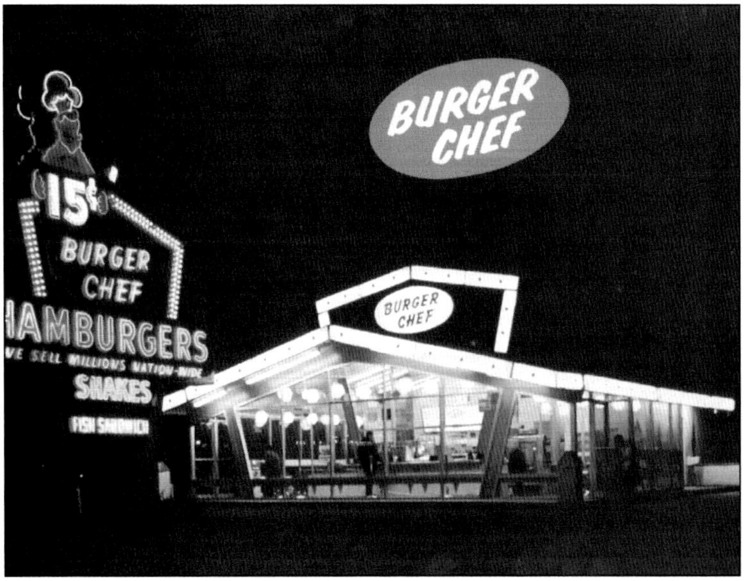

Seen is a 1960s Burger Chef restaurant featuring its innovative nighttime lighting. In 1968, the chain was purchased by the General Foods Corporation, which continued its rapid expansion. By 1970, there were nearly 2,400 locations and a redesigned building and logo. The chain's mascots were called Burger Chef and Jeff. (Alan E. Hunter collection.)

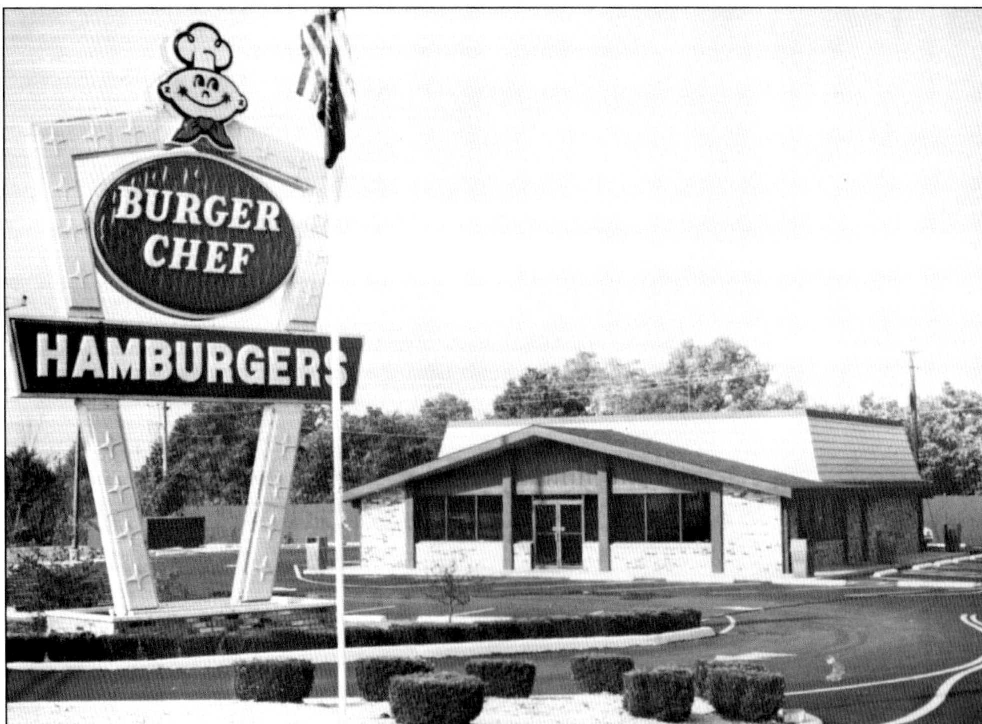

This is the Burger Chef restaurant design featured from the mid-1960s until the early 1970s. In the early 1970s, the chain introduced the Funburger, then the Funmeal, with specially printed packaging that included stories about Burger Chef and Jeff's adventures with riddles, puzzles, and small toys. Other premiums included flexi-disc recordings with more stories and a token that could be redeemed for a frozen treat. In 1982, Burger Chef was sold to the Hardee's food chain. The final Burger Chef closed in 1996, but many of the chain's original buildings survive as Hardee's or various other fast-food or retail establishments. (Alan E. Hunter collection.)

Signs stretched across Washington Street advertise the 1921 Industrial Fair at the Indiana State Fairgrounds. The fair featured 400 modern exhibits and drew an estimated 100,000 visitors. (Allan E. Hunter collection.)

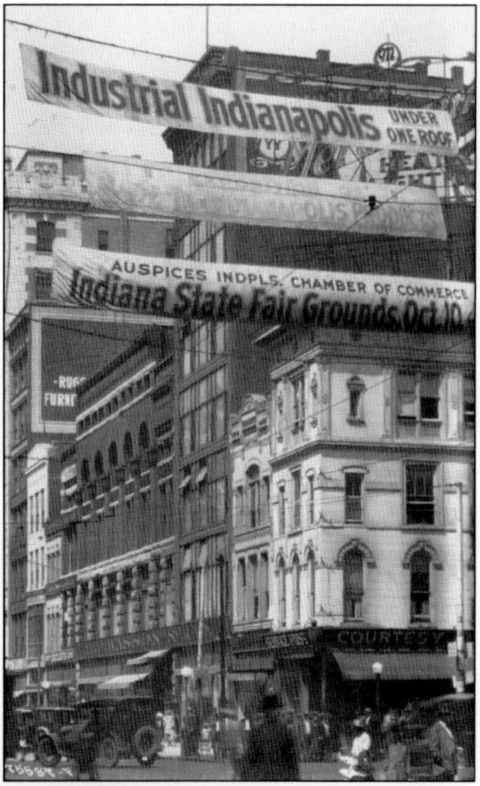

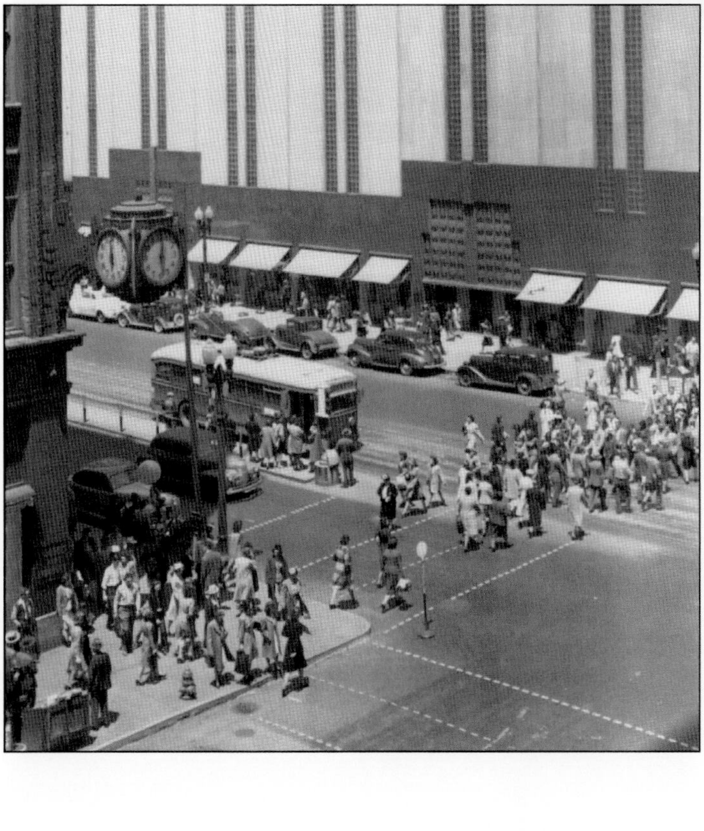

Here is a view of Washington and Meridian Streets in 1946. The sidewalks and intersections are bustling with shoppers experiencing the postwar boom. The L.S. Ayres clock, minus the cherub, can be seen in the left foreground. (Allan E. Hunter collection.)